D1551387

LACAN AND THE POLITICAL

Jacques Lacan is now acknowledged as the most influential and original psychoanalytic theorist since Freud and his work is increasingly being recognised for its relevance in socio-political analysis and philosophy. *Lacan and the Political* is the first book combining a presentation of the Lacanian conceptual and theoretical apparatus with a vigorous and systematic evaluation of its importance in contemporary political theory.

Yannis Stavrakakis moves beyond the standard applications of the Lacanian concept of the subject in treating social and political issues, towards an examination of Lacan's approach to the 'objective' side of human experience *per se*. He highlights Lacan's innovative understanding of the socio-political field and situates his thought within a theoretical terrain comprising deconstruction, discourse theory, the sociology of risk and recent developments in political theory and history.

Stavrakakis argues against the perception that Lacan's ideas are apolitical or even reactionary, by demonstrating that not only is a political reading of Lacan possible, but that it is capable of liberating and invigorating our political imagination. The author contends that a Lacanian perspective can free political thought from the strait-jacket of utopian politics on the one hand and ethical relativism on the other, in order to develop the radical potential of modern democracy.

Yannis Stavrakakis is teaching fellow at the department of Government at the University of Essex and Acting Director of the MA programme in Ideology and Discourse Analysis.

THINKING THE POLITICAL
General editors:
Keith Ansell-Pearson
University of Warwick
Simon Critchley
University of Essex

Recent decades have seen the emergence of a distinct and challenging body of work by a number of Continental thinkers that has fundamentally altered the way in which philosophical questions are conceived and discussed. This work poses a major challenge to anyone wishing to define the essentially contestable concept of 'the political' and to think anew the political import and application of philosophy. How does recent thinking on time, history, language, humanity, alterity, desire, sexuality, gender and culture open up the possibility of thinking the political anew? What are the implications of such thinking for our understanding of and relation to the leading ideologies of the modern world, such as liberalism, socialism and Marxism? What are the political responsibilities of philosophy in the face of the new world (dis)order?

This new series is designed to present the work of the major Continental thinkers of our time, and the political debates their work has generated, to a wider audience in philosophy and in political, social and cultural theory. The aim is neither to dissolve the specificity of the 'philosophical' into the 'political' nor evade the challenge that 'the political' poses the 'philosophical'; rather, each volume in the series will try to show it is only in the relation between the two that the new possibilities of thought and politics can be activated.

Volumes already published in the series are:

- *Foucault & the Political* by Jon Simons

- *Derrida & the Political* by Richard Beardsworth

- *Nietzsche & the Political* by Daniel W. Conway

- *Heidegger & the Political* by Miguel de Beistegui

LACAN AND THE POLITICAL

Yannis Stavrakakis

London and New York

First published 1999
by Routledge
2 Park Square, Milton Park, Abingdon, Oxon, OX14 4RN

Simultaneously published in the USA and Canada
by Routledge
270 Madison Ave, New York NY 10016

Routledge is an imprint of the Taylor & Francis Group

Transferred to Digital Printing 2005

©1999 Yannis Stavrakakis

Typeset in Times by Routledge

British Library Cataloguing in Publication Data
A catalogue record for this book is available from the British Library

Library of Congress Cataloging in Publication Data
A catalogue record for this title has been requested

ISBN 0–415–17187–3 (pbk)
ISBN 0–415–17186–5 (hbk)

CONTENTS

BIBLIOGRAPHICAL NOTE

Page references are to the English translations of the works of Jacques Lacan. In the case of the *Écrits* or Lacan's published seminars, I used the following abbreviations:

E
Jacques Lacan, *Écrits, A Selection*, trans. Alan Sheridan, London: Tavistock Publications, 1977.

I
Jacques Lacan, *The Seminar. Book I. Freud's Papers on Technique, 1953–4*, Jacques-Alain Miller (ed.), trans. with notes John Forrester, Cambridge: Cambridge University Press, 1988.

II
Jacques Lacan, *The Seminar. Book II. The Ego in Freud's Papers and in the Technique of Psychoanalysis, 1954–5*, Jacques-Alain Miller (ed.), trans. Sylvana Tomaselli, notes by John Forrester, Cambridge: Cambridge University Press, 1988.

III
Jacques Lacan, *The Seminar. Book III. The Psychoses, 1955–6*, Jacques-Alain Miller (ed.), trans. Russell Grigg, London: Routledge, 1993.

VII
Jacques Lacan, *The Seminar. Book VII. The Ethics of Psychoanalysis, 1959–60*, Jacques-Alain Miller (ed.), trans. Dennis Porter, notes by Dennis Porter, London: Routledge, 1992.

XI
Jacques Lacan, *The Seminar. Book XI. The Four Fundamental Concepts of Psychoanalysis, 1964*, Jacques-Alain Miller (ed.), trans. Alan Sheridan, London: Hogarth Press and the Institute of Psycho-Analysis, 1977.

XX
Jacques Lacan, *The Seminar. Book XX. Encore, On Feminine Sexuality, The Limits of Love and Knowledge, 1972–3*, Jacques-Alain Miller (ed.), trans. with notes Bruce Fink, New York: Norton, 1998.

Other published works by Lacan are cited in the text as dates only. References to the unpublished seminars of Jacques Lacan are indicated by the date of the seminar in brackets. In order to avoid any anachronisms, the seminars of Jacques Lacan are included in the Bibliography in the order of their composition. Since all quotations from the *Écrits* are indicated by the abbreviation E, and given the fact that many different papers are included in this collection, a decision was taken to include the following table so that readers can orient themselves more easily:

E, 1–7	The Mirror Stage as Formative of the Function of the I (1949).
E, 8–29	Aggressivity in Psychoanalysis (1948).
E, 30–113	The Function and Field of Language and Speech in Psychoanalysis (1953).
E, 114–45	The Freudian Thing (1955).
E, 146–78	The Agency of the Letter in the Unconscious or Reason since Freud (1957).
E, 179–225	On a Question Preliminary to any Possible Treatment of Psychosis (1957–8).
E, 226–80	The Direction of the Treatment and the Principles of its Power (1958).
E, 281–91	The Signification of the Phallus (1958).
E, 292–325	The Subversion of the Subject and the Dialectic of Desire in the Freudian Unconscious (1960).

ACKNOWLEDGEMENTS

Acknowledgements are due to Routledge and Norton for granting permission to quote from the following works of Jacques Lacan: *Écrits, A Selection*, London: Tavistock/Routledge, New York: Norton, 1977; *The Seminar. Book VII. The Ethics of Psychoanalysis, 1959–60*, London: Routledge, New York: Norton, 1992; *The Seminar. Book III. The Psychoses, 1955–6*, London: Routledge, New York: Norton, 1993. I am also indebted to Cormac Gallagher for granting me permission to use his private translations of the following unpublished seminars of Jacques Lacan: *The Formations of the Unconscious* (1957–8), *Desire and its Interpretation* (1958–9), *Transference* (1960–1), *Anxiety* (1962–3), *Crucial Problems for Psychoanalysis* (1964–5), *The Object of Psychoanalysis* (1965–6).

I would like to thank my teachers, friends and colleagues Ernesto Laclau, Chantal Mouffe, Thanos Lipowatz, Aletta Norval, David Howarth, Nicolas Demertzis and Jason Glynos. This book has benefited enormously from their valuable remarks on earlier versions of the manuscript. Many thanks are also due to Simon Critchley for his insightful comments on the final version of the draft and for his overall support for this project. Finally, I must not forget to thank my editor Tony Bruce for the meticulous supervision of this whole enterprise.

Some of the material included in this volume has been presented or has previously appeared elsewhere:

The first part of Chapter 4 was presented at the 1998 annual conference of the *Universities Association for Psychoanalytic Studies* which was held in London. An earlier version of the second part of the same chapter appeared in *The Letter* under the title 'On the Political Implications of Lacanian Theory: A Reply to Homer', no. 10, Summer 1997, pp. 111–22.

An earlier version of Chapter 5 was presented at the 1995 Learned Societies Conference held at the Université du Quebec à Montreal. My thanks go to the British Council and the Canadian Sociology and Anthropology Association for funding my trip to Canada. I would also like to thank Ellie Ragland and Benjamin Arditi for their helpful comments on this early draft. The paper was then included in the papers series of the Centre for Theoretical Studies in the Humanities and the Social Sciences of the University of Essex and was subsequently published under the same title 'Ambiguous Democracy and the Ethics of Psychoanalysis' in *Philosophy and Social Criticism*, vol. 23, no. 2, 1997, pp. 79–96.

INTRODUCTION

On some questions preliminary to any possible discussion on Lacan and the political

What does Lacan have to do with the political? Isn't Lacan that obscure mystical psychoanalyst turned philosopher who has nothing to do with any consideration of the political domain? This is one of the possible responses the title of this book can generate. In this kind of response we find at work two different objections to the project undertaken here. The first one is related to the general idea of bringing together psychoanalysis and the political. It is an idea that seems to be alien to both social scientists and psychoanalysts – although it is certainly hoped that the readership of this book will not be limited to these two professional categories. The first of these two categories of prospective readers is always suspicious of any reduction of the level of the social, the 'objective' level, to an analysis at the level of the individual, the 'subjective' level, and not without good reasons. There is no doubt that psychological reductionism, that is to say the understanding of socio-political phenomena by reference to some sort of psychological *substratum*, an essence of the psyche, is something that should clearly be avoided. As it has been correctly pointed out by Wrong, psychoanalytic reductionism in the study of socio-political problems (such as attributing war to outbreaks of repressed aggression, the Russian revolution to a revolt against 'the national father image' and 'German National Socialism' to a paranoid culture, that is to say, treating 'society as a patient' having a collective unconscious or superego and suffering from a psychopathological disorder) has deservedly given psychoanalysis a bad name among historians, sociologists and political scientists (Wrong, 1994: 172).[1] In that sense, Fredric Jameson is in principle right when he draws our attention to Durkheim's stern warning from *Les Règles de Méthode Sociologique* (*The Rules of Sociological Method*) that 'whenever a social phenomenon is directly explained by a psychological phenomenon, we may be sure that the explanation is false' (Durkheim in Jameson, 1982: 339).[2]

A similar objection is often articulated by psychoanalysts, who also seem to be sceptical about the confluence of psychoanalysis and socio-political analysis. 'How does a psychoanalyst have anything to say on these topics?'

1

asks Jacques-Alain Miller: 'You must ask yourself if it's not an abuse to speak of politics from the analytic point of view, because it is a highly individual act to enter analysis'. Analysis, however, is not a detached theory, the psychology of an isolated individual (Lacan opposed any such form of atomistic psychology), and the analysand is not a 'solitary wanderer': the analysand becomes an analysand within the analytic setting by being linked to another, to his/her analyst. This link constitutes a social bond in analysis, what Miller calls the minimum social bond. Hence 'Freud's groundwork was to show that the analytic relationship gives the nucleus of the social bond. And that is why he gives authorisation to our thought regarding the political sphere' (Miller, 1992: 8). The authorisation to which Miller refers can be also related to Freud's own exercises in a psychoanalytic socio-political analysis, most notably in *Group Psychology and the Analysis of the Ego* (*Massenpsychologie und Ich-Analyse*) (1920), but also in other works of the last period of his life, that is to say, in *The Future of an Illusion* (*Die Zukunft einer Illusion*) (1927) and in *Civilisation and its Discontents* (*Das Unbehagen in der Kultur*) (1930), as well as in his reply to Albert Einstein's invitation, sponsored by the League of Nations, to write a short piece on the phenomenon of war (*Why War – Warum Krieg –* 1933). Besides, as Lacan points out in 'The Freudian Thing' (1955), Freud regarded the study of languages and institutions, literature and art, that is to say, of the social world, as a necessary prerequisite for the understanding of the analytic experience itself: 'he derived his inspiration, his ways of thinking and his technical weapons from just such a study. But he also regarded it as a necessary condition in any teaching of psychoanalysis' (E: 144). In fact, Lacan goes so far as to argue that lack of such an interest, especially on the part of the younger analysts, entails the danger of a 'psycho-sociological objectification, in which the psychoanalyst will seek, in his uncertainty, the substance of what he does, whereas it can bring him no more than an inadequate abstraction in which his practice is engulfed and dissolved' (E: 144). Lacan himself was renowned for his interest and his creative borrowings from fields ranging from philosophical discourse (especially Plato, Aristotle, Descartes, Kant and Hegel), structuralist anthropology (Lévi-Strauss), linguistics (Saussure and Jakobson) and topology.

Nevertheless, the way in which Freud and Lacan deal with the relation between the individual and the collective level is far from identical. Here, one can point to similarities and differences. It is true that, as Lacoue-Labarthe and Nancy argue, psychoanalysis, 'the Freudian science, is by rights a science of culture, and consequently a political science' because in Freud's schema 'the contrast of the social and the individual falls within the limits of psychoanalysis' (Lacoue-Labarthe and Nancy, 1997: 9). As Freud himself points out in the beginning of *Group Psychology* 'individual psychology...is at the same time social psychology as well...in fact all the relations which have hitherto been the chief subject of psychoanalytic

2

research...may claim to be considered as social phenomena'. Accordingly, for Freud, 'the contrast between social and narcissistic...mental acts falls within the domain of individual psychology' (Freud, 1991: 95–6). In this respect, we can assert that psychoanalysis has the right to embark on social analysis exactly because the social itself is reduced to the individual: 'sociology...dealing as it does with the behaviour of people in society, cannot be anything but applied psychology. Strictly speaking there are only two sciences: psychology, pure and applied, and natural science' (Freud, 1973: 216).

Lacan, while in agreement with Freud on the plausibility and legitimacy of a psychoanalytically inspired analysis of the social, does not endorse such a strong 'reductionist' approach. He seems to be taking very seriously Freud's own remark that one

> should be very cautious and not forget that, after all, we are only
> dealing with analogies and that it is dangerous, not only with men
> but also with concepts, to tear them from the sphere in which they
> have originated and been evolved.
>
> (Freud, 1982: 81)

If Freud seems, at times, to ignore this danger,[3] Lacan is much more careful. As early as 1950 he made the following statement:

> It may be well that since its experience is limited to the individual,
> psychoanalysis cannot claim to grasp the totality of any sociologi-
> cal object, or even the entirety of causes currently operating in our
> society. Even so, in its treatment of the individual, psychoanalysis
> has discovered relational tensions that appear to play a fundamen-
> tal role in all societies, as if the discontent in civilisation went so far
> as to reveal the very joint of nature to culture. If one makes the ap-
> propriate transformation, one can extend the formulas of psycho-
> analysis concerning this joint to certain human sciences that can
> utilise them.
>
> (1996a: 14)

One should combine this approach – the movement from the individual to the social – with the more socio-centric statements included in Lacan's doctoral thesis (1932) and elsewhere – indicating an opposite movement from the social to the individual: 'We have admitted as explicative of the facts of psychosis the dynamic notion of social tensions, whose state of equilibrium or disequilibrium normally defines the personality in the individual' (Lacan in Borch-Jacobsen, 1991: 22). The implication is that, from the very beginning, Lacan was aware of a two-way movement between

3

the individual and the social level. As his work evolved and his approach radicalised, he was led to deconstruct the whole essentialist division between the two. As we shall see, he does so by introducing a novel conception of subjectivity, a 'socio-political' conception of subjectivity not reduced to individuality, a subjectivity opening a new road to the understanding of the 'objective'. That is why most contemporary attempts to articulate a Lacanian approach to the level of the collective or the socio-political, the objective level, are based on the premise of the Lacanian subject. But, as we shall argue, Lacan's importance for a consideration of the political does not stop there. The Lacanian subject can only be a starting point.

In this context, what is most important in Lacanian theory is that it permits a true implication or inter-implication – and not a mere 'application' – between psychoanalysis and socio-political analysis; it does not remain trapped within a traditional framework that 'applies' psycho-analysis to socio-political issues by simply adding a theory of subjectivity to the field of political analysis. As Ernesto Laclau has put it, Lacanian theory permits the confluence between these two fields

> neither as the addition of a supplement to the former by the latter, nor as the introduction of a new causal element – the unconscious instead of the economy – but as the confluence of the two, around the logic of the signifier as a logic...of [real] dislocation....The logic which presides over the possibility/impossibility of the construction of *any* identity.
>
> (Laclau, 1990: 96)

Beyond his 'socio-political' conception of subjectivity Lacan articulates a whole new view of the objective level,[4] of the level of social reality, as a level whose construction (the construction of social objectivity and political identity as a closed, self-contained structure) is ultimately impossible but, nevertheless, necessary (we are necessarily engaged all the time in identity construction exactly because it is impossible to construct a full identity). In this regard, Lacanian theory is indispensable in showing that understanding social reality is not equivalent to understanding what society is, but what prevents it from being (Laclau, 1990: 44). It is in the moment of this prevention which is simultaneously generating – or causing – new attempts to construct this impossible object – society – that the moment of the political is surfacing and resurfacing again and again.

Another objection implied in the scepticism against the confluence of Lacanian theory and the political has to do with the particular *status* of Lacanian theory. Here we can discern a number of separate, although related issues. The first one concerns the intricacies of Lacan's discourse, his baroque and complicated style. Lacan is generally considered a difficult reading. It seems, at least at first, that, like Nietzsche, he 'did virtually everything in his power to encourage confusion and misunderstanding' (Conway, 1997: 119). As a result, he has been repeatedly accused of being deliberately obscure in a cunning attempt to avoid critical evaluation.[5] Obviously, Lacanian discourse is not presented as a closed, coherent system, ready for piecemeal appropriation and application. It is also true that this is intentional: 'I am not surprised that my discourse can cause a certain margin of misunderstanding', but this is done 'with an express intention, absolutely deliberate, that I pursue this discourse in a way that offers you the occasion of not completely understanding it' (Lacan in Samuels, 1993: 16). In Lacan's view, it is a sign of *phronesis*, on the part of the reader, not to understand too quickly (XX: 79) and he seems determined to cultivate this new culture of reading in his audience – his text is a writerly and not a readerly text. In this context, Lacan was fully aware that his discourse was especially unsuitable for academic reappropriation: 'My *Écrits* are unsuitable for a thesis, particularly an academic thesis: they are antithetical by nature: either one takes what they formulate or one leaves them' (1977: vii).[6] Maybe then he was very optimistic when, in *Télévision* (1973), he was arguing that ten years would be enough for everything he wrote to become clear to everyone (1987: 49). It is absurd, however, to interpret such a strategy as an attempt to avoid criticism; in fact the opposite is true: this alleged obscurantism has been a major nodal point in the criticism addressed towards Lacanian theory. How are we then to interpret this strategy today? It seems that the difficulty in Lacan's discourse constitutes a protective device – not always successful, it has to be admitted – against an easy acceptance of his theory, an acceptance facilitated by an identification with Lacan as the *Absolute Master* (to borrow from the title of Borch-Jacobsen's book – Borch-Jacobsen, 1991).

The ambiguity of Lacan's discourse is, in fact, a challenge for every reader, a challenge that has to be accepted, a difficulty that has to be assumed; only by acknowledging the irreducible ambiguity and indeterminacy of his discourse can one develop a desire to work with it. This is the challenge Lacan addresses to us: 'you are not obliged to understand my writings. If you don't understand them so much the better – that will give you the opportunity to explain them' (XX: 34). Lacan always insisted that analysis is not aimed at adaptation through the identification of the analysand with the analyst as a role model embodying the socially acceptable or 'politically correct' good. As he has pointed out in *The Four Fundamental Concepts of Psychoanalysis* (1964), 'any analysis that one teaches as having to be terminated by identification with the analyst reveals, by the same token, that its true motive force is elided. There is a beyond to this identification' (XI: 271–2). Similarly, Lacan's teaching does not offer itself easily to such identifications, and rightly so. A further problem arises, however, at this point. What is not generally realised is that this particular *status* of Lacan's discourse does not legitimise the imitation of his style by

5

other 'Lacanian' commentators, a result of transferential idealisation. This way identification comes back through the back door. There is an obscurantist antisystematic tradition in Lacanian literature which, by attempting to imitate the intricacies of Lacan's own discourse is reproducing, on another level, the problems that Lacan himself criticised in Ego-psychology; it is in that sense that his strategy didn't prove to be entirely successful. Unfortunately, a considerable part of recent Lacanian bibliography – especially in the Anglo-Saxon world where, in contrast to the Continent, it has been, to a large extent, directed towards an exploration of the relevance of Lacan's work for research areas such as literature, film theory, feminism and, more recently, politics and political theory – belongs to this tradition.[7] The danger here is that, as Malcolm Bowie has put it, Lacan's importance could be obscured by the babbling of his unconditional admirers (Bowie, 1991: 203). In that sense, articulating a systematic, simple – but not simplistic and thus petrifying – account of Lacan's relevance for a consideration of the political domain is still pertinent, and this study is designed as a step in this direction.

A second difficulty related to the *status* of Lacanian discourse is its inherent instability due not only to Lacan's idiosyncratic style but also to its radical development in time; in Lacan's work the moments of struggle of a *Lacan contre Lacan* type are not that rare. But if it is possible to discern many different phases in Lacan's theoretical evolution, how then can we orient our analysis between them? Which constellation of concepts and definitions can one use without creating conceptual conflict and confusion? It seems that this problem – the shifting nature of Lacan's teaching – was already puzzling his audience from the early 1960s. In his unpublished seminar on *Anxiety* (1962–3) he states, as if responding to a widely held conviction, that he does not believe that there were ever two distinct phases in his teaching, one focusing on his conception of the 'imaginary', on the 'mirror stage', and another articulated around his conception of the 'symbolic'. Today it would be possible to add one more phase, the one starting with his seminar on *The Four Fundamental Concepts of Psychoanalysis*, in which it is the concept of the 'real' that becomes the nodal point of his discourse – the 'imaginary', the 'symbolic' and the 'real' being the three most important categories, or registers, through which Lacan maps human experience. Naturally, this tripartite schema is not the only mapping of Lacan's theoretical trajectory possible.[8] In any case we have no reason to believe that Lacan's response to all these attempts to spatialise and sediment his elusive discourse would be different today from what it was in 1962. Lacan argues, for instance, that references to the role of the signifier were present in his discourse and his papers from the 1940s – the same applies to the concept of the real which is already present in his first seminars.[9] The reason he didn't invest these dimensions with the same theoretical weight that he did with the imaginary is, according to his view, that his listeners were not yet ready to accept it at that time (seminar of 28 December 1962). Nevertheless, it would be very difficult to present Lacan's discourse as an easy-going linear development of a single set of theoretical insights, since Lacan himself, although sticking to the use of an almost fixed conceptual apparatus (with some notable exceptions), never ceases to provide multiple and even incompatible definitions for each of the concepts and categories contained in it. Once again, his work is inviting interpretation. The challenge for every reader of Lacan is to articulate his own reading without reducing the complexity of Lacan's thought to this particular sedimentation and without suturing a certain indeterminacy which has to be preserved as a trace of the real within representation. Simply put, instead of imitation we need interpretation, an interpretation which is not searching for the *real* definitive Lacan, and in order to avoid this lure of theoretical omnipotence, chooses to concentrate on the constitutivity of the Lacanian *real*, the element which interacts with the imaginary and the symbolic by disrupting the certainties we articulate through them.

Another impediment to a possible confluence of Lacan and the political is due to problems in the accessibility of Lacan's work. Besides the difficulties posed by the fact that Lacan presented his ideas mainly in his seminar – a cultural event in itself – and not in written papers of an academic sort (in the form of what he named *pubellecation*)[10], the implication being that the transcription of his oral performance has transmitted his teaching 'like the amber which holds the fly so as to know nothing of its flight' (1977: xv), these seminars – 27 in total – are not available yet in their majority, due to a slow process of editing that has been strongly criticised and even contested in the courts. This contestation reveals only a minor part of the 'political' struggles associated with the Lacanian project almost from its very beginning. It is not surprising then that for many people the only relation between Lacan and the political is incarnated in the sort of *Psychoanalytic Politics* (to borrow from another title of a relevant book by Sherry Turkle – Turkle, 1992) characteristic of Lacan's relation to the psychoanalytic establishment and his own followers, and of the endless debates concerning his legacy. And although this issue cannot be overlooked this whole book constitutes an attempt to show that Lacan's relevance for a consideration of the political is not, by any means, limited to it.

To recapitulate, our main hypothesis will be that Lacanian theory does not become relevant and, indeed, crucial for a reinvigoration of political theory and socio-political analysis, *only* by introducing a 'non-reductionist', 'socio-political' conception of subjectivity. Lacan adheres to the Freudian legacy of a psychoanalytically inspired socio-political analysis by articulating a set of concepts and logics that pertain to the 'objective' level *per se*, although this is an 'objective' not reducible to the traditional essentialist approaches to social objectivity. In that sense, what reveals the major political significance of Lacan's work is the fact that his split subject is coupled by a 'split object', a split in our constructions of socio-political objectivity. What is the nature of this split? What is its cause? In what sense exactly is it related to the political? How is this split administered in the socio-political world? What are the theoretical tools that Lacanian theory offers in our analysis of this whole domain? These are some of the main questions guiding our argumentation. Our answers to them do not pretend to be final, nor total. In fact, it must be stated from the beginning that the scope of this book is limited, in the sense that certain ways of linking Lacan and the political are not explored at all or not discussed in detail. For example, we are not referring to the Lacanian theory of the four discourses (one of them being the discourse of the master) which has been fruitfully used in a variety of political analyses (Lipowatz, 1982; Bracher, 1993, 1994; Verhaeghe, 1995). This type of exclusion in our political reading of Lacan in no way depicts a neglect of the theoretical tools or the research results in question, and is solely due to the space limitations of this volume, the particular interests of the author and the contingent articulation of the structure of this book. It is, however, important to be aware of these limits which are always constitutive since, as Lacan has put it, 'the condition of a [of any] reading is obviously that it imposes limits on itself' (XX: 65).

Although, as we have already argued, the danger of psychologism, when one works with Lacanian theory, is limited and can be clearly avoided, this does not mean that the difference between psychoanalysis and political theory can be eliminated, leading to some sort of unified meta-discourse, to a limitless fusion of politics and psychoanalysis. One warning then remains pertinent before we embark on our theoretico-political journey. Even if Lacanian theory can be made compatible with political theory, Lacan is clearly not a political theorist, not even a philosopher. This is what differentiates him from other major figures in our current terrain of theorising. He was first of all a psychoanalyst. As he points out in his unpublished seminar on *Identification* (1961–2), his teaching is determined by the paths of analytic experience (seminar of 30 May 1962), his whole ontology is founded on this experience (seminar of 27 June 1962). Although we shall not expand on this crucial clinical aspect of Lacanian theory it is important not to lose the provenance of Lacan's ideas from our argumentative horizon. In that sense, the title of this book should be read, first of all, as **Lacan** *and the Political*. Its first crucial dimension is to present some of the basic categories and theoretical insights which Lacan extracts primarily from his clinical experience. Our title, however, should also be read as *Lacan and the* **Political** in the sense that we are particularly interested in these Lacanian concepts that can be useful in approaching and accounting first for our socio-political reality, and then for the political *tout court*. Last but not least, our title should be read as *Lacan* **and** *the Political*. Precisely because Lacan is not a political theorist and because political pathways do

not necessarily lead to psychoanalytic cross-roads this 'and' is of prime
importance. It accounts for the work of a variety of theorists whose
interventions open the way for inter-implicating Lacan and the political
(and whose contributions will be acknowledged throughout this text) and
highlights the 'no man's land' nature of the terrain explored in this book.

As far as the concrete structure of my argument is concerned, I have tried
to introduce the reader step by step to a set of Lacanian concepts and
theories which gradually reveal the relevance of Lacan for our consideration
of the political. Simply put, the first three chapters of the book are laying
down the theoretical, epistemological and even ethical preconditions for the
confluence of Lacan and the political. The first chapter is devoted to the
Lacanian subject, the starting point in most socio-political appropriations of
Lacanian theory. Although immensely fruitful, this kind of approach is
sometimes masking what Lacan has really to contribute to a consideration
of the level of socio-political objectivity *per se*. Hence, in the second chapter,
our interest is focused on the Lacanian understanding of the 'objective'
level, the general field of socio-political reality (the Lacanian object in the
title of this chapter does not refer exclusively to the Lacanian category of
the *objet petit a* but to a multitude of concepts and theoretical schemas that
Lacan contributes to any study of social objectivity in general). The third
chapter is articulated around a Lacanian reading of political reality *stricto
sensu* and in the attempt to define a Lacanian conception of the political.
Needless to say, our attempt to present Lacan's relevance for all these issues
and research areas is not articulated in isolation or in opposition to all other
existing approaches; on the contrary, one of the main tasks of this study is
to discuss the relation of Lacanian theory to other theories, paradigms and
tools (including discourse theory, social constructionism, the sociology of
risk, deconstruction and others), to stress the similarities and agreements
and to pinpoint differences and divergences.

If the first three chapters aim at extracting the importance of the Lacanian conceptual and theoretical apparatus for political analysis and the
theory of politics, the two chapters that follow are designed to demonstrate
some of the ways in which this conceptual apparatus can lead to new
challenging approaches to areas which are crucial for contemporary
political theory and political praxis, namely the crisis of utopian politics and
the ethical foundation of a radical democratic project. Here again, we shall
argue that both a historical and theoretical analysis reveals that the politics
of utopia – which has for long dominated our political horizon – lead to a
set of dangers that no rigorous political analysis and political praxis should
neglect. Its current crisis, instead of being the source of disappointment and
political pessimism, creates the opportunity of 'liberating' our political
imagination from the strait-jacket imposed by a fantasmatic ethics of
harmony, and of developing further the democratic potential of this
imagination in an age in which all sorts of xenophobic, neofascist and

nationalist particularisms and fundamentalisms show again their ugly face. Lacanian theory can be one of the catalysts for these political 'liberations', simultaneously offering a non-foundational ethical grounding for their articulation.

Biographical sketch[11]

Jacques Marie Émile Lacan was born on 13 April 1901, one year after the publication of Freud's *Interpretation of Dreams*. He was the eldest of three children. His father, Charles Marie Alfred Lacan, was the Paris sales representative for a provincial oil and soap manufacturer, and his mother, Émilie Philippine Marie Baudry, a devout Christian who assisted her husband in his work. The Lacan family lived in comfortable conditions in the Boulevard du Beaumarchais before moving to the Montparnasse area. The young Jacques attended a prestigious Jesuit school, the Collège Stanislas where he began to study philosophy, especially the work of Spinoza.

In 1919 he started his medical training in the Faculté de Médecine in Paris. From 1926 onwards he began his specialisation in psychiatry and, in the same year, he co-authored his first publication which appeared in the *Revue Neurologique*. Very soon he becomes *interne des asiles* and then, in 1932, *Chef de Clinique*. He worked for three years in the area of forensic medicine and, in 1932, he received his doctorate diploma in psychiatry. He published his thesis which is entitled *De la psychose paranoiaque dans ses rapports avec la personnalité* (*On Paranoid Psychosis in its Relations to the Personality*). He posted a copy of his doctoral dissertation to Freud who acknowledged receipt by sending him a postcard. In the same year, his translation of Freud's article 'Some Neurotic Mechanisms in Jealousy, Paranoia and Homosexuality' was published in the *Revue Française de Psychanalyse*.

The 1930s marked the development of Lacan's relation to the psychoanalytic and the surrealist movement. He started his training analysis with Rudolph Loewenstein who later, after moving to the United States, became one of the founding fathers and champions of Ego-Psychology. He joined the Société Psychanalytique de Paris (SPP), the French psychoanalytic society officially recognised by the International Psychoanalytic Association (IPA), first, in 1934, as a candidate member, and then, in 1938, as a full member (*Membre Titulaire*). At the same time he became involved in the French surrealist movement. He developed a friendship with Breton and Dalí and published articles in a series of surrealist publications including the journal *Minotaure*. But his interest in intellectual matters did not end here. He met James Joyce and became well acquainted with the work of Jaspers and Heidegger and, of course, Hegel, by attending (together with Queneau, Bataille, Merleau-Ponty, Aron, Klossowski and others) the seminars on Hegel given by Alexandre Kojeve at the École Pratique des Hautes Études.

In 1936 he agreed to write, together with Kojeve, an article comparing Freud with Hegel which was planned to appear in the journal *Recherches philosophiques* with the approval of Koyré; this article was never published.

In 1934 he married Marie-Louise Blondin. Together they had three children; Caroline, born in 1934, Thibaut, in 1939, and Sibylle in 1940. Their marriage lasted until 1941. In 1939 Lacan began a relationship with Sylvia Bataille, an actress formerly married to George Bataille, and 1941 marked the birth of their daughter, Judith. He married Sylvia in 1953.

After the war, Lacan was recognised as one of the major theorists of the SPP and, as a member of its training committee, he introduced new statutes, making psychoanalytic training available to non-medical candidates. Eventually he was elected president of the SPP but this development produced a lot of controversy and a series of disagreements often focusing on Lacan's technique (including his introduction of analytic sessions of variable duration). The controversy led to the formation, mainly by Lagache, of a new psychoanalytic society, the *Société Française de Psychanalyse* (SFP). Lacan resigned from the SPP and joined the SFP in 1953. In the same year he started his public seminar (he was conducting a private seminar from 1951) at the Sainte-Anne hospital. In 1956 the SFP launched its journal; the first issue was devoted to the work of Lacan. He translated Heidegger's paper 'Logos' which was published in *La Psychanalyse*. The influence of his friend Claude Lévi-Strauss as well as that of structural linguistics (Saussure and Jakobson) was becoming increasingly apparent in his work.

The SFP applied for recognition by the International Psychoanalytic Association but the IPA asked for the termination of Lacan's training programme. In 1963 the SFP gave in to the demands of the IPA. Lacan was effectively forced to resign from the SFP and to stop his seminar at Saint-Anne. He was invited by Fernand Braudel to continue his seminar at the École Pratique, and, with the encouragement of Louis Althusser, he resumed his seminar in January 1964 at the École Normale Supérieure. Meanwhile, he acknowledged the importance of Foucault's book on *Madness and Civilization*. He founded the École Freudienne de Paris (EFP). A 900-page collection of his essays was published under the title *Écrits*, boosting his reputation both in France and internationally. While in his thesis he acknowledged the importance of Claude, Pinchon and others of his teachers in psychiatry for his development, now he considered Gaetan Gatian de Clerambault as his sole master in psychiatry, pointing out that he owed to him his encounter with the Freudian *corpus*. He was invited, in 1966, to visit the United States where he addressed the conference on 'The Languages of Criticism and the Sciences of Man' organised at the Johns Hopkins University. In 1969 a Lacanian department of Psychoanalysis was founded at the new and controversial Université de Paris VIII at Vincennes (later to be transferred to Saint-Denis).

Although Lacan was very critical of revolutionary action he was held by some as partly responsible for the events of May 1968 and was asked to leave the École Normale Supérieure. In fact, direct engagement in politics was always a problematic area in his personal life; he could be described as rather apolitical and sceptical in terms of his personal commitment to political action, although he was intrigued by political issues. This sceptical attitude brings to mind Freud's scepticism illustrated in his 'half-conversion' to Bolshevism: when he was told that communism would bring at first some hard years and then harmony and happiness, he answered that he believed in the first half of this programme.[12] During that period, though, Lacan for the first time added his signature to a petition asking for the liberation of Regis Debray, who was imprisoned in Bolivia, and on 9 May 1968 he signed a manifesto supporting the student movement. On 2 December 1969, however, speaking to hundreds of students he offered them the following statement: 'Revolutionary aspirations have only one possibility: always to end up in the discourse of the master. Experience has proven this. What you aspire to as revolutionaries is a master. You will have one!' (Lacan in Julien, 1994: 64). He moved his seminar to the Faculté de Droit at the Pantheon. In 1973, his first published seminar appeared, edited by Jacques-Alain Miller; it is his seminar of 1964, *The Four Fundamental Concepts of Psychoanalysis*.

In 1974, Lacan reorganised the Department of Psychoanalysis at Vincennes and authorised Jacques-Alain Miller to be its chairman. A two-part interview with Lacan was broadcast by French television and, in 1975, he travelled again to the United States, where he gave lectures at Yale, Columbia University and MIT. Five years later his son-in-law was elected to the board of directors of the EFP amid a lot of controversy and accusations of nepotism. As the protest mounted, Lacan decided to dissolve unilaterally the EFP (the dissolution is ratified by the EFP on 27 September 1980). He founded the École de la Cause Freudienne and travelled to Venezuela to open the first international congress of the Fondation du Champ Freudien, which had been founded by himself and his daughter, Judith Miller, in 1979. He died in 1981.

1

THE LACANIAN SUBJECT

The impossibility of identity and the centrality of identification

Prolegomena

Having drawn the attention of the reader to the problems involved and the precautions that are necessary in any project linking Lacanian theory and the political (problems that stem both from the difficulties entailed in all attempts at bringing together psychoanalysis and the political and from the particular *status* of Lacanian theory), but also having sketched some of the gains anticipated from such an enterprise – and after the brief summary of contents and Lacan's biography with which my introduction came to a conclusion – it is now time to start our exploration of Lacanian theory and its relevance for socio-political analysis, especially for a theory of the political. Our starting point, to which this first chapter is devoted, is the Lacanian conception of the subject. A subject that by being essentially split and alienated becomes the *locus* of an impossible identity, the place where a whole politics of identification takes place. It is this subject which is generally considered as Lacan's major contribution to contemporary theory and political analysis.

There is no doubt that poststructuralism is gradually but steadily hegemonising our theoretical and cultural milieu (especially as far as it concerns areas such as cultural studies and social theory). Lacan has been hailed as one of the cornerstones of this movement together with Jacques Derrida and others.[1] For Sam Weber, 'the writings of Lacan, together with those of Derrida, remain, today perhaps more than ever, two of the most powerful forces working to keep the alterity of language from being isolated and foreclosed', and thus to keep poststructuralism alive and kicking (Weber, 1991: xii). What seems to be the most interesting idea behind the poststructuralist appropriation of Lacan is that Lacanian theory can provide poststructuralism with a new conception of subjectivity compatible with its own theoretical foundations. And although to many poststructuralists such a project might seem self-defeating (since poststructuralism is supposed *per definitionem* not to need the subject any more), others lament 'the absence of an adequate poststructuralist (or should I say post-poststructuralist) theory of subjectivity' (Johnson in Bracher, 1993: 11). The Lacanian subject is celebrated as capable of filling this lack in poststructuralist theorisation.

This is not the case only with poststructuralism. It seems that the Lacanian subject can fill a lot of lacks and that lacks are increasingly proliferating around us (or maybe today we are becoming more aware of their presence and alert to their persistence). To provide only a few examples, giving particular attention to those having some political relevance, Rosalind Coward and John Ellis point out that 'Lacan's subject is therefore this new subject of dialectical materialism....The emphasis on language provides a route for an elaboration of the subject demanded by dialectical materialism' (Coward and Ellis, 1977: 93). Michele Barrett, for her part, argues that 'psychoanalysis [and she is mainly referring to Lacan] is the place one might reasonably start to correct the lamentable *lack* of attention paid to subjectivity within Marxism's theory of ideology' (Barrett, 1991: 118–19, my emphasis), while Mark Bracher concludes that 'Lacanian theory can provide the sort of account of subjectivity that cultural criticism needs' (Bracher, 1993: 12). To sum up, the core idea of this argument is that Lacan is relevant for contemporary socio-political analysis because of his vision of the human subject. As Feher-Gurewich states *à propos* of social theory: 'Lacan's psychoanalytic approach is founded on premises that are in sharp contrast to the ones which have led to the failure of an alliance between psychoanalysis and social theory'. And what are these premises? 'Lacan provides social theory with a vision of the human subject that sheds new light on the relations between individual aspirations and social aims' (Feher-Gurewich, 1996: 154).

Simply put, the Lacanian conception of subjectivity is called to remedy the shortcomings or 'supplement' – this term is not used here in its strictest Derridean sense, although a deconstructionist flavour is not entirely absent – poststructuralism, social theory, cultural criticism, theory of ideology, etc. But isn't such a move a reductionist move *par excellence*? Although our own approach, as it will be developed in the following chapters, is clearly located beyond a logic of supplementation, it would be unfair to consider the Lacanian subject as the point of an unacceptable reduction. This would be the case only if the Lacanian notion of subjectivity was a simple reproduction of an essentialist subject, of a subject articulated around a single positive essence which is transparent to itself and fully representable in theoretical discourse. But this essentialist subject, the subject of the humanist philosophical tradition, the Cartesian subject, or even the Marxist reductionist subject whose essence is identified with her or his class interests, is exactly what has to be questioned and has been questioned; it cannot be part of the solution because it forms part of the initial problem. The Lacanian subject is clearly located beyond such an essentialist, simplistic

14

notion of subjectivity. Not only is Lacan 'obviously the most distant from those who operate with essentialist categories or simplistic notions of psychic cause or origin' (Barrett, 1991: 107), but the Lacanian subject is radically opposing and transcending all these tendencies without, however, throwing away the baby together with the bath water, that is to say, the *locus* of the subject together with its essentialist formulations.

For Lacan it is 'true that the philosopher's *cogito* is at the centre of the *mirage* that renders modern man so sure of being himself even in his uncertainties about himself' (E: 165). But this essentialist fantasy, reducing subjectivity to the conscious ego, cannot sustain itself any more: 'the myth of the unity of the personality, the myth of synthesis...all these types of organisation of the objective field constantly reveal cracks, tears and rents, negation of the facts and misrecognition of the most immediate experience' (III: 8). It is clear that the Freudian discovery of the unconscious, of an agency splitting the subject of this whole tradition, cannot be overlooked; it brings to the fore something that this tradition had to foreclose in order to sustain itself. As Lacan formulates it in the 'Freudian Thing', as a result of Freud's discovery the very centre of the human being is no longer to be found at the place the humanist tradition had assigned to it (E: 114). It follows that, for Lacan, any project of asserting the autonomy of this essentialist free ego is equally unacceptable – which is not the same, of course, with promoting heteronomy as a general theoretical or political principle: 'I designated that the discourse of freedom is essential to modern man insofar as he is structured by a certain conception of his own autonomy. I pointed out its fundamentally biased and incomplete, inexpressible, fragmentary, differentiated, and profoundly delusional character [which should not be confused with psychosis but, nevertheless, operates 'in the same place']' (III: 145). Lacan argues that Freud's discovery of the unconscious is more radical than both the Copernican and the Darwinian revolutions in that they both left intact the belief in the identity between human subject and conscious ego. In his view, we owe to Freud the possibility of effecting a subversion of this conception of the subject. It is the subversion of the subject as *cogito* which, in fact, makes psychoanalysis possible (E: 296): psychoanalysis opposes 'any philosophy issuing directly from the *cogito*' (E: 1).[2]

But if Lacan dynamitises the essentialist conception of subjectivity, if he moves beyond the metaphysics of a conscious (present) subjectivity, what does he introduce in its place? (Because in opposition to poststructuralists who, in reality, eliminate the *locus* of the subject by reducing it to a set of subject positions, Lacan does introduce something.) 'We are told that man is the measure of all things. But where is his own measure? Is it to be found in himself?' he asks in his first seminar (I: 68). And the answer is no. If there is an 'essence' in man it is not to be found at the level of representation, in his representation of himself. The subject is not some sort of psychological *substratum* that can be reduced to its own representation. Once this is granted the way is open to develop an alternative definition of subjectivity. If there is an essence in the Lacanian subject it is precisely 'the lack of essence' (Chaitin, 1996: 196). And this lack may acquire a quasi-transcendental structure but it does not reproduce traditional metaphysics as some commentators seem to imply (see, in this respect, the discussion of Lacoue-Labarthe and Nancy's *The Title of the Letter* (1992) in Chapter 3).

The roots of this conception of subjectivity can be traced back to the Freudian idea of a *Spaltung* (splitting) characteristic of the human condition. Freud never elevated this idea to an epicentre of his theories, but he uses the term from time to time in order to refer to the internal division of the psyche, as in the separation between different psychical agencies (unconscious and conscious/pre-conscious systems) (Laplanche and Pontalis, 1988: 427–8). In addition, within Freudian theory the conception of the 'Splitting of the Ego' (*Ich-spaltung*) is primarily used with reference to fetishism and psychosis. Lacan, for his part, sees this split as something constitutive of subjectivity in general. It is clear, therefore, that Lacan's standpoint differs in two crucial respects from Freud's. While Freud does not refer to the concept of the subject which has mainly philosophical relevance, Lacan, from the very start of his teaching, focuses his theoretical edifice on the idea of subjectivity, which he understands as fundamentally split, thus generalising Freud's idea of the *Ich-spaltung*.

Lacan always presented the idea of an irreducible split in subjectivity as the most crucial truth discovered by Freud. No matter how often – or how rarely – Freud used the term *Spaltung*, it cannot be denied that the discovery of the unconscious itself is a sufficient basis for its formulation and legitimisation, as well as for the generalisation that Lacan is promoting. In his own words:

> But if we ignore the self's radical ex-centricity to itself with which man is confronted, in other words, the truth discovered by Freud, we shall falsify both the order and methods of psychoanalytic mediation; we shall make of it nothing more than the compromise operation that it has, in effect, become, namely, just what the letter as well the spirit of Freud's work most repudiates.
>
> (E: 171).[3]

In his seminar on *The Formations of the Unconscious* (1957–8) Lacan reaffirms that the subject of psychoanalysis is not the subject of knowledge as it is constructed in the tradition of philosophy, that is to say, as corresponding to consciousness, but the subject as structured around a radical split, the Freudian *Spaltung* (seminar of 14 May 1958). Since the Lacanian conception of subjectivity has been widely acknowledged as the starting point *par excellence* for the socio-political appropriation of Lacan, our aim in this chapter will be to trace the formulation of this lacking subject within Lacanian theory and to map some of its socio-political implications.

Alienation in the imaginary: 'the ego is essentially an alter ego'

As with most Lacanian concepts it is easier to approach the concept of the subject in Lacan by pointing out not what it is but what it is not, that is to say through a certain *via negativa*.[4] The Lacanian subject becomes relevant for every philosophical discussion of the political exactly because it is not identical to the 'individual' or the 'conscious subject' presupposed in everyday discourse, but also implied in traditional Anglo-American philosophy and political analysis, from Rawls to rational choice theories.[5] Most of these accounts of subjectivity reduce the subject to the ego. And the Lacanian subject, as we have already pointed out, is definitely not reducible to the ego. Distinguishing the subject from the ego has been a fundamental orientation of Lacanian theory ever since Lacan's first seminar. It is necessary at this point to clarify this important distinction. In Lacan's view, the ego can only be described as a sedimentation of idealised images which are internalised during the period Lacan names the 'mirror stage'.[6] Before this phase the self as such, as a unified whole, does not exist. In the mirror stage, during the period from the sixth to the eighteenth month of the infant's life, the fragmentation experienced by the infant is transformed into an affirmation of its bodily unity through the assumption of its image in the mirror. This is how the infant acquires its first sense of unity and identity, a spatial imaginary identity.

At first, the infant appears jubilant due to its success in integrating its fragmentation into an imaginary totality and unity. Later on, however, the joyous affirmation of imaginary unity is replaced by a resurfacing of the distance between this new unity and the continuing fragmentary, uncoordinated and lacking character of the infant's lived experience of its real body. Besides, the image in the mirror could never be identical to the infant since it is always of different size, it is inverted as all mirror images are, and, most importantly, it remains something alien — and thus fundamentally alienating:

> The fact is that the total form of the body by which the subject anticipates in a mirage the maturation of his powers is given to him only as a *Gestalt*, that is to say, in an exteriority in which this form is certainly more constituent than constituted, but in which it appears to him above all in a contrasting size (*un relief de stature*) that fixes it and in a symmetry that inverts it, in contrast with the turbulent movements that the subject feels are animating him. Thus,

this *Gestalt*...by these two aspects of its appearance, symbolises the mental permanence of the I, at the same time as it prefigures its alienating destination.

(E: 2)

The ego, the image in which we recognise ourselves, is always an alien *alter ego*: we are 'originally an inchoate collection of desires – there you have the true sense of the expression *fragmented body* [very well depicted, according to Lacan, in the art of Hieronymus Bosch] – and the initial synthesis of the ego is essentially an alter ego, it is alienated. The desiring human subject is constructed around a centre which is the other insofar as he gives the subject his unity' (III: 39). In this regard, the Lacanian theory of the mirror stage is probably one of the first instances in which the radical ex-centricity of human subjectivity is recognised within our cultural terrain.

What is most important here is that in the mirror stage, the first jubilant moment is anticipating its own failure. Any imaginary unity based on the mirror stage is founded on an irreducible gap: 'the human being has a special relation with his own image – a relation of gap, of alienating tension' (II: 323). Unity in the imaginary is a result of captivation, of a power relation between the infant and its image. But this captivation, the anticipation of synthesis, can never eliminate the real uncoordination of the body of the infant, it can never erase the external and alienating character of its own foundation. This ambiguity is never resolved. One important consequence of this is that narcissism starts appearing in a different light, as constituting the basis of aggressive tension: the imaginary is clearly the prime source of aggressivity in human affairs.[7] What characterises every narcissistic relation is its deep 'ambiguity' (III: 92–3). The ambiguity of the imaginary is primarily due to the need to identify with something external, other, different, in order to acquire the basis of a self-unified identity. The implication is that the 'reflecting specular image' in imaginary relations, 'always contains within itself an element of difference': what is supposed to be 'ours' is itself a source of 'alienation'. In that sense, 'every purely imaginary equilibrium or balance with the other is always marked by a fundamental instability' (Lacan in Wilden, 1968: 481). This alienating dimension of the ego, the constitutive dependence of every imaginary identity on the alienating exteriority of a never fully internalised mirror image, subverts the whole idea of a stable reconciled subjectivity based on the conception of the autonomous ego. It is not surprising then that when Lacan discusses the idea of the autonomous ego in the 'Freudian Thing' it is enough for him to say 'It is autonomous! That's a good one!' (E: 132).

If the imaginary representation of ourselves, the mirror image, is incapable of providing us with a stable identity, the only option left for acquiring one seems to be the field of linguistic representation, the symbolic register. In fact, the symbolic is already presupposed in the functioning of the mirror

stage (which highlights the fact that, for Lacan, the passage from the
imaginary to the symbolic is a theoretical abstraction pointing to a certain
logical and not strictly speaking chronological order). From the time of its
birth, and even before that, the infant is inserted in a symbolic network
constructed by its parents and family. The infant's name is sometimes
chosen before it is born and its life is interwoven, in the parents' imagination, with a pre-existing family mythology. This whole framework, while the
new-born is not aware of it, is destined to influence its psychic development.
Even the images with which we identify in the mirror stage derive from how
our parents see us (thus being symbolically sanctioned) and are linguistically
structured, which explains why the mirror stage takes place around the
period the child is first inserted into language and starts developing its own
linguistic skills. In his unpublished seminar on *Anxiety* (1962–3) Lacan
explicitly points out that the articulation of the subject to the imaginary and
the symbolic Other do not exist separately. Already in the first jubilant
moment of the mirror stage, when the infant assumes itself as a functioning
totality in its specular image, already at that point of inaugural recognition,
it turns back towards the one who is carrying it, who is supporting and
sustaining it, to the representative of the big Other (parent, relative, etc.), as
if to call for his or her approval (seminar of 28 November 1962). In that
sense, the specular image has to be ratified by the symbolic Other in order to
start functioning as the basis of the infant's imaginary identification: every
imaginary position is conceivable only on the condition that one finds a
guide beyond this imaginary order, a symbolic guide (I: 141).[8] Lacan
illuminates further this particular relation of the imaginary to the symbolic
in his seminar on *The Psychoses*: 'While the image equally plays a capital
role in our domain [a role dominant, although not absolute, during the
mirror stage], this role is completely taken up and caught up within,
remoulded and reanimated by, the symbolic order. The image is always
more or less integrated into this order' (III: 9). It is the symbolic that 'binds
and orients', that gives consistency to the imaginary instances of human
experience (III: 28). If the ego emerges in the imaginary the subject emerges
in the symbolic.[9]

Alienation in the symbolic[10]: 'the subject takes a structure
from the signifier'

Let us now focus on the passage from the imaginary to the symbolic
dimension of identity; it is, first of all, a passage depicting the chronological
development of Lacanian theory, but it is also a way of introducing Lacan's
theoretical insights in a logically coherent and pedagogically accessible

manner. If the imaginary, the field of specular images, of spatial unities and totalised representations, is always built on an illusion which is ultimately alienating for the child, his or her only recourse is to turn to the symbolic level, seeking in language a means to acquire a stable identity.[11] By submitting to the laws of language the child becomes a subject in language, it inhabits language, and hopes to gain an adequate representation through the world of words: 'the symbolic provides a form into which the subject is inserted at the level of his being. It's on this basis that the subject recognises himself as being this or that' (III: 179). As Lacan puts it in his unpublished seminar on *Identification* (1961–2), the signifier determines the subject, the subject takes on a structure from it (seminar of 30 May 1962). In *The Four Fundamental Concepts of Psychoanalysis* this thesis is reiterated with clarity: 'the subject is the subject of the signifier – determined by it' (XI: 67). The subject comes to being as long as it agrees to be represented by the signifier: 'it is the symbolic order which is constitutive for the subject' (II: 29). In that sense, it depends on the signifier, it is located in a secondary position with respect to the signifier. This is what Lacan, in his seminar on Poe's *Purloined Letter*, describes as the 'pre-eminence of the signifier over the subject' (1988: 51).

But instead of transgressing alienation in the direction of acquiring a solid identity, the subject of the signifier, the subject constituted on the basis of the acceptance of the laws of language, is uncovered as the subject of lack *par excellence*. Already this is indicative of the political relevance of the Lacanian category of the lacking subject. This lack can only be thought as a trace of the ineliminable act of power at the root of the formation of subjectivity, as the trace of an *ex nihilo* decision entailing the loss of certain possibilities or psychic states (the imaginary relation with the mother, for example) and the formation of new ones. As mentioned above, the subject can only exist on the condition that it accepts the laws of the symbolic. It becomes an effect of the signifier. In that sense it is a certain subordination, an exercise of power, that constitutes the condition of possibility for the constitution of subjectivity. Judith Butler is right when, in her recent book *The Psychic Life of Power*, she argues that there is no formation of subjectivity without subordination, the passionate attachment to those by whom she or he (the subject in question) is subordinated (Butler, 1997: 7). It seems however that she remains within the limits of a somewhat traditional conceptualisation of power when she is personalising her account (those to whom we are subordinated are presumably our parents, especially during our early formative years). In Lacan, it is the signifier that is revealed as the *locus* of this power forming the subject: 'power is coterminous with the logic of the signifier' (Dyrberg, 1997: 130). This power of the signifier cannot be reduced to the physical presence or the behaviour of the biological parents. As we shall shortly see, it is the Name-of-the-Father, the symbolic and not the real father, who is the agent of this power, the agent of symbolic Law.

Obviously, this symbolic dimension of power is different from its imaginary dimension.[12] Imaginary power is limited within a destructive game of rivalry between equals. Symbolic power, on the other hand, is based on the recognition of difference, and makes possible the institution of a certain order: the imaginary destruction of the other can be replaced by a coexistence by pact (Julien, 1994: 55). The Other, the field of the symbolic, is the order of a Master and a Guarantor (seminar of 9 May 1962); coexistence is never a natural given but an effect of symbolic power. To this symbolic dimension of power we will return in a while; for the time being, and this is a prerequisite for any further elaboration of the symbolic dimension of power within the Lacanian problematic of subjectivity, let us concentrate on the Lacanian conception of the symbolic.

Lacan's radical decentrement of subjectivity with respect to the signifier depends on a particular understanding of this symbolic level, the register of the signifier, the big Other. This conception of the symbolic is developed through Lacan's encounter with structural linguistics. It is to this encounter that we have to turn our attention now. To start with, we know that the main aim of Lacan's return to Freud was to reinvigorate analytic theory by taking into account developments in the vanguard of the scientific thought of his age. He considered linguistics, as founded by Saussure – since Saussure 'can truly be said to be the founder of modern linguistics' (E: 125) – as the guide in such an enterprise, a role he would later assign to mathematics and topology:[13] 'Linguistics can serve as a guide here, since that is the role it plays in the vanguard of contemporary anthropology, and we cannot possibly remain indifferent to it' (E: 73). Linguistics is of great importance for psychoanalysis for two main reasons. First of all, it can assist in the development of analytic theory, a development which depends, for Lacan, on its adequate formalisation:

> Psychoanalysis has played a role in the direction of modern subjectivity, and it cannot continue to sustain its role without bringing it into line with the movement in modern science that elucidates it. This is the problem of the grounding that must assure our discipline its place among the sciences: a problem of formalization, which, it must be admitted, has not got off to a very good start.
>
> (E: 72)

And, of course, linguistics is suitable for this psychoanalytic reappropriation because analysis operates through language: psychoanalysts are 'practitioners of the symbolic function', and it would thus be astonishing if they should 'turn away from probing deeper into it, to the extent of failing to recognise (méconnâitre) that it is this function that situates us at the heart of the movement that is now establishing a new order of the sciences' (E: 72). Lacan's advice 'Read Saussure' (E: 125) is furthermore legitimised by

21

the fact that Freud himself saw language as the grounding of his discovery of the unconscious. Lacan's argument is that Freud had anticipated Saussure since his main interest, from the time of *The Interpretation of Dreams* (1900) is not to articulate a psychology of dreams but to explore their elaboration, that is to say their linguistic structure (E: 259). Lacan makes very clear that what Freud presents as formations of the unconscious – jokes, dreams, symptoms – are nothing but the result of his ability to discern the primary *status* of language.

Thus, Lacan's strategy is to use modern linguistics in order to 'recover' the truth of the Freudian enterprise, a truth long lost for analytic theory. Is this, though, his sole motivation? There is no doubt that this is a two-way movement. By searching in Freud for a certain linguistic element, Lacan reconstructs Freud in a way influenced by modern linguistics. The strategic genius of Lacan's move is that while interpreting Freud according to his view of modern linguistic theory he can also claim to recover the lost meaning of Freud.[14] This is not to say that, for Lacan, psychoanalysis is reducible to linguistics. As we shall see, it is a particular reading of linguistic theory which can be made relevant for analytic theory. This is again a two-way movement. In other words, the linguistic insights which are of interest for psychoanalysis are already constructed and defined through a particular analytic reading of structural linguistics. What psychoanalysis discovers in linguistics becomes equivalent only to what linguistics can mean within a psychoanalytic framework. The nodal points of Lacanian theory emerge as the points that over-determine the specific terms of the relation between the two domains. Within this dialectic Lacan seems almost to be fulfilling Saussure's own thesis that psychology will determine the proper use of semiology, although in a way that Saussure was certainly in no position to foresee. In *Encore* (1972–3) it becomes clear that, in Lacan's schema, Saussure's *langue* is effectively substituted by Lacan's *lalangue*, that Lacan's linguistic insights do not really belong to linguistics but institute a separate terrain of *linguistérie*: 'The fact that I say (*Mon dire*) that the unconscious is structured like a language is not part and parcel of the field of linguistics' (XX: 15).[15]

Lacan starts his exploration of structural linguistics with the founding stone of modern linguistics, the concept of the sign. For Saussure, language is a formal system which is constructed on the basis of pure difference: 'In the language itself there are only differences' (Saussure, 1983: 118). The content of a word is not determined by what it contains but by what exists outside it. The value of a concept is purely differential: concepts are defined negatively by contrast with other items in the same linguistic system (Saussure, 1983: 115). Accordingly, defining one unit demands taking into account the whole structure of language, a structure that classical structuralism accepts as a closed system – this closure will later on be disputed and deconstructed by poststructuralism. But Saussure retains the concept of difference as applicable only to the levels of the signifier (the 'sound pattern') and the signified (the 'concept') when viewed independently from one another. Viewed together they produce something positive: the sign. Lacan is not keen in retaining this isomorphism characteristic of the Saussurean schema. In that he is in agreement with developments in linguistics towards a greater formalism; he seems to be in touch, for example, with the theoretical progress from Saussure to Jakobson and Hjelmslev: if all language is form and not substance and if an isomorphism exists between these two levels, then it becomes very difficult to differentiate them without reintroducing some conception of substance. If, for Saussure, isomorphism functioned as a trap, Lacan is clear from the beginning that there is no isomorphism between the two domains, that of the signifier and that of the signified. Their relation is not a relation of two equivalent levels.

There is, however, one more problem with the Saussurean schema beyond the form/substance relation in its strict sense. Saussure, despite his efforts to avoid such a development, appears to be reintroducing a representationalist conception of signification. In Saussure, the distinction between signifier and signified can be described as 'a relic, within a theory allergic to it, of a representationalist problematic of the sign' (Borch-Jacobsen, 1991: 175). It is clear that Lacan's reformulation of Saussurean linguistics moves beyond any such kind of representationalism. Lacan articulates a refined position which seems to take into account the critique of the Saussurean idea of the arbitrariness of the sign. For Saussure, arbitrariness is a defining characteristic of the relation between signifier and signified, a relation which is conceived as alien to any kind of natural connection. It is this idea of the absence of any natural connection that puzzles Benveniste. If by signified we mean the concept and not the referent (as Saussure was keen to point out from the beginning) then what is the meaning of Saussure's statement that there is no natural connection between the two domains? Why would one think something like that?

> It is clear that the argument is falsified by an unconscious and sur-
> reptitious recourse to a third term which was not included in the ini-
> tial definition. This third term is the thing itself, reality. Even
> though Saussure said that the idea of 'sister' is connected to the sig-
> nifier *s-ö-r*, he was not thinking any the less of the *reality* of the no-
> tion. When he spoke of the difference between *b-ö-f* and *o-k-s*, he
> was referring in spite of himself to the fact that these two terms ap-
> plied to the same *reality*. Here, then, is the *thing*, expressly excluded
> at first from the definition of the sign, now creeping into it by de-
> tour, and permanently installing a contradiction there.
>
> (Benveniste, 1966: 44)

This contradiction is never resolved in Saussure's work, since the problem of external reality is never elaborated in length. There is a certain realist representationalism still haunting Saussure's work or some of its many applications:[16] between the lines it seems to be presupposed that the signified precedes the emergence of the signifier which is there only in order to express and communicate it; meaning springs from the signified to the signifier (Barthes, 1990); language is conceived as standing in for or as being identical with the real world (Coward and Ellis, 1977: 47). As Derrida has put it, in such a schema,

> not only do signifier and signified seem to unite, but in this confusion, the signifier seems to be erased or to become transparent so as to let the concept [a concept linked to external reality] present itself, just as if it were referring to nothing but its own presence.
>
> (Derrida, 1981: 32–3)

For Lacan, a theory of meaning founded on a recourse to some kind of referent, to a supposedly accessible order of objective reality, is clearly insufficient. Lacanian theory offers a tentative solution to this problem by subverting the relation between the signifier and the signified. Instead of the unity between the signifier and the signified, Lacan stresses their division; if unity prioritises the signified, division gives priority to the signifier over the production of the signified, a production which only now becomes fully elucidated.

Thus, although starting from a Saussurean angle, Lacan draws a very different distinction between signifier and signified from that of Saussure. What is most important here is that, although this second order interacts historically on the first, it is the structure of the first that governs the direction of the second (E: 126) – this position will be further radicalised in the course of Lacan's teaching. In 'Agency of the Letter' (1957) Lacan makes a crucial move with reference to the Saussurean algorithm, which he presents as S/s. This is an algorithm regulating the relation between signifier and signified. Lacan attributes this primordial position of the signifier to Saussure himself although it seems quite clear from his presentation that he is aware that this is not the way it is found in Saussure's schemas; he thinks nevertheless that this is a legitimate interpretation. It is certainly one which permits him to adapt the Saussurean concept to the analytic framework, and, at the same time, lay his claim on Saussure's legacy (a strategy he used successfully in his reading of Freud). Here, the signifier (S) is located over the signified (s), this 'over' corresponding to the bar separating them, a barrier resisting signification. This barrier is exactly what makes possible 'an exact study of the connections proper to the signifier, and of the extent of their function in the genesis of the signified' (E: 149). If the dominant factor here is the bar which disrupts the unity of the Saussurean sign, then the unity of signification can only be an illusion. What creates this illusion (the effect of the signified) is the play of the signifiers: 'the signifier alone guarantees the theoretical coherence of the whole as a whole' (E: 126).

In Lacan's schema then, the signifier is not something which functions as a representation of the signified; nor is the meaning of the algorithm S/s that there is a parallelism between the two levels, between that of the signifier and that of the signified. Simply put, meaning is produced by signifiers; it springs from the signifier to the signified and not vice versa (as argued by realist representationalism). It is this idea that Lacan captures with his famous example of the toilet doors. In this case the signified – loosely defined as external reality – is the same – two identical doors presumably leading to two identical toilets. What creates the different meaning in each case, what creates the difference between the ladies' toilet and the gentlemen's toilet is the different signifier, that is to say the fact that each door carries a different label ('Ladies' and 'Gentlemen'). The signifier manifests the presence of difference and nothing else, making impossible any connection between signs and things. In other words, reference to signs implies a reference to things as guarantees of signification, something which Saussure himself was ultimately unable to avoid, while the notion of the primacy of the signifier breaks with such representationalist connotations. If an intuitive theory of meaning is usually based on a 'picturing' or denotative schema, as exhibited in the Augustinian picture of language according to which words signify objects,[17] Lacan clearly subverts this simplistic theory. At this point, however, it is crucial to avoid a common misconception. This subversion is not effected through the elimination of the structural position of the signified.

What happens then to the signified in the Lacanian schema? Lacan understands the signified as an effect of transference. If we speak about the signified it is only because we like to believe in its existence. It is a belief crucial for our construction of reality as a coherent, 'objective' whole; a belief in something that guarantees the validity of our knowledge, sustaining the fantasy of an *adaequatio* between language and the world. But for Lacan, as he argues in his seminar on *The Psychoses* (1955–6), even 'the transference of the signified, so essential to human life, is possible only by virtue of the structure of the signifier' (III: 226). Put another way, 'the supposed realism of describing the real by details is only conceivable in the register of an organized signifier...the formal articulation of the signifier predominates with respect to transference of the signified' (III: 229). Lacan then is radicalising the semiological idea, implicit in Saussure and expressed by Barthes, that 'it appears increasingly more difficult to conceive a system of images and objects whose signifieds can exist independently of language....The world of signifieds is none other than that of language' (Barthes, 1973: 10). The signified is never a full presence constituted outside language. Lacan's radicalisation, however, entails the definitive break with the isomorphism between signifier and signified and a refined resolution of the problem of external reality. The archimedian point of his solution is the following: the symbolic is not the order of the sign, as in Saussurean linguistics, but the order of the signifier. Meaning is produced by the signifier: 'It's the signifier that creates the field of meanings' (III: 292). An example from socio-political analysis may serve to elucidate this point. As Pierre Bourdieu points out, it is evident that the constitution of an organised social or political movement out of the mass of a dominated group, through, for example, the act of symbolisation by which the spokesperson of the movement is chosen, coincides with the constituting of the group *per se*:

> the sign creates the thing signified, the signifier is identified with the thing signified which would not exist without it, and which can be reduced to it. The signifier is not only that which expresses and represents the signified group: it is that which *signifies* to it that it exists, that which has the power to call into visible existence, by mobilizing it, the group that it signifies.
>
> (Bourdieu, 1991: 207)

In Lacan, who is more radical in this respect than Bourdieu, the signifier is capable of producing meaning due to the fact that it does not refer to any 'signified' object. It is the sign of an absence (III: 167). Every signification refers to another one and so on and so forth; the signified is lost in the metonymic sliding characteristic of the signifying chain. As Lacan suggests, 'Our starting point, the point we keep coming back to, since we shall always be at the starting point, is that every real signifier is, as such, a signifier that signifies nothing' (III: 185).

This disappearance of the signified (not as a structural position but as the real point of reference of signification) is due to a complex and even paradoxical but effective strategy designed to avoid Sausssure's cul-de-sacs (or the dangers of a simplistic representationalism in general). Surprisingly enough, for Lacan, the signified disappears because it is no longer associated with the concept, as in Saussure, but is conceived as belonging to the order of the real; that's why the bar dividing signifier and signified, instead of constituting an intimate link between them, instead of creating the unity of the sign, is understood as a barrier resisting signification, as a limit marking the intersection of the symbolic with the real (Boothby, 1991: 127). Put another way, Lacan accepts from the beginning what Saussure denied but was forced to introduce through the back door. In Lacan, however, this relation between the signified and the real is accepted only to be located at the limit of signification and not in its kernel. The signified disappears as such, that is to say as the epicentre of signification, exactly because in its real dimension it is situated beyond the level of the symbolic. What is retained is the *locus* of the signified which is now designated by a constitutive lack. What is also retained is the promise or the aspiration of attaining the lost/impossible signified, to fill in the vacuum in the *locus* of the absent signified. Signification is articulated around the illusion of attaining the signified; but this illusion itself is a result of the signifying play. The signified, as we have pointed out, is an effect created by the signifier in the process of signification. The conceptual content of an utterance, as Jameson points out, has to be seen as a meaning effect; it is the relationship between signifiers that produces the objective mirage of signification (Jameson, 1991: 26). It is the signifier, in other words, that determines the illusory effect of the signified: 'the signifier has an active function, while the signifiable – that which can be signified – endures its mark. The signified is caused by the signifier' (Klotz, 1995: 94). The illusion of a stable meaning is an effect of the play of signifiers; Lacan's theory of meaning is thus situated beyond any representationalist problematic. What he means by this is that if there is a signified it can only be a signifier to which we attribute a transferential signified function. The signified is a linguistic 'subject supposed to know', or rather 'object supposed to know' what a signifier signifies for a subject.

But now a certain confusion seems to contaminate our argument. What is the exact *status* of the signified? Is the signified real or imaginary? At first we argued that the signified is the effect of transferential illusion, an imaginary entity. Later on we introduced the signified as pertaining to the real order, an order beyond signification. Lacan seems to be accepting two opposite definitions of the signified. A more careful examination reveals however that this is not the result of some kind of conceptual confusion but Lacan's ingenious solution to the problem of meaning. A rigorous Lacanian approach to the terrain of meaning and signification has to take into account all the three dimensions involved; the real, the imaginary and the symbolic register. According to Lacan, the signified, what is *supposed* to be, through its links to external reality, the source of signification, indeed belongs to the real. But this is a real that resists symbolisation – this is the definition of the real in Lacan; the real is what cannot be symbolised, the impossible. Surely, if this real is always absent from the level of signification it *cannot* be in itself and by itself the source of this same signification. Its absence however, the constitutive lack of the signified as real, *can*. This lack constitutes something absolutely crucial for signification. This absence has to be compensated if signification is to acquire any coherence. It is the absence of the signified in its real dimension which causes the emergence of the transference of the signified. What emerges is the signified in its imaginary dimension. There is, however, one more dimension to this signifying play. This transference of the signified, the emergence of the imaginary signified can only be the result of the play between signifiers. This is how the third dimension, the dimension of the symbolic, determines signification. It is the predominance of the signifier that produces the imaginary signified in order to cover over the absence of the real signified or rather of the signified as real.[18]

Now, let us return, after this necessary semiotic diversion, to our initial concern: one conclusion that follows is that the priority of the signifier is crucial for the Lacanian conceptualisation of the subject as articulated in the symbolic. If there is always something missing in the order of language, if there is always something lacking in the signifying chain, it is because the signified always slips out of reach, because signification is never complete – the illusion of the signified, the play of the signifiers can never eliminate the absence, the lack of the impossible real. It is possible to approach this lack from a variety of angles within Lacanian theory. At this point, and since we are discussing the constitution of subjectivity, let me concentrate on the issue of the subject's singularity, a real singularity which occupies the position of a signified that can never be signified. In *The Psychoses* Lacan argues that

> there is, in effect, something radically unassimilable to the signifier. It's quite simply the subject's singular existence. Why is he here? Where has he come from? What is he doing here? Why is he going to disappear? The signifier is incapable of providing him with an answer, for the good reason that it places him beyond death. The signifier already considers him dead, by nature it immortalizes him.
>
> (III: 179–80)

This is then the paradoxical role of the signifier: on the one hand, and due to the 'universality' and 'objectivity' of language, the signifier offers to the subject an almost 'immortal', stable representation, only this representation is incapable of representing, for the same reasons, the singularity of the subject, this signified is missing; immortality presupposes the subject's death: the word is the murder of the thing. Entering the order of the signifier entails a certain mortification. Insofar as life has meaning only within a symbolic universe then life presupposes a continuous death: *Media vita, in morte sumus*. The subject is petrified and alienated exactly in the place where it seeks the birth of itself.

Alienation is thus constitutive of the subject: as Lacan points out in 'Position of the Unconscious' (1964), 'alienation constitutes the subject as such' (1995: 268). At this point an irreducible lack is inscribed within the subjective structure, a lack due to the priority of the signifier and the nature of the symbolic order; the subject becomes identical to this lack: 'by being born with the signifier, the subject is born divided' (Lacan in Soler, 1995: 43). As Lacan states in his unpublished seminar entitled *Crucial Problems for Psychoanalysis* (1964–5), in determining the subject, the signifier bars it (seminar of 7 April 1965). The fact that we speak itself divides the subject: the gap between the subject of the enunciation and the subject of the statement can never be bridged. As argued earlier, what stands at the origin of the subject is nothing but a signifying *Spaltung*. Slavoj Žižek has described very successfully this dialectic by which the symbolic identity of the subject is simultaneously affirmed and suspended:

> In short, by means of the Word, the subject finally *finds* itself, comes to itself...in the Word, the subject directly attains itself, posits itself as such. The price for it, however, is the irretrievable *loss* of the subject's self-identity: the verbal sign that stands for the subject, that is, in which the subject posits itself as self-identical, bears the mark of an irreducible dissonance; it never 'fits' the subject.
>
> (Žižek, 1997a: 43)

The failure of its own symbolic self-representation is the condition of possibility for the emergence of the subject of the signifier, for representation in general.

From identity to identification: imaginary and symbolic dimensions

What are the implications of the constitutive alienation in the imaginary and the symbolic for a theory of subjective identity? The fullness of identity that the subject is seeking is impossible both in the imaginary and in the symbolic level. The subject is doomed to symbolise in order to constitute her- or himself as such, but this symbolisation cannot capture the totality and singularity of the real body, the close-circuit of the drives. Symbolisation, that is to say the pursuit of identity itself, introduces lack and makes identity ultimately impossible. For even the idea of identity to become possible its ultimate impossibility has to be instituted. Identity is possible only as a failed identity; it remains desirable exactly because it is essentially impossible. It is this constitutive impossibility that, by making full identity impossible, makes identification possible, if not necessary. Thus, it is rather misleading to speak of identities within a Lacanian framework. What we have is only attempts to construct a stable identity, either on the imaginary or the symbolic level, through the image or the signifier. The subject of lack emerges due to the failure of all these attempts. What we have then, if we want to be precise and accurate, is not identities but identifications, a series of failed identifications or rather a play between identification and its failure, a deeply political play.

The concept of identification becomes crucial then for any understanding of the Lacanian conception of subjectivity; it was already crucial in Freudian theory. In Freud, identification emerges as a concept of major importance as it refers to the mechanism through which subjectivity is constituted. Identification refers to the 'psychological process whereby the subject assimilates an aspect, property or attribute of the other and is transformed, wholly or partially, after the model the other provides. It is by means of a series of identifications that the personality is constituted and specified' (Laplanche and Pontalis, 1988: 205). What Lacan adds to this picture is two qualifications. First of all the distinction between imaginary and symbolic identification, which clarifies a lot of ambiguities in Freud's account, and, second, the important emphasis on the idea that identification cannot result in a stable subjective identity: The ontic horizon of identification is that of ultimate failure; its ontological horizon that of impossibility.[19] Yet this is not, strictly speaking, a failure of identification, but a failure of identity, that is to say a failure to achieve identity through identification. It is, however, this same impossibility to achieve identity (substance) that makes identification (process) constitutive. This is not only true for the life of the child but for the life of the adult as well, something which reveals the relevance of the concept of identification for social and political analysis. Since the objects of identification in adult life include political ideologies and other socially constructed objects, the process of identification is revealed as constitutive of socio-political life. It is not identity which is constitutive but identification as such; instead of identity politics we should speak of identification politics.

In this section we will enrich and rearticulate the points presented up to now by bringing into play the central Lacanian concept of identification. Lacan formulates a detailed understanding of identification for the first time in his mirror stage paper. In defining the mirror stage he depicts identification as the transformation that takes place in a subject when she or he assumes an image of her- or himself: 'We have only to understand the mirror stage as an identification, in the full sense that analysis gives to the term: namely, the *transformation* that takes place in the subject when he assumes an image' (E: 2). This primary identification is what produces the ego. As we have pointed out, this identification cannot provide the subject with a stable identity; it is irreducibly alienating, based on the *méconnaissance* of the 'dehiscence at the heart of the organism, a primordial Discord betrayed by the signs of uneasiness and motor unco-ordination of the neo-natal months' (of the prematurity of birth), on a short-lived illusion of autonomy:

> the mirror stage is a drama whose internal thrust is precipitated from insufficiency to anticipation – and which manufactures for the subject, caught up in the lure of spatial identification,[20] the succession of phantasies that extends from a fragmented body-image to a form of its totality that I shall call orthopaedic – and, lastly, to the assumption of the armour of an alienating identity, which will mark with its rigid structure the subject's entire mental development.
>
> (E: 4)

Symbolic identification differs from imaginary identification in a variety of respects. According to the orthodox interpretation, alienated in the image, the child attempts to emerge as a subject on the symbolic level. At this point – at this logical conjecture – the alienating ensemble of the child's imaginary identifications, as developed in the mirror stage, is properly situated within the surrounding socio-linguistic system. Symbolic identification emerges as a solution to the ambivalence of the imaginary. We must not, however, paint too rosy a picture for symbolic identification: 'The symbolic order has to be conceived as something superimposed' (III: 96). How is the symbolic imposed on the subject, opening at the same time the road for the symbolic representation of herself? This is done through the intervention of the Name-of-the-Father, of a primary signifier which supports the whole matrix of signification. Before this intervention the infant is locked in an imaginary relation to its mother. The 'invasion' of the 'Name-of-the-Father' destroys this incestuous imaginary relation between the mother and 'her' child:

> The Oedipus complex means that the imaginary, in itself an inces-
> tuous and conflictual relation, is doomed to conflict and ruin. In
> order for the human being to be able to establish the most natural
> of relations, that between male and female, a third party has to in-
> tervene, one that is the model of something successful, the model of
> some harmony. This does not go far enough – there has to be a law,
> a chain, a symbolic order, the intervention of the order of speech,
> that is, of the father [the Name-of-the-Father].
>
> (III: 96)

The invasion of the Name-of-the-Father makes possible a new kind of identification – in the symbolic – that attempts to suspend the ambiguity in the imaginary. The tensions entailed in the imaginary are resolved one way or the other. In other words the mirror stage, the hegemony of the imaginary, has an end (E: 5), an end marked by the invasion of the symbolic. The reason we use words like 'imposition' and 'invasion' is because entering the symbolic register presupposes a certain loss, or rather a prohibition, the prohibition of the mother. It presupposes, in other words, the imposition of symbolic Law. If the subject is to emerge in and through language, the symbolic has to be accepted, the laws of language have to be recognised. For that to happen the idea of Law has to be instituted. As mentioned above, the agent of Law is here the Name-of-the-Father, that is, not the real existing father but a signifier which disrupts the imaginary relation between mother and child, by erecting the prohibition of incest: 'It is in the name of the father that we must recognize the support of the symbolic function which, from the dawn of history, has identified his person with the figure of the law' (E: 67). Simply put, the father introduces the idea of a new order. This is, according to Lacan, the most striking dimension of the function of the father. The paternal function introduces an order, but an order structurally different from the natural order, an order instituting human society, a certain community of meaning (III: 320). In that sense, the role of the signifier instituting the symbolic order for the subject, the role of the Name-of-the-Father, is both prohibitive, since it demands something from the subject, but also productive, since it makes possible the emergence of the subject of the signifier in its relation to the order of symbolic reality.

If the laws of language presuppose, in order to function at all, the acceptance of Law as such, for Lacan this Law is clearly articulated at the level of the signifier. Signification, the articulation of signifiers in certain orders, is grounded on the fact that there is a Law. If, with regard to the family drama, Law is introduced with the prohibition of incest, in terms of the general dialectic of identity formation the Law is introduced with the sacrifice of all unmediated access to a pre-symbolic real, a sacrifice entailed in the advent of language. In other words, the function of language in general, the social order itself as distinct from the natural order, is supported by the Name-of-the-Father as the bearer of symbolic Law.[21] The question of the importance of this signifier can be also approached in a negative way. We can ask for example 'What happens when the signifier in question, the organising centre, the point of significant convergence that it constitutes, is evoked but fails to appear [fait défaut]?' (III: 283). When the Other is excluded what concerns the subject is expressed through the little other, the shadows of others (III: 53). The lack of the symbolic is covered by imaginary constructions which take the form of delusions.

> In psychosis it's the signifier that is in question, and as the signifier is never solitary, as it inevitably forms something coherent – this is the very meaningfulness of the signifier – the lack of one signifier necessarily brings the subject to the point of calling the set of signifiers into question.
>
> (III: 203)

What stands at the root of psychosis is the foreclosure of this signifier, the Name-of-the-Father:

> It is in an accident in that register and in what takes place in it, namely the foreclosure of the Name-of-the-Father in the place of the Other, and in the failure of the paternal metaphor, that I designate the defect that gives psychosis its essential condition, and the structure that separates it from neurosis.
>
> (E: 215)

It is exactly this lack of the Name-of-the-Father, the lack of the signifier that supports the symbolic Other, that explains the linguistic disturbances noticed in psychotics, such as the inability to construct creative metaphors, etc.[22]

In its particularity, the Name-of-the-Father introduces a certain lack, it demands the 'sacrifice' of the child's incestuous relation with the mother. At a more general level, this lack constitutes an affirmation of the symbolic laws of language, it permits the subject to enter into the social world in which he or she can constitute him- or herself as a desiring subject at the level of language. In this sense 'social structures are symbolic' (Lacan in Evans, 1996: 193). Oedipus is a necessary factor of security for every neurotic subject since it erects a defence against the threatening and anxiety-provoking real of the absorption by the mother which would lead to psychosis. In order to gain the ability to symbolise (and to live a normal, neurotic life) what is presupposed is to sacrifice something, to accept that symbolisation can never be total, that something will be forever excluded if the world is to have meaning. What we have here is the inclusion (*Bejahung*), the acceptance, of an exclusion, as a condition of possibility for symbolisation. Entering the symbolic world entails this dual movement. In order to gain the symbolic world we have to sacrifice the essence of what we are seeking in it, in order to gain the signifier we have to sacrifice the signified. Symbolic identification is an identification structured around the acceptance of this constitutive lack.

Central to this argument is the idea that something has to be excluded if something else is to function properly; thus, by excluding certain alternatives, symbolic identification forms the kernel of decision in human life. As I mentioned above, the signifier, the general function Lacan attaches to the Name-of-the-Father, constitutes the prime *locus* of power in human life; the signifier introduces the symbolic dimension of power. This is a power both negative and positive. One could note here a certain homology with Foucault's conception of power as something not only prohibitive but also productive. It seems that Lacan's paternal function is exemplifying this power *à la* Foucault especially since the prohibitive function of the father is exactly what makes possible the development of sexual desire and Foucault's conception of power is articulated *vis à vis* the history of sexuality; as Jon Simons suggests in *Foucault and the Political*, 'It is in regard to the domain of sexuality that Foucault most dramatically asserts that power is productive as well as repressive' (Simons, 1995: 33).[23] Another crucial aspect of this symbolic dimension of power is the fact that, in opposition to imaginary power, it presupposes the complicity or rather the acceptance, of the subject. The Law of language has to be accepted by the subject if psychosis is to be avoided. This is a schema very close to Bourdieu's conception of symbolic power in which symbolic power is legitimised by the acceptance of those who are subjected to it (Bourdieu, 1991). In both cases this acceptance is never very easy; in psychoanalysis this difficulty in accepting the Name-of-the-Father stands at the root of neurosis, while regarding the social level, the difficulty is surfacing in all the socio-political struggle around the idea of order in society, a question which will be further discussed in other parts of this book.

What should be stressed at this point is that what is at stake here is not only subjective identification but the constitution of reality itself: 'in order for there to be reality, adequate access to reality, in order for the sense of reality to be a reliable guide, in order for reality not to be what it is in psychosis, the Oedipus complex has to have been lived through' (III: 198). As we shall see in Chapter 2, reality is symbolically constructed and articulated in language. Once again, linguistic articulation presupposes a certain loss, the exclusion of something through an act of decision: power is revealed as an inherent element of the logic of the signifier.[24] There is no society and social reality without exclusion; without it the world collapses into a psychotic universe. But what is it exactly that is sacrificed in the world of language? We said that it is the mother, the maternal Thing. On a more general level, it is also our access to an unmediated level of need relating to all animal life. It is to the constitutivity of the symbolic in human life that we owe the fact that need becomes demand and instinct becomes drive and then desire. What is happening in all these transformations is the loss of a primordial level of the real. What is lost is all unmediated access to this real. Now we can only try to encounter the real through symbolisation. We gain access to reality, which is mainly a symbolic construct, but the signified of the signifier 'reality', the real itself, is sacrificed for ever.[25] No identification can restore it or recapture it for us. But it is exactly this impossibility that forces us to identify again and again. We never get what we were promised but that's exactly why we keep longing for it.

In other words, any identity resulting from identification is always an unstable identity, a split or even non-identity, since every identification is marked by an alienating dimension. As argued earlier, although imaginary identification offers the subject a sense of identity it also entails a radical ambiguity, it introduces a certain antagonistic tension. The same alienation is characterising symbolic identification: in *The Four Fundamental Concepts of Psychoanalysis*, Lacan refers to a lack which 'emerges from the invasion of the symbolic, by the fact that the subject depends on the signifier but the signifier is first of all in the field of the Other' (XI: 204–5). Here we are confronted with an ambivalence similar to the one that led to the failure of imaginary identification. What belongs to the socio-symbolic Other can never become totally ours; it can never become us: it will *always* be a source of ambivalence and alienation and this gap can never be bridged. The ultimate result of symbolic identification is a further alienation in language, in the social world: 'The paradox of the Word is therefore that its emergence resolves the tension of the pre-symbolic antagonism, but at a price: the Word...involves an irretrievable externalization-alienation' (Žižek, 1997a: 42). To recapitulate our argument so far, both imaginary and symbolic identification fail to provide us with a stable identity. A lack is continuously re-emerging where identity should be consolidated. All our attempts to cover over this lack of the subject through identifications that promise to offer us a stable identity fail, this failure brings to the fore the irreducible character of this lack which in turn reinforces our attempts to fill it. This is the circular play between lack and identification which is marking the human condition; a play that makes possible the emergence of a whole politics of the subject.

In this regard we have to be very clear, assuming at the same time the risk of a certain repetition: the politics of the subject, the politics of identity formation, can only be understood as a politics of impossibility. If the ego is based on the imaginary misrecognition of the impossibility of fullness and closure, it also entails a constitutive alienation, making visible a certain lack. This lack also constitutes an irreducible element of the symbolic order in which the subject turns for its representation; here lack is elevated to the position of a precondition for symbolic representation. In the symbolic, the subject is properly constituted but as the subject of lack; something is again missing. Identification is thus revealed as, by constitution, alienating (Laclau and Zac, 1994: 14). It can never realise its aim, it can never achieve full identity, it can never bring back our lost fullness since it was its own institution that introduced this loss. Identification is always an identification doomed to fail. One has to agree with Laclau and Zac that the proper answer to Lacoue-Labarthe's rhetorical question 'Why, after all, should the problem of identification not be, in general, the essential problem of politics?' is that the problem of politics is identification and its failure (Laclau and Zac, 1994: 35). Beyond identity politics, identification politics is revealed as the politics of impossibility.

Politics of the subject: identification with what?

Lack is clearly central in the Lacanian conception of the subject as the space where the whole 'politics' of identification takes place. Yet lack is neither hypostasised nor essentialised in Lacanian theory. The idea of the subject as lack cannot be separated from the recognition of the fact that the subject is always attempting to cover over this constitutive lack in the level of representation, through continuous identification acts. On the contrary, it is this same lack – the characteristic mark of subjectivity – which makes necessary the constitution of every identity through a process of identification: 'one needs to identify with something because there is an originary and insurmountable lack of identity' (Laclau, 1994: 3). In that sense the notion of the subject in Lacan does not only invoke lack but also all our attempts to eliminate this lack which, however, does not stop re-emerging. Here we are shifting our attention from the subject of lack to the attempts of the subject to represent herself, these two moments being two sides of the same coin that reveal the dialectic between the subject and the social in Lacanian theory. It is precisely the nature of identification that reproduces this lack within subjective structure. The subject meets lack and alienation where it seeks fullness and identity. It must have become clear that this non-reductionist conception of subjectivity opens the way for a first confluence between Lacanian theory and political analysis. The constitution of every (ultimately impossible) identity can be attempted only through processes of identification with socially *available* discursive constructions such as ideologies, etc.

We can now dispel the confusion which accompanies many discussions on the relation between psychoanalytic theory and socio-political analysis, a confusion which is open to accusations of a certain psychoanalytic reductionism. We may approach this issue through the question: 'What serves to unite these two approaches?' The most common but totally misleading answer is the following: 'But surely, the role of the individual actor in politics'. Such a view has been articulated by Bellamy as a criticism of the use of Lacanian theory in Laclau's and Mouffe's work:

> In order to render more meaningful their invoking of psychoanalytic terms Laclau and Mouffe would need to be more specific about the precise nature of the intersection between the social...and the psychic which however fragmented, alienated and deconstructed is surely a major factor in the implementing of political actions. Their use of psychoanalytic terms to further elucidate certain ideological and political phenomena is too broadly deployed to allow for a consideration of the *individual psyche* as a factor in the operations of ideology.
>
> (Bellamy, 1993: 34–5, my emphasis)

Here I would like to question the conception of 'individual psyche' that Bellamy has in mind. For her formulation seems to betray a certain resistance to giving up an ultimately essentialist perspective. What must be emphasised once more here is that, for Lacan, this psyche is nothing other than the pure substanceless subject as lack. The object of Lacanian psychoanalysis is not the individual, it is not man. It is what he is lacking (1978: 26). In that sense, all attempts to present the Lacanian notion of the subject as related to what 'used to be called individuality', every attempt to reduce it to 'the one who suffers' or to a 'biological' channel of discourse, simultaneously reducing analysis to its 'therapeutic action' (Alcorn, 1994: 28)[26] or to 'a science of the individual' (Feher-Gurewich, 1996: 164) are not only incapable of providing a link between Lacan and the political or a 'new alliance between psychoanalysis and social theory' (ibid.: 151) but are completely misplaced; Lacan is extremely clear in this respect:

in the term subject...I am not designating the living substratum needed by this phenomenon of the subject, nor any sort of substance, nor any being possessing knowledge in his pathos, his suffering, whether primal or secondary, nor even some incarnated logos.

(XI: 126)

It is the Lacanian subject of the signifier, the lacking subject, that provides the first link between psychoanalysis, society and politics, and this precisely because it highlights its dependence on the socio-symbolic order:

> Psycho-analysis is neither a *Weltanschauung*, nor a philosophy that claims to provide the key to the universe. It is governed by a particular aim, which is historically defined by the elaboration of the notion of the subject. It poses this notion in a new way, by leading the subject back to his signifying dependence.

(XI: 77)

By locating, at the place previously assigned to an essence of the individual psyche, a constitutive lack, Lacanian theory avoids the essentialist reductionism of the social to the individual level and opens the way to the confluence of psychoanalysis and socio-political analysis, since this lack can only be filled by socio-political objects of identification. The point here is that analytic theory is not only concerned with lack but also with what attempts to fill this lack: 'Psychoanalysis is otherwise directed at the effect of discourse within the subject' (III: 135). In that sense, 'Lacan...believed in the priority of social discourses, of language, over the subject' (Copjec, 1994: 53). This is the meaning of the constitutivity of the symbolic in the emergence of the subject that we have been describing up to now. Michelman is correct then when asserting that 'Durkheim and Lacan are thus allied in their critiques of various forms of psychological and biological reductionism that deny the existence and efficacy of facts of this order [the symbolic/social order]' (Michelman, 1996: 127). Thus Lacan not only seems aware of the dangers pointed by Durkheim and reiterated by Jameson – with which we started this book – but avoids them in the most radical way: 'there is no subject according to Lacan which is not always already a *social* subject' (Lacoue-Labarthe and Nancy, 1992: 30).[27]

Nonetheless, there is still an obvious problem with this argument; namely, there is nothing very radical or innovative about it. Simply put, it is not Lacanian theory alone that stresses this role of the 'objective', of the social factor. Freud himself, despite all his reductionist tendencies, had, from the very beginning, pointed out that 'in the individual's mental life someone else is invariably involved, as a model, as an object, as a helper, as an opponent...the relations of an individual to his parents and to his

37

brothers and sisters, to the object of his love, and to his physician', all these social relations are crucial for the individual identity (Freud, 1985: 95–6). Nowadays it is commonplace in analytic theory and theory in general to argue that the social constitutes the depository of the representations the psyche uses, that it is the place from where objects of identification originate. It is also generally accepted that this process is not limited to our early years but determines the whole of our life (Leledakis, 1995: 166–77). But then what new is Lacan introducing? Certainly, Lacan's conception of subjectivity should be seen as a radicalisation and elaboration of this Freudian position, and in fact, a radicalisation of ground-breaking proportions. In Lacan this vague idea is grounded on a firm conceptual apparatus and a rigorous theoretical basis. But, as we shall see, and this is what is most important, Lacan's relevance for socio-political analysis is not limited to this radicalisation.

What else can Lacanian theory be offering? Let us try to answer this question by simultaneously summarising our argumentation up to now. Our first point was that Lacanian theory can be relevant for socio-political analysis because it offers a 'socio-political' conception of subjectivity. The subjective is no longer 'subjective' in the traditional sense of the word which presupposes the identification of the subject with the conscious ego. The subject is equivalent to the lack which stands at the root of the human condition. This view of subjectivity permits the development of a psycho-analytic approach to the socio-political level, to social reality, since social reality is the *locus* in which the subject as lack seeks its absent fullness. One should not get the impression, though, that this fullness can be reconstructed through identification in the socio-symbolic level; this level is also lacking. And this is perhaps the most radical thesis that Lacanian theory offers to a reconsideration of the socio-political plane. If the subjective is no longer 'subjective', the objective is also no longer 'objective' in the sense of a closed structure, of an entity capable, under certain circumstances, of filling the lack in the subject. The field of representation is itself revealed as lacking because it attempts the impossible, that is to say, the representation of something ultimately unrepresentable. Representation is the representation of a real fullness which is always beyond our grasp.

Simply put, lack is not marking only the Lacanian subject:

> the most radical dimension of Lacanian theory lies not in recognis-
> ing ['that the Lacanian subject is divided, crossed-out, identical to a
> lack in a signifying chain'] but in realising that the big Other, the
> symbolic order itself, is also *barré*, crossed-out, by a fundamental
> impossibility, structured around an impossible/traumatic kernel,
> around a central lack.
>
> (Žižek, 1989: 122)

This is the *big secret of psychoanalysis,* as Lacan called it as early as his 1958–9 seminar. Something is missing in the Other; there is no Other of the Other (seminar of 8 April 1959). As he further points out in *Anxiety,* the structure of the Other is revealed as a certain void, the void of its lack of guarantee in the real (seminar of 5 June 1963). Meaning is always based on semblance; precisely because 'there is no last word'; meaning always indicates the direction toward its failure (XX: 79), its failure to anchor itself on the real. This effectively translates into the split character of every object of identification – what Laclau calls the ultimate *impossibility of society.* In that sense, Lacan's major contribution to contemporary theory is 'a new picture of the social' (Michelman, 1996: 129). The social field is revealed as a discursive field of representation which is articulated on the basis of the repression, the exclusion, the reduction of an ultimately unrepresentable real; a real which is however resurfacing, making thus visible the irreducible failure inscribed at the heart of the Other of meaning: 'there is a fault, hole or loss therein [in the Other]' (XX: 28). If Lacan introduces such a radical view of the socio-political level then surely our own argumentation cannot remain fixed or exclusively focused on his conception of subjectivity. To be able to extract all Lacan has to offer to political theory we need to pass from the subjective to the objective. This is the purpose of the next chapter.

2

THE LACANIAN OBJECT

Dialectics of social impossibility

The objective is also lacking

My starting point in this chapter is that although the Lacanian subject is of great importance for socio-political theory (some of its political implications were explored in the previous chapter), it is Lacan's insights on the objective level which reveal the importance of his work for political theory. What must be stressed from the beginning, however, is that this is not some kind of zero-sum game; obviously, one doesn't have to concentrate either on Lacan's comments on the subjective or on his treatment of the objective, these are not two incompatible approaches. In fact, it is the Lacanian conception of the subject itself which permits the articulation of Lacan's novel approach to the objective level; precisely because it ultimately entails the deconstruction – but not the 'destruction' – of the dominant bipolarities individual/collective and subjective/objective, and moves beyond all subject–object imaginary relations (seminar of 23 May 1962).[1] In his seminar on *The Psychoses* Lacan pointed out that it is an illusion that the subjective is the opposite of the objective (III: 80) and in *Anxiety* he locates the split subject, the subject as marked by the signifier, on the objective side, the side of the Other (seminar of 21 November 1962).[2] These two levels are not, of course, identical but in any case they are not antithetical; there is something linking the individual to the collective, the subjective to the objective, the universal to the particular; but this is not a fundamental essential identity, an identity already realised or in the making. It is exactly the opposite: it is the subject, symbolic lack itself, which splits the essentialist conceptions of individuality; it is the same subject as lack that introduces division into human collectivity. Hence Lacan's position:

> let me simply say that this is what leads me to object to any reference to totality in the individual, since it is the subject who introduces division into the individual, as well as into the collectivity that

40

is his equivalent. Psychoanalysis is properly that which reveals both
the one and the other to be no more than mirages.

(E: 80)

This is then the radical view that Lacan introduces to our conceptions of
collectivity, reality, social objectivity. All these mirages, that capture social
imagination and guide political praxis, are revealed as lacking; this lack is
located at the centre of the dialectic between the subjective and the
objective, the individual and the collective, revealing it as a dialectic of
impossibility.

'Objectivism' and 'subjectivism' are symmetrical expressions of the desire
for a fullness that is ultimately impossible (Laclau and Mouffe, 1985: 13).[3]
The individual seeks a strong subjective identity in identifying with collective
objects but the lack on the objective level means that every such identification is only reproducing the lack in the subject, being incapable of providing
the lost real fullness of the individual subject. When, in *Transference* (1960–
1), Lacan argues that the individual and the collective are one and the same
level, what he means is that what is true at the one level is also true at the
other, and this truth can only be the lack marking both domains, the
constitutive impossibility proving both domains to be no more than
mirages. One lack is no lack at all; it is necessary to take into account both
these lacks – the lack in the subject and the lack in the Other – in order to
avoid the neutralisation of Lacan's radical insights. This play, however, the
play between the subjective and the objective as two lacking domains, is not
leading to a collapse of the distinction between the subjective and the
objective. It definitely leads to the deconstruction of the traditional
opposition between these two fields; what unites them now is their lacking
character: in the Lacanian universe the subject of lack meets the lack in the
Other and the split subject meets the split object. Within this framework
what remains of great interest for a philosophical reconsideration of the
political is the lack in the Other, the split in the 'objective' side of experience,
and its socio-political administration. In short, although Lacanian theory
conceives the lacking subject as depending on the identification with socio-
symbolic objects and thus accepts, in a certain sense, the priority of the
'objective' on the subjective, at the same time it introduces an anti-
objectivist conception of social reality. If I need to identify with something it
is not only because I don't have a full identity in the first place, but also
because all my attempts to acquire it by identifying with a supposedly full
Other are failing. Identification becomes thinkable only as a result of the
lack within the structure, the structure of the social Other. The objective as a
closed totality is a semblance; the objective Other is lacking.

How should we view the *status* of this lack in the Other? Surely, every
lack has to be a lack of something. So is this Lacanian lack also the lack of
something? And what can this 'something' be? In Lacan, this lack is, first of

all, a lack of *jouissance*, the lack of a pre-symbolic, real enjoyment which is always posited as something lost, as a lost fullness, the part of ourselves that is sacrificed/castrated when we enter the symbolic system of language and social relations:[4] 'to be more specific, the lack inscribed in the signifying chain through which the Other, as the only possible site of truth, reveals that it holds no guarantee, is in terms of the dialectic of desire a lacking in *jouissance* of the Other' (Lacan and the École Freudienne, 1982: 117). As Lacan has formulated it, the subject is symbolically deprived of it for ever. The subject is deprived of what she or he believes to be the most intimate part of themselves:

> Therein lies the primordial 'decentrement' of the Lacanian subject: much more radical and elementary than the decentrement of the subject with regard to the 'big Other', the symbolic order which is the external place of the subject's truth, is the decentrement with re-gard to the traumatic Thing-*jouissance* which the subject can never 'subjectivise', assume, integrate.
>
> (Žižek, 1997b: 49)

This is because as soon as the subject emerges in language the pre-symbolic real – what is impossible to integrate in the symbolic – is posited as an external prohibited object. The universality of language cannot capture the singular real of the pre-symbolic mythical subject. The most intimate part of our being is experienced as something lost. But is this the whole truth? Or is it a strategy for the perpetuation of *desire* in a world marked by the lack in the Other? Desire is of course the key word in our last sentence, and this is where we must turn our attention now and search for an answer to these questions.

The emergence of desire cannot be conceived independently of the family drama of the subject. Not surprisingly, it is the Name-of-the-Father, the paternal metaphor, that demands the sacrifice of *jouissance*. The primordial Thing, the mother, has to be sacrificed if desire is to be articulated.[5] This loss, however, the prohibition of *jouissance*, is exactly what permits the emergence of desire; a desire that is structured around the unending quest for the lost/impossible *jouissance*. The paradox here is that what is prohibited is something by definition impossible:

> The paradox (and perhaps the very function of the prohibition as such) consists of course in the fact that, as soon as it is conceived as prohibited, the real impossible changes into something possible, i.e. into something that cannot be reached, not because of its inherent impossibility but simply because access to it is hindered by the ex-ternal barrier of a prohibition. Therein lies, after all, the logic of the most fundamental of all prohibitions, that of incest: incest is inher-

ently impossible (even if a man 'really' sleeps with his mother: 'this is not that'; the incestuous object is by definition lacking), and the symbolic prohibition is nothing but an attempt to resolve this deadlock by a transmutation of impossibility into prohibition. There is One which is the prohibited object of incest (mother), and its prohibition renders accessible all other objects.

(Žižek, 1993: 116)

This is exactly the point Lacan makes in his unpublished seminar on *Anxiety*: desire for the mother, is identical to the function of the law. The same law that prohibits having her is what imposes desiring her, because in itself the mother is not such a desirable object (seminar of 16 January 1963). The trick of the Law is that it creates desire as a result of the lack imposed by the prohibition of incest. In that sense one can argue that it is the prohibition itself, the performative institution of symbolic Law, that makes possible the desire to 'recapture' this impossible *jouissance*. This is the nodal point of the Oedipus complex: 'the Oedipus complex constitutes *jouissance* as forbidden by relying on the paternal law' (Lacan and the École Freudienne, 1982: 117). The Law makes us believe that what is impossible really exists and it is possible for us to encounter it again:

if the paths to *jouissance* have something in them that dies out, that tends to make them impassable, prohibition, if I may say so, becomes its all-terrain vehicle, its half-track truck, that gets it out of the circuitous routes that lead man back in a roundabout way toward the rut of a short and well-trodden satisfaction.

(VII: 177)

What is revealed here is the dialectic between desire and the Law. The prohibition of an impossible *jouissance* creates the desire for its attainment: 'what we see here is the tight bond between desire and the Law' (VII: 177). Desire is always presented as a will to *jouissance*. In *Identification*, Lacan makes clear that it is in the fact that the impossible *jouissance* is prohibited, suspended, *aufgehoben*, that lies the supporting plane for the constitution of desire (seminar of 4 April 1962). Accordingly, in *The Ethics of Psychoanalysis* he articulates a similar logic in relation to the Thing. The object is not really lost: 'the object is by nature a refound object. That it was lost is a consequence of that – but after the fact. It is thus refound without our knowing, except through the refinding, that it was ever lost' (VII: 118). The lost object is an object which is not lost as such but is posited as lost *après coup*. What does that in effect mean? It means that it is lack that introduces the idea of fullness and not vice-versa. It means that it is an act of power, an act of exclusion, that retroactively produces the fullness we attribute to what was excluded, to that unknown impossibility. No doubt, it is common sense to think that something was there before exclusion, otherwise exclusion would make no sense at all; the only problem is that we can't really know what it was. To think that it was a state of fullness is a retroactively produced fiction. This is made clear when Lacan refers to the Heideggerian vase. What the vase does, for Lacan, is that by creating a void, it also introduces the possibility of its filling:

> It creates the void and thereby introduces the possibility of filling it. Emptiness and fullness are introduced into a world that knows not of them. It is on the basis of this fabricated signifier, this vase, that emptiness and fullness as such enter the world...if the vase may be filled, it is because in the first place in its essence it is empty.
>
> (VII: 120)

In other words it is the signifier as such, as instituted through symbolic castration, that introduces the idea of recapturing fullness, a fullness which is desired exactly because it is posited as lost/sacrificed. This fullness is in fact impossible to recapture because it was never part of ourselves. Even the pre-symbolic real in which nothing is lacking should not be conceived as a stage of fullness. In *Crucial Problems for Psychoanalysis* it is clearly stated that the real should not be understood as a raw and opaque mass (seminar of 2 December 1964). As Lacan also points out in his seminar on *Anxiety*, the non-lacking character of the real does not mean that the real is always full. On the contrary, it is plausible to conceive the real as full of holes. What it means is that it does not lack anything (seminar of 20 March 1963). There is no lack or absence in the real (II: 313).[6] Lack is introduced then at the intersection of the real with the symbolic. It is the symbolic that entails lack. Lack emerges in and through the symbolisation of the real. Before the introduction of the symbolic there is no lack and that's why we know that the real is not lacking; if it was lacking, lack would be introduced without the symbolic or before the introduction of the symbolic. The real is related to lack exactly because in the process of symbolisation, the signifier produces the signified, creating the imaginary illusion of attaining the lost real. Sooner or later, the illusory character of this fixation of meaning is revealed. If the real is the domain of the inexpressible, the domain of death and inexpressible enjoyment (*jouissance*) then its presence, the encounter with the real, can only have as a consequence the revelation of the lack of our imaginary/symbolic constructs, of their inability to represent death and *jouissance*, to be 'real'.

Desire, the desire to capture the real, is thus an effect of the signifier: 'The function of desire is a last residuum of the effect of the signifier in the subject. *Desidero* is the Freudian *cogito*' (E: 154). Desire arises as a consequence of the imposition of the symbolic order through the signifier of the Name-of-the-Father; in this respect, desire is always socially conditioned. When the Name-of-the Father appears on the horizon, as the support of the symbolic itself, it prohibits the mother which, as a result of this same prohibition, becomes the lost 'signified' around which sexual desire is structured: 'The signifier being a father is what creates the highway in sexual relations with a woman' (III: 293). This desire is never satisfied, it is always metonymically transposed. Desire is illusory, says Lacan in *Anxiety*, precisely because it is always addressed elsewhere (seminar of 15 May 1963), exactly because the imaginary signified can never become real.

If, however, failure constitutes the horizon of identification, if full identity is proven ultimately impossible, what makes us identify again and again? In other words, if lack and failure is the destiny of every identification act then what is the driving force behind our continuous attempts to transcend this constitutive alienation, what is the ontological horizon of this play? What stimulates our *desire* for new identification acts? We are now in a position to answer all these questions which are, as we shall see, of crucial political significance. Desire, the element that keeps everything going, is animated by the quest for a lacking/impossible fullness, around the promise of encountering *jouissance* – and *jouissance* always has 'the connotation of fullness' (Forrester, 1990: 100). Whenever we reach the object of our desire, any *jouissance* we get is nothing compared to what we were expecting: ' "That's not it" is the very cry by which the *jouissance* obtained is distinguished from the *jouissance* expected' (XX: 111). If no object can provide us with our lost/impossible *jouissance*, it follows that the fragile equilibrium of desire can only be maintained by the continuous displacement from object to object: strangely enough it is the prevention of *jouissance* that sustains desire, a prevention which keeps the dream of attaining it alive (seminar of 17 December 1958). It is this repetition of failure that sustains desire as a promise to attain the mythical *jouissance*; if the realisation, the full satisfaction of desire is impossible, then the promise of this realisation becomes necessary; without it no desire can be sustained. But what is the exact nature of this promise? It cannot be strictly symbolic although it is animated by the introduction of symbolic lack, since it is promising the imaginary elimination of this lack by recapturing the lost real. It seems that in Lacanian theory the name for this promise is fantasy.

Fantasy and the promise of fullness

The subject identifies with the Other, but the Other is lacking, unable to offer a stable identity and thus unable, by itself, to sustain the desire to identify, a desire that depends on the constitutivity of lack but also on the urge to suture this lack. Nothing in the symbolic can provide us with a solution for our division, an exit from this frustrating state. Thus we are led to bring something in from another register, the quasi-imaginary *objet petit a*, the field of fantasy. As Lacan claims in *Desire and its Interpretation*, at the moment when the subject 'faints' before the lack of the signifier corresponding to his place at the level of the big Other, she or he finds support in the object, the kernel of fantasy (seminar of 20 May 1959). In a last attempt to fill this lack in the Other, the lack crossing our socio-political world, the subject then resorts to fantasy. Fantasy is a construction that stimulates, that causes desire, exactly because it promises to cover over the lack in the Other, the lack created by the loss of *jouissance*. Since this lack is an effect of castration, of the introduction of language and symbolic Law, then fantasy is also revealed as a defence against castration. Fantasy is a scenario that veils the lack in the Other effected by castration. In Lacan, the structure we always find in fantasy is this relation between the split subject, the lacking subject and the promise of the elimination of this lack or of a compensation for it amounting to its structural neutralisation. If the human condition is marked by a quest for a lost/impossible enjoyment, fantasy offers the promise of an encounter with this precious *jouissance*, an encounter that is fantasised as covering over the lack in the Other and, consequently, as filling the lack in the subject.[7]

This is articulated as a total operation and thus can be thought of as being essentially imaginary. In fact Lacan, at several points in his work, stresses the imaginary character of fantasy. Fantasy however is not purely imaginary.[8] As it is shown in *The Formations of the Unconscious*, fantasy is an imaginary involved in a signifying function (seminar of 21 May 1958); a statement which is repeated one year later (seminar of 28 January 1959). This is because fantasy emerges as a support exactly in the place where the lack in the Other becomes evident; it functions as a support for the lacking Other of the symbolic. It becomes a simulacrum of what in the order of the signifier resists signification, that is to say of the real, of what presents itself as lost. In short, it attempts to take the place of the lacking Other of the Other, of the missing signification that would, this is our mythology, represent our sacrificed enjoyment. It is because reality is articulated at the symbolic level and the symbolic is lacking, that reality can only acquire a certain coherence and become desirable as an object of identification, by resorting to fantasy; the illusory nature of fantasy functions as a support for the desire to identify.

What Lacan suggests in *Anxiety* is that through symbolic identification we try to constitute ourselves as the mythological or hypothetical subject which depends on the closure of the Other, of the order of the signifier. There is a 'Subject' insofar as there can be an 'Other' (seminar of 23 January 1963). The problem is that, as experience and ontological reflection show, the full Other does not exist; the guarantee of the Other is missing, the Other can only be a barred Other. There is no signified or transcendental signifier to hold together signification, guaranteeing its coherence and fullness. What we have is a lack in the Other; the final signification of the Other fails to appear, there is no Other of the Other. What follows is that the subject can only be a barred subject since the full Other that would guarantee the full constitution of the subject is absent.[9] The barred subject, however, doesn't stop desiring its absent fullness – it is the fact that it is barred that posits fullness as lost (prohibited) but possible in principle, that is to say possible to be desired.

The role of the object is crucial in sustaining this desire. The object appears as the remainder of the lost mythological subject of *jouissance* that promises to provide what the Other lacks and thus unify us as subjects. The subject is thus *caused* by this object (1982: 165). The mythological subject, the subject before the sacrifice of enjoyment, is what Lacan calls the subject of *jouissance*. What remains of this fiction after the invasion of the symbolic is a remainder, something which cannot be in itself symbolised, albeit being a performative by-product of the prohibition itself. In this sense, the *objet petit a*, the remainder of the constitution of the subject as a barred subject, functions as a metaphor for the always absent (impossible) mythological subject of *jouissance*. Fantasy attempts to remedy the fundamental deficiency (impossibility) of the big Other, to 'restore' the fullness of the Other, so that we can believe that it is possible for this full subject (S) to be constituted through signification and identification (identification has to be made with the object of desire, as Lacan points out in his seminar on *Identification* – seminar of 24 January 1962; *a* is an object of identification as it is made clear in *Anxiety* – seminar of 23 January 1963). To sum up, fantasy attempts to make bearable the lack in the Other – which is not the same as filling it up, something ultimately impossible; it attempts to achieve a 'forgetting of origins' of reality, that is to say of the act of decision/exclusion which stands at its genesis, to sediment an objectivity suturing the distance between the real and reality. It attempts to do so by offering us the object as a metaphor of our lacking fullness. This promise, however, can only be sustained if its realisation is deferred. Its realisation is always lacking. Thus, the object is ineradicably related to lack. It can only be manifested as lacking. By promising an always absent fullness it positivises symbolic lack.[10] If, as Lacan points out, *a* 'is related to the imaginary and the Other [A] to what is related to the symbolic' (XX: 83), it could be argued that the object performs a symbolic function (supporting the lacking fullness of the symbolic) by promising an imaginary mastery of the impossible real. If identification (in its dominant symbolic dimension) is fundamentally played out at the symbolic plane, fantasy reintroduces an imaginary promise as an answer to the anomaly emerging at the intersection of this symbolic and the persisting real.

At this point it seems impossible to develop further our argumentation without discussing and encircling the traces of the Lacanian real. One of the possible ways to approach this elusive but persisting real is to present a 'chronological' account. Bruce Fink, for example, and he is not alone here – his comments build on Miller's class *Orientation lacanienne* – develops a distinction between a first real, the pre-symbolic real, real$_1$ as he calls it, and the real as it is surfacing after the introduction of the symbolic, the real 'after the letter', real$_2$. The first real which is not accessible as such, undergoes a progressive symbolisation in the child's life without ever being totally absorbed by the symbolic. There is always a certain remainder which cannot be symbolised and persists alongside the symbolic. Although it is the 'primitive' real which is the epicentre of all our symbolic constructions, although it is the quest for this inaccessible real that motivates our desire, it is impossible to say anything about it; in fact this real is 'our own hypothesis' (Fink, 1995a: 28), a hypothesis founded on the careful evaluation of the play between symbolisation and its failure: if symbolisation is never total then something must be always escaping it.

Since *jouissance* emerges as one of the most important modalities of the real, Fink introduces a similar schema in his approach to *jouissance*. He distinguishes *jouissance*$_1$ from *jouissance*$_2$, that is to say *jouissance* 'before the letter', from *jouissance* as it is 'refound' or restaged in fantasy, as the remainder of symbolisation:

> this second order of *jouissance* takes the place of the former 'wholeness' or 'completeness' [the real unity between mother and child] and fantasy – which stages this second order *jouissance* – takes the subject beyond his or her nothingness, his or her mere existence as a marker at the level of alienation, and supplies a sense of being.
>
> (Fink, 1995a: 60)

It is certain that such an approach is legitimate, pedagogical and fruitful; it is, furthermore, based on some of Lacan's own insights. The only problem is that by approaching things in chronological terms we risk the danger of projecting what we know of the second order phenomena (real$_2$ and *jouissance*$_2$) onto the first order phenomena of which we know nothing (at least nothing positive or concrete). In a first approach, it is certainly true that in the alienated world of language *jouissance* is posited as a lost, pre-symbolic state of bliss, unity and fullness; but this is not a picture of the pre-symbolic *jouissance per se*, it is only our retroactive construction of it, a construction due to the castrating intervention of the symbolic.

I take my lead in this regard from the Lacanian idea that 'the signifier is the cause of *jouissance*' (XX: 24). Once this is granted, one quickly realises that this chronological presentation of the real and *jouissance* should be accepted only as a view of the terrain in question from within the frame of symbolisation. The fact that the symbolic instituting human reality circles around an impossible real, an impossible/lost *jouissance*, 'doesn't mean that *jouissance* is prior to reality' (XX: 55). In any case it does not give us any indication of the nature of this pre-symbolic state. Such an idea (for which

Freud is perhaps to blame) presupposes a certain 'developmentalism' which is unacceptable for Lacan. In other words, the second order real, real$_2$, and the second order *jouissance*, *jouissance$_2$*, are produced by the introduction of the symbolic to a pre-symbolic state, to a terrain which cannot be approached adequately any more. *Jouissance$_2$*, as it is staged in fantasy, is a false real, a domesticated real that cannot indicate what the pre-symbolic real is (Lacan himself alludes to these imitations of *jouissance* – seminar of 2 May 1962). It only shows our projection of it, our hypothesis of it, which is always a retroactive effect of symbolic castration. Symbolic lack, the lack of *jouissance* in the Other, creates the desire for an imaginary fullness which is projected onto our representation of the real. Once the symbolic order is introduced it creates the illusion that it has always been there, since 'we find it absolutely impossible to speculate on what preceded it other than by symbols' (II: 5), symbols which are supported by a fantasmatic frame. For this reason it is impossible to inquire into the nature of any pre-symbolic state. The closest we can get to that pre-symbolic or non-symbolisable real is through the points of failure of the symbolic,[11] but this again doesn't provide us with any positive description of what the pre-symbolic real 'really' is.

So far in this section we have been mainly focusing on an examination of the concept of fantasy in its relation to the real and *jouissance*. It is now time to turn to the Lacanian category of the *objet petit a* around which every fantasy is articulated. It is exactly because no object can embody the real as such that *a* can only function as cause if it is posited as an outside, an exteriority before internalisation (simultaneously concealing the fact that this internalisation is ultimately impossible). The object can only function as object of desire when it is absent, it can cause and perpetuate desire only if it is lacking, making the satisfaction of this desire impossible (when the object embodying the *objet petit a* function is acquired then desire is fixed on another lacking object). In that sense, the *objet petit a* is another modality of the necessary/impossible couple in Lacanian theory. *Objet petit a* is also defined by Lacan, in *Identification*, as the object of castration. Here the intimate relation between desire and lack is fully revealed. This object of castration takes the place of the nodal point of the missing ultimate signification of the Other. The *objet petit a*, emerging at the point of failure of the Other, embodies this lack of the Other together with the promise of its filling, thus creating the illusory consistency of the world. In other words, the object is exactly what links desire and *jouissance*. Desire is stimulated by lack and can never be fulfilled, it aims at its reproduction as such; in that sense desire keeps us away from *jouissance* (seminar of 23 March 1966). *Jouissance*, on the other hand, is something total but impossible, it is what desire can never reach. The object is exactly what unites these two dimensions. It provides desire with a certain consistency by embodying the impossible *jouissance* as a prohibited fullness. This metaphor of *jouissance* is what sets in motion the metonymic sliding of desire.

In that sense, *objet petit a* designates the effects of a signified or a transcendental signifier binding together signification, a lacking entity whose presence is always deferred. It is only a reference to an absent/sacrificed *jouissance* that can perform this task. Before introducing the concept of the *objet petit a* Lacan had assigned this role to the phallus as the signifier of desire:

> That there must somewhere be *jouissance* of the Other is the only possible check on the endless circulating of significations – but this can only be ensured by a signifier, and this signifier is necessarily lacking. It is as his payment to this place that the subject is called upon to make the dedication of his castration – the negative mark bearing on the organ at the imaginary level (the lack of phallic image in the image desired) is positivised as phallic symbol, the signifier of desire.
>
> (Lacan and the École Freudienne, 1982: 117)

The imaginary phallus has to be sacrificed in order for the symbolic phallus to appear, as the signifier of desire. The phallus, as the signifier of desire, is the signifier of the *Aufhebung* which it inaugurates by its disappearance (Lacan and the École Freudienne, 1982: 82). The phallus is a signifier, the signifier of all signifiers, the point around which signification centres: 'For the phallus is a signifier...the signifier intended to designate as a whole the effects of the signified, in that the signifier conditions them by its presence as a signifier' (E: 285).

It could be argued that the concept of the *objet petit a* gradually takes, in the work of Lacan, the place of the symbolic phallus. The object-cause of desire takes the place of the signifier of desire. It could even be possible to consider these two terms as identical. In *Desire and its Interpretation* Lacan notes that the object of desire should be understood primarily as a signifier (seminar of 1 July 1959). And in his seminar on *The Formations of the Unconscious*, although at first he declares that the phallus is a signifier and not an object, later on, however, he uses the two concepts interchangeably. In fact, it could be argued that when he differentiates the phallus from the object he has in mind a particular definition of the object. This point is made clear in the *Écrits*: 'Nor it is [the phallus] as such an object, (part-, internal, good, bad, etc.) in the sense that this term tends to accentuate the reality pertaining in a relation' (E: 285). In that sense, it would be plausible to argue that both the phallus and the *objet petit a* correspond to the same field but viewed from different angles, from the angle of the signifier and from the angle of the object, something which signifies the shift in Lacan's interest from the symbolic aspect of desire to its real dimension. The symbolic phallus is produced through the castration of the imaginary one which is nothing but the elevation of the real phallus to an imaginary state (the false real to which we referred earlier). The object, on the other hand, is related to the recognition of the fact that the symbolic is also marked by a fundamental impossibility, by a radical lack. This is a lack of real *jouissance*. The object aims to cover over this lack, it is promising to bring back the real; this is an imaginary promise which can be supported only when the object is posited as missing. As Colette Soler has put it 'the object of fantasy has a twofold status: It is the object that is lacking in the subject, and the object that fills the lack in the subject' (Soler, 1995: 267). Here, there is a certain symbolic dimension entering the field of the object. In other words, both the phallus and the object support desire by promising an encounter with the castrated real but the phallus is a promise in which the symbolic dimension is dominant (since it is seen as an answer to the disintegration of imaginary unity) while what is dominant in the object is the real *as lacking* (this is again the symbolic dimension) and being represented by an *imaginary* fullness.

This section examined, albeit in a brief and elliptical manner, the way concepts such as 'fantasy' and *'objet petit a'* function within Lacanian theory. But in what sense are these concepts relevant for socio-political analysis? Is not fantasy, for example, a strictly individual entity? What has to be stressed once more at this point is that the domain of fantasy does not belong to the individual level; fantasy is a construction that attempts, first of all, to cover over the lack in the Other. As such it belongs initially to the social world; it is located on the objective side, the side of the Other, the lacking Other. Even in Freud fantasy involves the subjective registration of normative symbolic structures:

> although the subject regards his fantasy as his private property and
> his most intimate and idiosyncratic possession, the fantasy is the
> precipitate in the subject of formations which are beyond the limits
> of subjectivity and intersubjectivity – formations which are present
> in myths, legends, fairy tales, stories and works of art of different
> times and civilisations.
>
> (Rodriguez, 1990: 101)

In that sense, fantasy belongs to these Lacanian scandals in which the standard form of the opposition between the subjective and the objective is subverted. If fantasy is not 'objective' (it does not exist outside subjective perception), it is also not 'subjective' (it is not reducible to subjective consciousness). It belongs to what Žižek calls the 'objectively subjective' level (Žižek, 1997b: 118). Fantasy is located on the side of reality, it sustains our sense of reality (Žižek, 1997b: 66). Our social construction of reality acquires its ontological consistency due to its dependence on a certain fantasy frame. When this frame disintegrates, the illusion – the promise – of capturing the real that sustains reality, the illusion that closes the gap between the real and our symbolisations of it, between signifier and signified, is dislocated.

What is, however, the exact political significance of the fantasmatic promise? From millenarianism to the *Communist Manifesto* and up to Green ideology, we know that every political promise is supported by a reference to a lost state of harmony, unity and fullness, a reference to a pre-symbolic real which most political projects aspire to bring back. Once again, the constant presence of this idea of a lost past is not revealing anything about the true nature of such a state; it is a retroactive projection conditioned by the intervention of symbolic lack. If social reality is lacking, if enjoyment is only partial, then the pre-symbolic state we long for has to be a state of fullness, a state without limits; *'jouissez sans entrants'* was one of the slogans of *les événements* of May 1968 as it is revealed in the famous photograph taken by Cartier-Bresson. The attributes of this state as articulated in political fantasy are a retroactive effect of symbolisation: symbolisation makes us believe that what is impossible was prohibited and thus can also be recaptured. Psychoanalysis, as we shall see, recognises the importance of such fantasies without affirming their empirical plausibility or sanctioning their imaginary projections. In that sense, although Freud's 'pre-civilisation state of happiness', characteristic of the primal horde, goes against all available ethnographic and archaeological material (Leledakis, 1995: 175), it is a 'necessary fiction', a myth bringing to the fore the utopian structure of human fantasy. This state of happiness, embodying the lost/impossible *jouissance*, has to be posited as lost (and thus as pre-existing our current state) if our life in the socio-symbolic world is to have any meaning; without it no desire for social and political identification would arise. This does not mean, of course, that psychoanalysis accepts the possibility of an adequate embodiment of this pre-symbolic real.[12]

To summarise my argument so far in this chapter, this is then the paradox of the human condition in Lacan. The field of discursive representation, a field extending from the linguistic to the social in general, is constitutive in all our doomed attempts to achieve a perfect identity with ourselves. But the central feature of language, of the symbolic, is discontinuity: something is always missing in language, the symbolic itself is lacking. Words can never capture the totality of the real, they can never fully represent us. As Lacan points out in *Television* (1973), language cannot say the whole truth. The words to do it are missing; it is *materially impossible* (these are Lacan's exact words) to achieve it and this is a source of alienation in which what emerges is the lack in every representation. This is also why entering into the field of linguistic representation permits the development of our desire and a certain structuration of our identity; but this identity can never be full since the symbolic is never full. Entering into language entails a loss of immediacy, the loss of a direct unmediated fulfilment of need. It entails symbolic castration. We are forced to approach the real through its symbolisation, by attempting to represent it, but thus we loose it for ever. Entering into the social world entails a loss of this register of the real, it entails the emptying out of *jouissance* from the body. 'And what is the agent of this castration?' asks Darian Leader, 'What creates lack that in turn gives rise to creative efforts to suture lack?' asks Ellie Ragland-Sullivan: 'the symbolic register as such, language. The organisms passage through and into language is castration, introducing the idea of loss and absence into the world' (Leader, 1996: 148). It is language that murders the referent, things as full presence (Ragland-Sullivan, 1991: 4). This is the meaning of the Lacanian *dictum* 'there is no Other of the Other' (E: 316). The Other cannot offer what we demand from him, that is to say our lost/impossible *jouissance*; precisely because the Other is structured around the prohibition, the sacrifice of this *jouissance. Jouissance* is forbidden, this is the Law of the Other. It is foolish to believe that this absence is due to the particular social and political configuration (E: 317). Alas, it is a structural irreducible feature of the Other, of the symbolic as such: 'We must insist that *jouissance* is forbidden to him who speaks as such' says Lacan (E: 319).

We can also approach this issue from the point of view of the relation of the signifier to the Thing. The Thing is what has to be represented by the signifier, but this representation is not a smooth enterprise:

> the Thing is that which in the real, the primordial real, I will say, suffers from the signifier – and you should understand that it is a real that we do not yet have to limit, the real in its totality, both the real of the subject and the real he has to deal with as exterior to him.

> (VII: 118)

This representation 'involves flocculation, the crystallisation into signifying units'. The Thing can only be sought in the paths of the signifier, it can only be represented in the field of the Other, and only as represented by something else, as veiled (ibid.). Thus we are revealed as divided between our representations of ourselves and our real *jouissance*. In our representations we are continuously searching for this lost-impossible real but this quest is doomed to failure since it is our attempts to symbolise the real that force us to lose it for ever.[13] And the reason we still symbolise, we still represent, we still identify, is that every symbolisation, every representation of reality is articulated around a fantasy frame, a promise of encountering our lost *jouissance*. Fantasy creates this illusion by offering us the *objet petit a* as embodying, in its absence, this fullness. Fantasy, however, cannot fulfil desire – since it cannot capture the unknown pre-symbolic real; it can only sustain it, revealing human experience as a dialectics of impossibility. The promise of fullness that sustains desire is generated in a performative way by symbolic lack. The objective level is thus revealed as the level of a structural lack but also as the level in which fantasmatic, futile attempts to neutralise this lack are taking place. If, however, symbolisation and fantasy are crucial in every such attempt to produce the impossible object 'society' doesn't that mean that Lacanian theory is but another version of social constructionism, of the idea that reality as a coherent whole is socially constructed?

Lacan and the social construction of reality: posing the problem

At first it is indeed possible to confuse the anti-objectivist dimension of Lacanian theory with the standard social constructionist argumentation recently in vogue. Lacan suggests that social reality is not a stable referent, a depository of identity, but a semblance created by the play of symbolisation and fantasmatic coherence. Reality is lacking and, at the same time, attempting to hide this lack through the symbolic and imaginary means at its disposal. Social constructionism is also articulated on the basis of the critique of objectivist and essentialist conceptions of reality. If, in the past, it was thought possible to acquire an objective representation or symbolisation of reality, even of the deep essence of things, constructionism argues that the failure of all these attempts, the historical and social relativity of human representations of reality, show that this reality is always the result of a process of social construction. What we accept as (objective) reality is nothing but a social construction with limited duration. Reality is always constructed at the level of meaning and discourse.[14]

The importance of constructionism is very clearly shown in our representation of nature since nature is something we usually perceive as objectively real. Nature, in everyday discourse, refers to the idea of an objective externality which can be absolutely intelligible through the mediation of sensation and without the intervention of social meaning. This is a belief still widely shared by natural scientists, Green activists and lay people. But how natural is nature? In order to answer this question social constructionists focus their attention on the coexistence, in the same social terrain, of different, if not contradictory, representations of nature. It is obvious that in our societies a Green activist and an industrialist do not share the same conception of nature. Social constructionism is based on the recognition of this social relativity of knowledge. As Berger and Luckmann have pointed out, what is real for a Tibetan monk may not be real for an American businessman (Berger and Luckmann, 1967: 15). The same applies to the level of diachrony. Our perception of reality is not only socially relative but also historically relative. As Collingwood and Kelsen have shown, the ancient Greek conception of nature differs from the Renaissance and the modern conception, while the primitive attitude towards nature is markedly different from modern scientific conceptions of nature (Collingwood, 1945; Kelsen, 1946).

What social constructionism concludes from the social and historical relativity of human knowledge is that reality is socially constructed; that it is impossible, for example, to pin down once and for all the essence of nature. For humans, reality comes to existence as a meaningful whole only within a network of meaning, within the level of discourse in which the elusive 'objective' reality is articulated with the meaning with which it becomes visible for us. This shift from a naturalist to a culturalist paradigm signifies a change of perspective: it is not social meaning that is reduced to nature but nature that is revealed as socially constructed at the level of meaning. Within the naturalist framework, real nature (as represented in the 'objective' discourse of the naturalist) is accepted as the signified of all social meaning. Social constructionism introduces an important reversal: nature is only a signifier and its signified is society, which sets the rules according to which we understand the world (Eder, 1996: 31). Not only nature is a signifier and not an object or a signified, but its own signified, the signified of 'nature', is not reality (as a hard extra-discursive entity), but the level of construction, of the production of social meaning. The signified is itself a signifier; in a very Lacanian manner signification refers only to another signification, and so on and so forth. Today that social constructionism is hegemonising the terrain of the social sciences, it is standard textbook knowledge (normal science in Kuhn's vocabulary) that 'nature is increasingly being seen as a social construction. Social science can no longer suppose the objectivity of nature as an unchanging essence' (Delanty, 1997: 5).

This stress on the loss of an objective, natural anchor of meaning, the reversal of constructionism, seems, as we have already hinted, very close to the Lacanian conceptualisation of signification. The signified, the real object implied in signification, is ultimately absent in both cases and a replacement constructed through a signifying process. In Lacan, it is also the case that reality is always precarious (III: 30). The reality with which psychoanalysis is concerned 'is upheld, woven through, constituted, by a tress of signifiers'; reality, in other words, 'implies the subject's integration into a particular play of signifiers' (III: 249). It is the signifier that produces reality:

> Day and night, man and woman, peace and war – I could enumer-
> ate more oppositions that don't emerge out of the real world but
> give it its framework, its axes, its structure, that organize it, that
> bring it about that there is in effect a reality for man, and that he
> can find his bearings therein. The notion of reality that we bring to
> bear in analysis presupposes this web, this mesh of signifiers.
>
> (III: 199)

In short, reality is always discursively constructed. In *Crucial Problems for Psychoanalysis*, Lacan points out that any reference to reality, to reality as an objective whole, should generate a certain mistrust (seminar of 24 February 1965); elsewhere he refers to the myth of reality. And, in *Encore*, he concludes: 'There isn't the slightest prediscursive reality, for the very fine reason that what constitutes a collectivity – what I called men, women, and children – means nothing *qua* prediscursive reality. Men, women, and children are but signifiers' (XX: 33). Existence depends on linguistic representation; what cannot be articulated in language, strictly speaking, does not exist. The emphasis here tends to be on symbolic construction. It seems then legitimate to reduce the Lacanian position to a pure constructionist one. Or not?

On a fairly simple level, one can even point to a series of direct links between Berger and Luckmann's influential book on *The Social Construction of Reality* (Berger and Luckmann, 1967) and analytic theory. For example, they seem to argue that the internalisation of the socially constructed reality, in the first years of our life, is achieved through a process of primary socialisation. This process is, in fact, based on the identification with our parents and through them with what Berger and Luckmann call the 'base-world', our first conception of the world as a structured unity. We can easily see the similarity between this identification that structures our conception of reality and Lacanian imaginary identification that, in a sense, initially structures our subjective reality. Berger and Luckmann talk about a secondary socialisation also. This process seems to be similar to the Lacanian symbolic identification. This second socialisation is achieved through the identification with sub-worlds, that is to say, partial symbolic structures such as the rules of a game, a certain professional attitude, etc. Here the dimension of imaginary unity is replaced by a conception of symbolic rules and norms.

These analogies, however, are only superfluous. Furthermore, they are limited to an exploration of the relation between the socially constructed reality and the individual, an opposition ultimately subverted in the Lacanian schema. Having already established that Lacan breaks with this sort of opposition, our main interest will be to examine the relevance of Lacanian theory for the analysis of the process through which reality is constructed in the first place. In fact, Lacan has a lot to contribute on the issue of explaining the particular ways in which this 'objective' reality is socially produced.

Exploring reality

We have already shown that the Lacanian conceptualisation of the symbolic offers a plurality of angles through which we can approach the ways in which meaning is produced at the level of the signifier. First, social construction is possible exactly because meaning and signification do not depend on some stable signified or transcendental signifier. Starting from the deconstruction of the relation between signifier and signified, Lacan ends up with a novel theory of meaning which has important implications for the construction of reality. As we shall see in the next chapter, this Lacanian theory of construction is also crucial in revealing the political implications of constructionist argumentation. Second, central to his conception of reality is the notion of fantasy. If a symbolically constructed reality can only be a lacking reality, fantasy is crucial in supporting this reality by creating the illusion of covering over this lack by staging, for example, a domesticated scenario of castration, a reduction with suturing effects.[15] We can summarise the basic parameters of Lacan's argument as follows:

Metaphor and metonymy   As we saw in Chapter 1, Lacan suggests that it is the signifier which is of prime importance in signification. The laws of the signifier are primary, in their autonomy, with regard to the production of meaning. Signification is produced through the relations between signifiers, through the formation of linguistic chains, chains that refer to other chains. Signification never indicates the real *per se*, but always refers back to another signification (E: 126). Lacan uses the term 'signifying chain' exactly because it 'gives an approximate idea: rings of a necklace that is a ring in another necklace made of rings' (E: 153). These necklaces, the signifying chains, exhibit a set of properties. In fact, Lacan's reference to rings and necklaces reveals the dual dimension of linguistic and discursive chains. Which are these two dimensions implied in the articulations of signifiers? The first one is the dimension of continuity and concatenation, the property of combination, while the second one is the dimension of the possibility of substitution, applying to each signifier in the chain. These two properties are not only the key for the production of meaning in general but also for the possibility of the articulation of ever new meanings. Following Jakobson, Lacan names the first one metonymy: 'it is in the word-to-word connection that metonymy is based. I shall designate as metonymy, then, the one side (*versant*) of the effective field constituted by the signifier, so that meaning can emerge there' (E: 156). The second property of signification he names metaphor: '*One word for another*: that is the formula of metaphor' (E: 157). In 'Direction of the Treatment' (1958) Lacan restates that what is at stake in metaphor is the substitution of one term *for* another, while in metonymy we have the combination of one term *with* another (E: 258). In other words, in Saussurean terms (and although Jakobson is radicalising the Saussurean schema and Lacan seems to be radicalising Jakobson's contribution), metonymy accounts for the syntagmatic/diachronic axis of language whereas metaphor accounts for its paradigmatic/synchronic axis.

Given this context, any exploration of the Lacanian theory of metaphor and metonymy has to start from Lacan's relation to Jakobson's linguistic insights. Lacan builds on two particular aspects of Jakobson's theory of metaphor and metonymy. In a first approach we could say that it is Jakobson himself who initiates the link between linguistics and the psychic level and thus opens the road to the Lacanian reappropriation of his theory. If, for Saussure, 'the linguistic sign is...a two-sided psychological entity' (Saussure, 1983: 66), for Jakobson also the theory of metaphor and metonymy is articulated at the cross-roads of linguistics with psychopathology; his whole theory is formed with reference to the various forms of aphasic disorder (the indicative title of Jakobson's article is 'Two Aspects of Language and Two Types of Aphasic Disturbances' – Jakobson, 1998: 31–54). Moreover, in developing the opposition between metaphor and metonymy, Jakobson is aiming at the formulation of a general theory of meaning and not just of a set of tools for linguistic analysis. Lacan also points out that the production of meaning through metaphoric and metonymic processes is very rich in its various implications for the analysis of many aspects of human experience. These two types can be discerned in all forms of semiotic systems including painting (according to Jakobson, cubism is metonymically oriented while realism is metaphorically oriented), cinema, story-telling, and psychic processes (Jakobson, 1998: 51–3). What is astonishing is that psychic processes and psychoanalysis are implicated in Jakobson's argument in two instances. First, they are presupposed, since metaphor and metonymy are formulated with reference to aphasia; and second, they are one of the semiotic fields in which this distinction can be made useful.

Yet, although it is Jakobson who makes the link between the two semiotic aspects and the Freudian *corpus* (*The Interpretation of Dreams* in particular), Lacan is more explicit in this respect. His argument is that what Freud describes as the formations of the unconscious – and here Lacan is referring again to the work of Freud on dreams, jokes and the psychopathology of everyday life – are produced through these mechanisms:

> The opposition between metaphor and metonymy is fundamental, since what Freud originally drew attention to in the mechanisms of neurosis, as well as in the mechanisms of the marginal phenomena of normal life or of dreams, is neither the metaphorical dimension nor identification. It's the contrary. In general what Freud calls condensation is what in rhetoric one calls metaphor, what one calls displacement is metonymy. The structuration, the lexical existence of this entire signifying apparatus, is determinant for the phenomena present in neurosis, since the signifier is the instrument by which the missing signified expresses itself. It's for this reason that

in focusing attention back onto the signifier we are doing nothing other than returning to the starting point of the Freudian discovery.

(III: 221)

At this point, however, one can point to a set of problems in Jakobson's theory and divergences from the Lacanian perspective. First of all, Jakobson and Lacan are not advocating exactly the same approach to metaphor and metonymy. As is the case with Saussure, Lacan incorporates Jakobson's terminology into his own *linguistérie*. Thus, Lacan has repeatedly been accused of using Jakobson's concepts in the wrong way. His answer to these accusations is epitomised in the following statement:

> When, beginning with the structure of language, I formulate metaphor in such a way as to account for what he calls condensation in the unconscious, and I formulate metonymy in such a way as to provide the motive for displacement, they become indignant that I do not quote Jakobson (whose name would never have been suspected in my gang – if I had not pronounced it) [Jakobson connects displacement with metonymy – Jakobson, 1998: 53].
> But when they finally read him and notice that the formula in which I articulate metonymy differs somewhat from Jakobson's formula in that he makes Freudian displacement depend upon metaphor [according to Jakobson's view, as it is expressed in 'Linguistics and Poetics', metonymy has a metaphoric dimension and metaphor a metonymic one – Jakobson, 1998], then they blame me, as if I had attributed my formula to him.
> They are, in a word, playing about.

(1977: xiv)

In this light, it becomes clear that Lacan's approach differs from Jakobson's in the sense that, by connecting them to the Saussurean legacy, he locates metaphor and metonymy in two different axes; as a result, the Lacanian opposition is much more sharp. Furthermore, in the Lacanian schema, both metaphor and metonymy become parts of a 'unified' theory of meaning. They are not lost in an ocean of polysemy but understood as two dimensions within a framework which although not reduced to them depends on their function in order to constitute itself.

What is a point de capiton? Stressing the importance of the laws of metaphor and metonymy does not mean that Lacan subscribes to the postmodern idea of an unending fluidity of meaning. It is true that each signification refers to another one and so on and so forth, and that both metaphoric substitution and metonymic combination can, in principle, be described as infinite, but, for Lacan, this endless movement of signification

59

is stopped by the prominent role attributed (retroactively) to certain signifiers. These signifiers he calls *points de capiton*: the *point de capiton* is the signifier which 'stops the otherwise endless movement (*glissement*) of the signification' (E: 303).[16] In his seminar on *The Psychoses* it is clear that the *point de capiton*, the quilting point, is the point with which all concrete analysis of discourse must operate (III: 267). These signifiers fix the meaning of whole chains of signifiers:

> Everything radiates out from and is organised around this signifier, similar to these little lines of force that an upholstery button forms on the surface of material. It's the point of convergence that enables everything that happens in this discourse to be situated retroactively and retrospectively.
>
> (III: 268)

Thus meaning is produced in the relations between signifiers through the establishment of certain *points de capiton*. Since it is indeed impossible to attach a definite signification to a signifier, what the *point de capiton* does is link signifiers to signifiers. The *point de capiton* fixes the signifier to a signifying knot and not to an object. Although without the retroactive (and retrospective) function of the *point de capiton* there would be no meaning, on the other hand, the existence of *points de capiton* never produces an eternally stable meaning, only a relative and temporary – albeit necessary[17] – fixation; nevertheless, this fixation is, most of the time, mythically invested with the properties of a final one. As Lacan points out in *The Formations of the Unconscious*, the sedimentation of meaning effected by the *point de capiton* is of a mythical nature.

This is where the difference between Lacan and most postmodern conceptions of meaning becomes apparent. Although Lacan accepts the priority of the signifier in the formation of meaning he also focuses on the ways this signifier mythologically attempts to embody the real, the ways in which it constructs the imaginary illusion of anchoring our symbolic being to a pre-symbolic level of immediate fulfilment of need. In other words, prioritising the signifier is coupled with exploring the complex ways in which this signifier produces the effect of the signified. The *point de capiton* is one of these ways. The *point de capiton* is directly implicated in the production of a signified or a transcendental signifier as the point of reference for signification. Without the reference to this structural position all meaning would be impossible. Let me illustrate the practical importance as well as some of the political implications of this operation with the example of the solution of the longitude problem, a story which currently became topical through the publication of Dava Sobel's popular science best-seller *Longitude* (Sobel, 1996).

These are, in brief, the basic parameters of the longitude problem: before the construction of suitable timekeepers by the English inventor John Harrison (1693–1776) it was impossible for seamen to calculate their exact longitude. This created so many obstacles to long-distance travel that, for more than two centuries, the quest for a 'scientific' solution of the longitude problem assumed legendary proportions 'on a par of discovering the Fountain of Youth, the secret of perpetual motion, or the formula for transforming lead into gold' (Sobel, 1996: 8). Although it was posed as part of a quest to master the real, the exact nature of the problem was related to the lack of a first reference point (the zero degree longitude) from which it would be possible to calculate any other longitude. What was missing then was a point of reference, a *point de capiton*. When Harrison perfected his timekeepers it became possible to keep a record of the distance from this first point. Its exact location, however, remained disputed. The crucial point not to be missed here is that this *point de capiton* was not a signifier directly representing a fixed signified, a real presence. There was no such signified; there was no natural anchor in the real. There was no geographical location embodying by nature the zero degree longitude. This anchor had to be constructed, and, in fact, it could be constructed in a plurality of ways: the zero-longitude, the prime meridian, had been identified with the Azores, Cape Verde, Rome, Copenhagen, Jerusalem, Pisa, Paris and other places. It could be put wherever one liked.

What does that reveal? It reveals that what was necessary for the stability and practical usefulness of a certain signification (the calculation of longitude) was the structural ordering introduced by a certain point of reference; this point of reference was a signifier whose signified could be produced in a variety of ways, all of them having comparable implications in terms of symbolising the real. What is also very important is that the structural role of the *point de capiton* in the production of meaning introduces a certain political element. What becomes evident in our example is that 'the placement of the prime meridian is a purely political decision' (Sobel, 1996: 4). If the role of the *point de capiton* is necessary (or universal) in structural terms, its particular content (the signified produced by its signifying predominance) is not a matter of mirroring a pre-existing objective reality but of hegemonic struggle. It is not surprising then that the final decision to declare the Greenwich meridian as the prime meridian of the world was taken at an international gathering, the International Meridian Conference held in Washington in 1884. It is also worth mentioning that this decision was partly the result of the gradual hegemonisation of the use of nautical tables for navigation at sea by the *Nautical Almanac* which was printed in England and used the Greenwich Meridian as the universal reference point. This hegemonic struggle resulted not only in the solution of the longitude problem but also in the solution of another problem, that of organising international time zones. Greenwich became the reference point for the calculation of time all over the world: 'Since time is longitude and longitude time...time zones the world over run a legislated number of hours ahead of or behind Greenwich mean time (GMT)' (Sobel, 1996: 168). One cannot underestimate the practical importance of these solutions: 'with the development of travel (mail-coach services and railway) during the nineteenth century there was growing concern for the standardization of time reckoning on a supralocal level. GMT became the basis for the formalization of a standardized railway timetable' (Thompson, 1995: 33). Today, even astronomers use GMT which they call *universal time*.[18]

Fantasy supports reality This signified function of the nodal point is not, however, solely reduced to its discursive position. It is supported by a whole fantasy construction. As Lacan argues in *Identification*, the object of fantasy comes to occupy the place of the lacking significance marking the nodal point around which the Other is structured (seminar of 27 June 1962). The construction of reality, the illusion of the world as a well-structured whole, would not be possible without the intervention of this element of fantasy. In Lacan's view, 'everything we are allowed to approach by way of reality remains rooted in fantasy' (XX: 95). As Jacques-Alain Miller has put it with a touch of exaggeration, 'reality is fantasy' (Miller, 1995: 12). Although in common sense usage and even in some psychoanalytic writing fantasy is opposed to reality, such a view of fantasy cannot be sustained within psychoanalytic theory; this is clear from the beginning in Lacan's theory of fantasy. As I have already pointed out, reality is not some kind of unproblematic given which can be perceived in one and only one objectively correct way, but something which is discursively constructed (Evans, 1996a: 59). The fantasmatic dimension of reality is also revealed in the link Lacan draws between reality and desire. In Lacan, the construction of reality is continuous with the field of desire. Desire and reality are intimately connected, argues Lacan in *The Logic of Fantasy* (seminar of 16 November 1966). The nature of their link can only be revealed in fantasy.

In order to illustrate further this point let us return to the example of our constructions of nature, a nature which is still generally thought as a hard reality, existing and being accessible independently of any fantasmatic scenario. This idea of nature is closely associated with an overwhelming consensus, forming the foundation of the science of ecology, that the 'natural', original state of nature was balance (a consensus that was hegemonic until a new generation of ecologists began to question all these old ideas and metaphors and to assert that nature is inherently unbalanced or chaotic – Worster, 1994: 389). The fact that this view of nature had to repress all the evidence for any other representation of nature, until that proved to be impossible (when chaos kept boiling out from nowhere, breaking down order and balance – Worster, 1994: 389), shows that, for humans, reality needs to be coherent, and since it does not seem to be by itself it has to be constructed as a coherent harmonious whole (at least a harmonious whole in the making). Of course, this harmony can be of many different forms. In the construction of nature, for example, one can trace a movement from the divine order of nature in Linnean ecology to the romantic holistic and animistic conception of nature. This trajectory culminates, within modern ecology, in the organismic idea of a climax of nature introduced by Clements, in Odum's 'ecosystemic' view and Love-lock's *Gaia*. No matter how different these representations of nature were they are all positing a harmonious nature. Take for example Worster's point about Odum and Clements, two of the most important figures in the science of ecology:

> Eugene Odum may have used different terms than his predecessor Frederic Clements, and he may even have had a radically different picture of nature; but he did not depart from Clements' notion that the law of organic nature was to bring order and harmony out of the chaotic materials of existence.
>
> (Worster, 1994: 367)

Mac Arthur, Odum and Clements, like Isaac Newton, 'had tried to make nature into a single, coherent picture where all the pieces fitted firmly together'. All of them tried to reduce the disorderliness or the unknown qualities of nature to a single all-encompassing metaphysical idea (Worster, 1994: 400). Even conceptions of nature stressing the element of conflict, such as the Darwinian one, sometimes feel the need to subject this non-perfect image to some discernible goal of nature (for example the 'constantly increasing diversity of organic types in one area' – Worster, 1994: 161) which introduces a certain harmony through the back door.

What constantly emerges from this exposition is that when harmony is not present it has to be somehow introduced in order for our reality to be coherent. It has to be introduced through a fantasmatic social construction.[19] One should not get the impression though that this is a mere philosophical discussion. In so far as our constructions of reality influence our behaviour – and this is what they basically do – our fixation on harmony has direct social and political consequences. Reality construction does not take place on a superstructural level. Reality is forced to conform to our constructions of it not only at the spiritual or the intellectual, but also at the material level. But why does it have to be forced to conform? This is due, for instance, to the gap between our harmonious fantasmatic constructions of nature and nature itself, between reality and the real. Our constructions of reality are so strong that nature has to conform to them and not they to nature; reality is conceived as mastering the real. But there is always a certain leftover, a disturbing element destabilising our constructions of nature. This has to be stigmatised, made into a scapegoat and exterminated. The more beatific and harmonious is a social fantasy the more this repressed destabilising element will be excluded from its symbolisation – without, however, ever disappearing.

In this regard, a vignette from the history of nature conservation can be revealing. As is well known nature conservation was developed first in the United States; what is not so well known is that 'a major feature of the crusade for resource conservation was a deliberate campaign to destroy wild animals – one of the most efficient, well-organized, and well-financed such efforts in all of man's history' (Worster, 1994: 261). All this, although not solely attributable to it, was part of a 'progressive' moralistic ideology which conceived of nature together with society as harbouring ruthless exploiters and criminals who should be banished from the land (Worster, 1994: 265).The driving force behind this enterprise was clearly a particular ethically distinctive construction of nature articulated within the framework of a conservation ideology. According to this construction what 'was' had to conform to what 'should be' and what 'should be', that is to say nature without vermin (coyotes and other wild predators), was accepted as more natural – more harmonious – than what 'was': 'These conservationists were dedicated to reorganizing the natural economy in a way that would fulfil their own ideal vision of what nature should be like' (Worster, 1994: 266). This construction was accepted by the Roosevelt administration in the USA (1901–9) and led to the formation of an official programme to exterminate vermin. The job was given to a government agency, the Bureau of the Biological Survey (BBS) in the Department of Agriculture, and a ruthless war started (in 1907 alone, 1,700 wolves and 23,000 coyotes were killed in the National Parks and this policy continued and expanded for years) (Worster, 1994: 263).

What is this dialectic between the beatific fantasy of nature and the demonised vermin doing if not illustrating the Lacanian dialectic between the two sides of fantasy or between fantasy and symptom? Since we will explore the first of these two Lacanian approaches to fantasy in Chapter 4, we will concentrate here on the fantasy/symptom axis.[20] As far as the promise of filling the lack in the Other is concerned, fantasy can be better understood in its relation to the Lacanian conception of the symptom; according to one possible reading, fantasy and symptom are two inter-implicated terms. It is the symptom that interrupts the consistency of the field of our constructions of reality, of the object of identification, by embodying the repressed *jouissance*, the destabilising part of nature excluded from its harmonious symbolisation. The symptom here is a real kernel of enjoyment; it is the repressed *jouissance* that returns and does not ever 'stop in imposing itself [on us]' (Soler, 1991: 214). If fantasy is 'the support that gives consistency to what we call reality' (Žižek, 1989: 49) on the other hand reality is always a symptom (Žižek, 1992). Here we are insisting on the late Lacanian conception of the symptom as *sinthome*. In this conception, a signifier is married to *jouissance*, a signifier is instituted in the real, outside the signifying chain but at the same time internal to it. This paradoxical role of the symptom can help us understand the paradoxical role of fantasy. Fantasy gives discourse its consistency because it opposes the symptom (Ragland-Sullivan, 1991: 16). Hence, if the symptom is an encounter with the real, with a traumatic point that resists symbolisation, and if the discursive has to arrest the real and repress *jouissance* in order to produce reality, then the negation of the real within fantasy can only be thought in terms of opposing, of stigmatising the symptom. This is then the relation between symptom and fantasy. The self-consistency of a symbolic construction of reality depends on the harmony instituted by fantasy. This fantasmatic harmony can only be sustained by the neutralisation of the symptom and of the real, by a negation of the generalised lack that crosses the field of the social.

But how is this done? If social fantasy produces the self-consistency of a certain construction it can do so only by presenting the symptom as 'an alien, disturbing intrusion, and not as the point of eruption of the otherwise hidden truth of the existing social order' (Žižek, 1991a: 40). The social fantasy of a harmonious social or natural order can only be sustained if all the persisting disorders can be attributed to an alien intruder. To return to our example, the illusory character of our harmonious construction of nature is shown in the fact that there is a part of the real which escapes its schema and assumes a symptomatic form (vermin, etc.); in order for this fantasy to remain coherent, this real symptom has to be stigmatised and eliminated. It cannot be accepted as the excluded truth of nature; such a recognition would lead to a dislocation of the fantasy in question. When, however, the dependence of fantasy on the symptom is revealed, then the play – the relation – between the symptom and fantasy reveals itself as another mode of the play between the real and the symbolic/imaginary nexus producing reality.

From reality to the real: Towards a realist constructionism or a constructionist realism?

Having presented some of the angles Lacanian theory provides constructionist argumentation, let us now return to our initial question: is it legitimate to reduce the Lacanian position to a constructionist one (either of a sociological, poststructuralist or postmodern kind)? Well, not really. What is the crucial difference? The difference is that, from a Lacanian perspective, exploring the symbolic and fantasmatic dimensions of social objectivity does not exhaust the whole debate on the nature of human experience. The increasing hegemony of constructionist argumentation does not mean that the argument of the social construction of reality is marking the end of the debate on the nature of the real. In fact, when constructionists are led to believe that the universe of social construction includes the totality of the real, that there is nothing outside social construction, a certain essentialism starts contaminating the constructionist argument, since construction acquires the structural position of the essence of our world, an essence the social constructionist claims to know. It is of course an essentialism paradoxically entailing the danger of solipsism, but this fact makes no real difference. Thus the anti-essentialist, anti-objectivist character of constructionism is dynamitised. The problem is similar to the one highlighted by Žižek *vis à vis* the non-existence of meta-language. Everybody seems to agree today that there is no meta-language; Lacan, Derrida, Gadamer appear to be in agreement (Žižek, 1987: 31). The same applies to constructionism insofar as constructionist argumentation denies the existence of a meta-language (scientific or other) capable of eliminating the distance between language and reality. But, as Žižek points out:

> The position from which the deconstructionist [and the constructionist] can always make sure of the fact that 'there isn't any meta-language', that no utterance can say precisely what it intended to say [that no utterance can say the truth about reality]; that the process of enunciation always subverts the utterance [that reality is always socially constructed], is the *position of metalanguage* in its purest, most radical form.
>
> How can one not recognize in the passionate zeal with which the post-structuralist insists that every text, his own included, is caught in a fundamental ambiguity and flooded with the 'dissemination' of the inter-textual process, the signs of an obstinate denial...a hidden acknowledgement of the fact that one is speaking from a safe position, a position not nuanced by the de-centred textual process?
>
> (Žižek, 1987: 33)

The blind spot of constructionism, according to this reading, is that on the one hand it reduces everything to the level of construction and, on the other hand, it occupies a meta-linguistic or essentialist position outside construction. This tension reveals one thing: the urge (the desire) of constructionism to occupy a position which is not reduced to construction.[21] It reveals, in other words, the existence, within the field of constructionist theorisation itself, of a position (although this is a position ultimately impossible to occupy) which is denied by the constructionist argument. Thus, in order to de-essentialise constructionist argumentation we need to relate the production of reality constructions to something external to the level of construction itself. This exteriority, however, cannot be a transparent exteriority, a new essence which is objectively accessible. If that was the case we would have a return to traditional essentialism and objectivism. In other words, this 'outside' cannot be a base on which the superstructure of reality constructions is erected. It has to be an exteriority *impossible* to represent, to construct at the level of symbolic meaning, but also *impossible* to avoid. If it is impossible to avoid it in the construction of our arguments it is all the more impossible to avoid it in our reflections on the nature of reality *per se*. But why is that exteriority necessary? It is not only because otherwise social constructionism becomes essentialist. It is also because any tautological entrapment into the world of social construction is incapable of providing an account of the cause that governs the productions of social constructions of reality. The crucial question that social constructionism is incapable of answering is the following: if the level of construction is engulfing the totality of the real, what stimulates the production of new social constructions? What stimulates the desire to articulate new constructions of reality? This cause has to be something external to the level of construction itself otherwise the argument enters into a tautological spiral. We have established then so far that in order to de-essentialise the constructionist argument and reveal the logic that governs its production and articulation, without however reoccupying a traditional essentialist position, we have to locate an exteriority which serves as the cause of our social constructions,[22] an exteriority which is in itself unrepresentable but constitutive of the play of representation. What can this element be? Let's start by exploring its traces within the level of representation itself.

Indeed it is possible to trace in constructionist argumentation a certain moment when something external to social construction makes its presence felt. It is the moment in which a 'problem' or a 'crisis' dislocates our social constructions (Berger and Luckmann, 1967: 39). This is much more evident in B. Holzner's study of *Reality Construction in Society* where he speaks of 'reality shocks', meaning the moments in which we come face to face with the impossible (Holzner, 1968). A. P. Cohen in his *Symbolic Construction of Community* seems, more or less, to share Holzner's views (Cohen, 1989). This conceptualisation of the moment of the meaningless *event*, of the accident or the disaster that destroys a well-ordered social world and dislocates our certainties, representing a crisis in which we experience the limits of our meaning structures, is something we cannot neglect. In fact, the resonance of the phrase 'social construction of reality' to young sociologists influenced by protest movements in the 1960s stemmed from its recognition of the vulnerability of the social order (Wrong, 1994: 45). Social construction presupposes the need for new constructions of reality and this need can only arise if social destruction is not only possible but constitutive. On the other hand, however, Berger and Luckmann, Holzner and Cohen do not recognise the tremendous importance of this moment. It is only in Laclau's argumentation that this moment of negativity acquires central importance. What Laclau shows is that the level of the objective, social reality itself as a sedimentation of meaning, exists in an irreducible dialectic with the moment(s) of its own dislocation. Social reality is eccentric to itself because it is always threatened by a radical exteriority which dislocates it. Further-more, this moment of dislocation is exactly what causes the articulation of new social constructions that attempt to suture the lack created by dislocation. Since dislocation denotes the failure and subversion of a system of representation (be it imaginary or symbolic) by not being representable, since dislocation creates a lack in the place of a discursive order, dislocation can be conceived as an encounter with the real in the Lacanian sense of the word. The lack, however, created by dislocation produces the need (rather the desire in our Lacanian vocabulary) for its filling. Hence the dual character of dislocations: 'If on the one hand, they threaten identities, on the other, they are the foundation on which new identities are constituted' (Laclau, 1990: 39).

This dual role is also characteristic of the effects of the Lacanian real. The real is not reality: it is a 'real that has nothing to do with what traditional knowledge has served as a basis for, which is not what the latter believes it to be – namely, reality – but rather fantasy' (XX: 131). The real is exactly what destroys, what dislocates this fantasmatic reality, what shows that this reality is lacking. The real is close to Ambrose Bierce's definition of calamity as the unmistakable reminder that the affairs of this life are not of our own ordering; it is whatever one cannot make what one wishes (seminar of 5 January 1966). In a continuous circular movement, however, disloca-tion and real lack stimulate the desire of their own subversion through an act of trying to found a 'new harmony' (Žižek, 1989: 193). If reality constitutes the symbolically constructed and fantasmatically supported part of objectivity, the real also belongs to the objective level, it is what exceeds the domesticated portion of the objective. It is exactly what accounts for the failure of all symbolic representations of objective reality: 'the object which accounts for the failure of every neutral-objective representation' (Žižek, 1997b: 214). The real is not an ultimate referent of external reality but the limit which hinders the neutral representation of external (symbolic) reality (Žižek, 1997b: 214). It is thus revealed in the failure of symbolisation itself. It is the radical externality which does not permit the internalisation of the socially constructed reality, it is exactly what keeps identification from resulting in full identity. Nonetheless, the real cannot be conceived independently of signification: it is revealed in the inherent failure/blockage of all signification, it is exactly what reveals all symbolic truth to be 'not-all', it can only be thought as the internal limit of the symbolic order. The real cannot be symbolised *per se* but is shown in the failure of every attempt to symbolise it (Žižek, 1997b: 217). It is an internally shown exteriority surfacing at the intersection of symbolisation with whatever exceeds its grasp.

As soon as we recognise the centrality of dislocation in our experience, we can easily understand the play between possibility and impossibility governing the field of social construction. If it is construction that makes possible the sedimentation of social reality, this reality is always threatened by an encounter with impossibility, with the part of the real that escapes the boundaries of construction. What is also shown in this reading of our experience is that dislocation and the lack it creates in our representations of reality, is exactly what stimulates our new attempts to construct new representations of this real. This play between possibility and impossibility, construction and dislocation, is structurally equivalent to the play between identification and its failure which marks the subjective level. However, this argumentation is still located at the level of a certain phenomenology of the social. How can we further approach the *status* of this element which stimulates our desire to represent it through social construction, but which, due to the impossibility to represent it fully, returns to dislocate all our social constructions? It is here that Lacanian theory can be of great help. In Lacan, the cause of this play between possibility and impossibility is, of course, the real. This is then the paradox of Lacan's relation to constructionist argumentation. Lacan is not a mere constructionist because he is a real-ist; that is to say, in opposition to standard versions of constructionism Lacanian theory of symbolic meaning and fantasmatic coherence can only make sense in its relation to the register of a real which is radically external to the level of construction. This Lacanian real-ism is, however, alien to all other standard versions of epistemological realism in the sense that this real is not the ultimate referent of signification, it is not something representable, but exactly the opposite, the impossible which dislocates reality from within. The real does not exist in the sense of being adequately represented in reality; its effects however are disrupting and changing reality, its consequences are felt within the field of representation. Lacan would be a constructionist if he was not a real-ist; or maybe he can be a true constructionist (since his constructionism avoids the solipsist, essentialist and objectivist dangers of traditional constructionism) exactly because he is a real-ist.[23]

This chapter, which is now coming to its conclusion, uncovered some of the ways in which Lacanian theory disrupts the homogeneity of the objective level both in its essentialist and its constructionist versions. The objective in Lacan includes the symbolic Other as a lacking structure, the pre-symbolic real which escapes this Other and the symbolic and fantasmatic ways through which we are compensated for this lack and attempt to repress it, to make it bearable. Only thus is social reality constructed – as an attempt to master the real through symbolisation. On the one hand, acknowledging the symbolic and fantasmatic dimensions of this and every reality disrupts essentialist objectivism while, on the other hand, recognising, within the objective level, the trace of an unrepresentable kernel of the extra-discursive real disrupts constructionist objectivism. To return to our example, it is now possible to identify two different natures: nature as reality, as a social construction, and nature as real, as that which is always located outside the field of construction and has the ability to dislocate it by revealing its limits. Evernden draws a relevant distinction between 'Nature', that is to say our signifying construction through which we attempt to represent nature, and 'nature' as the 'amorphous mass of otherness that encloaks the planet' (Evernden, 1992: xi). Nature, that is to say the representations articulated in the course of civilisation, is not reflecting nature. This is a utopian naturalisation of meaning. A naturalisation attempting to transform otherness to identity, the real to reality. Yet the opposite is true. What is thought to be a specular representation of nature (the mirror of nature to use Rorty's vocabulary) is revealed in the long run as mere construction (with all its real implications). When we encounter the real of nature, 'nature' in Evernden's vocabulary, when what was excluded from our symbolisations of reality is resurfacing, then our constructions are dislocated. The real dislocates social objectivity. This dislocation is introducing a strong political element, the element of radical rupture, into social constructionism and makes possible the approach to political reality articulated in the next chapter.

3

ENCIRCLING THE POLITICAL
Towards a Lacanian political theory

Politics v. the political

Chapter 2 examined the various ways in which Lacanian theory transforms our view of the objective side of human experience. If up to now our main focus was reality in general (especially in the last part of Chapter 2), I will start Chapter 3 by rearticulating some of the conclusions of the previous chapter but this time with particular reference to the field of political reality. Naturally, what we said about reality in general is also applicable to political reality.[1] But what is this political reality for which Lacan is relevant? In fact what exactly is political reality in general? We know that in mainstream political science, politics and political reality are associated with citizenship, elections, the particular forms of political representation and the various ideological families. Politics is conceived as constituting a separate system, the political system, and is expected to stay within the boundaries of this system: people, that is to say, politicians, social scientists and citizens, expect to find politics in the arenas prescribed for it in the hegemonic discourse of liberal democracies (these arenas being parliament, parties, trade unions, etc.), and also expect it to be performed by the accordingly sanctioned agents (Beck, 1997: 98). Although this well-ordered picture is lately starting to show signs of disintegration, with the politicisation of areas previously located outside the political system (as Beck has put it 'if the clocks of politics stop there [within the official arenas of the political system], then it seems that politics as a whole has stopped ticking' – Beck, 1997: 98), politics can only be represented in spatial terms, as a set of practices and institutions, as a system, albeit an expanding one. Politics is identical to political reality and political reality, as all reality, is, first, constituted at the symbolic level, and, second, supported by fantasy.

But if reality in general can only make sense in its relation to a real which is always exceeding it, what can that real associated with political reality be? If reality cannot exhaust the real it must be also the case that politics cannot exhaust the *political*. Not surprisingly then, it is one of the most exciting

71

developments in contemporary political theory, and one promoted by theorists such as Laclau, Mouffe, Beck and Lefort, that the political is not reducible to political reality as we have been describing it:

> The political cannot be restricted to a certain type of institution, or envisaged as constituting a specific sphere or level of society. It must be conceived as a dimension that is inherent to every human society and that determines our very ontological condition.
>
> (Mouffe, 1993: 3)

In order to illustrate this 'emancipation' of the moment of the political let us examine very briefly the relevant argument put forward by Claude Lefort. Lefort's project entails the reinterpretation of the political. He considers both the Marxist and the strictly scientific definitions of the political inadequate. Marxism regards the political as a mere superstructure determined by a base consisting of the supposedly real level of relations of production, and thus is unable to recognise any substantial specificity to the political. Political sociology and political science, on the other hand, attempt to delineate political facts in their particularity, as distinct from other social facts which are considered as belonging to other separate levels of social reality: the economic, the aesthetic, the juridical, the scientific, the social itself. Such an approach claims to provide an objective reconstruction of reality as consisting of all these strict differentiations and thus does not realise that its own constructs derive from social life and are, consequently, historically and politically conditioned – our discussion on constructionism becomes relevant again. In the definition of politics (as the space of political institutions, such as parties, etc.) what is lost is the political itself, meaning the moment in which the definition of politics, the organisation of social reality, takes place:

> The political is thus revealed, not in what we call political activity, but in the double movement whereby the mode of institution of society appears and is obscured. It appears in the sense that the process whereby society is ordered and unified across its divisions becomes visible. It is obscured in the sense that the *locus* of politics (the *locus* in which parties compete and in which a general agency of power takes shape and is reproduced) becomes defined as particular, while the principle which generates the overall configuration is concealed.
>
> (Lefort, 1988: 11)

The point here is that the institution of political reality presupposes a certain repression of the constitutivity of the political. It entails an impossible attempt to erase the political ontology of the social. In Lefort's view, for example, and here he draws from traditional political philosophy in which what distinguishes one society from another is its regime, its shaping of human existence, the political is related to what generates society, the different forms of society. It is precisely because the very idea of society contains a reference to its political definition that it becomes impossible to localise the political within society. The political is thus revealed as the ontological level of the institution of every particular shaping of the social (this expression denoting both giving meaning to social relations and staging them) (Lefort, 1988: 217–19). When we limit our scope within political reality we are attempting a certain domestication/spatialisation of the political, we move our attention from the political *per se* (as the moment of the disruption and undecidability governing the reconstruction of social objectivity including political reality) to the social (as the result of this construction and reconstruction, as the sedimented forms of objectivity) (Laclau, 1990: 35). This sedimentation of political reality (as a part or a subsystem of the social) requires a forgetting of origins, a forgetting of the contingent force of dislocation which stands at its foundation; it requires the symbolic and fantasmatic reduction of the political. Yet, 'to negate the political does not make it disappear, it only leads to bewilderment in the face of its manifestations and to impotence in dealing with them' (Mouffe, 1993: 140). What constantly emerges in these currents of contemporary political theory is that the political seems to acquire a position parallel to that of the Lacanian real; one cannot but be struck by the fact that the political is revealed as a particular modality of the real. The political becomes one of the forms in which one encounters the real.

The field of social construction and political reality is the field in which the symbolisation of this real is attempted. Chaitin is correct when asserting that symbolisation 'has the creative power to produce cultural identities, but at a price, the cost of covering over the fundamental nothingness that forms its foundation...it is culture, not nature, that abhors a vacuum, above all that of its own contingency' (Chaitin, 1996: 4–5), of its ultimate inability to master and symbolise the impossible real: 'there is a structural lack in the symbolic, which means that certain points of the real can't be symbolised in a definite manner....The unmitigated real provokes anxiety, and this in turn gives rise to never-ending, defensive, imaginary constructs' (Verhaeghe, 1994: 60). Following from this, 'all human productions [Society itself, culture, religion, science]...can be understood in the light of that structural failure of the symbolic in relationship to the real' (ibid.: 61). It is the moment of this failure, the moment of our encounter with the real, that is revealed as the moment of the political *par excellence* in our reading of Lacan. It is the constitutivity of this moment in Lacanian psychoanalysis that proves our fantasmatic conception of the socio-political institution of society as a harmonious totality to be no more than a *mirage*. It is this traumatic moment of the political *qua* encounter with the real that initiates again and again a process of symbolisation, and initiates the ever-present hegemonic play between different symbolisations of this real. This play leads to the emergence of politics, to the political institution of a new social fantasy (or of many antagonistic fantasies engaged in a struggle for hegemony) in the place of the dislocated one, and so on and so forth. In this light, Lacan's insistence on the centrality of the real, especially in the latter part of his teaching, acquires major political importance. Lacan himself, in his seminar on *The Four Fundamental Concepts of Psychoanalysis* uses noise and accident as metaphors or examples of our encounter with the real. It might be possible to add the political to this chain of equivalences. Lacan's schema of socio-political life is that of a play, an unending circular play between possibility and impossibility, between construction and destruction, representation and failure, articulation and dislocation, reality and the real, *politics and the political.*

It is this constitutive play which can help illuminate a series of political questions and lead to a novel approach to political analysis. As an illustration let us examine a concrete problem of political analysis. How are we, for example, to account for the emergence and the hegemonic force of apartheid discourse in South Africa? Is this emergence due to a positively defined cause (class struggle, etc.)? What becomes apparent now, in light of the structural causality of the political, is that the reasons for the resurgence of Afrikaner nationalism in the 1930s and 1940s are not to be found in some sort of 'objective' conditions (Norval, 1996: 51). Apartheid can be traced back to the dislocations that conditioned the emergence of this Afrikaner nationalist discourse (associated, among others, with the increasing capitalisation of agriculture, the rate of urbanisation and events such as the Great War). The articulation of a new political discourse can only make sense against the background of the dislocation of the preceding socio-political order or ideological space. It is the lack created by dislocation that causes the desire for a new discursive articulation. It is this lack created by a dislocation of the social which forms the kernel of the political as an encounter with the Lacanian real. Every dislocatory event leads to the antagonistic articulation of different discourses that attempt to symbolise its traumatic nature, to suture the lack it creates. In that sense the political stands at the root of politics, dislocation at the root of the articulation of a new socio-political order, an encounter with the real moment of the political at the root of our symbolisation of political reality.

Underlying Lacan's importance for political theory and political analysis is his insistence on the split, lacking nature of the symbolic, of the socio-political world *per se.* Our societies are never harmonious ensembles. This is only the fantasy through which they attempt to constitute and reconstitute themselves. Experience shows that this fantasy can never be fully realised. No social fantasy can fill the lack around which society is always structured. This lack is re-emerging with every resurfacing of the political, with every encounter with the real. We can speak about the political exactly because there is subversion and dislocation of the social. The level of social construction, of human creativity, of the emergence and development of socio-political institutions, is the level in which the possibility of mastering the real makes itself visible but only to be revealed as a chimera unable to foreclose a moment of impossibility that always returns to its place. Given this context, the moment of the political should be understood as emerging at the intersection of our symbolic reality with this real, the real being the ontological horizon of every play between political articulation and dislocation, order and disorder, politics and the political.[2]

Let us summarise our Lacanian commentary on the concept of the political. The political is not the real *per se* but one of the modalities in which we experience an encounter with the real; it is the dominant shape this encounter takes within the socio-objective level of experience. The moment of the political is the moment made possible by the structural causality of this real, a moment linked to the surfacing of a constitutive lack within our fantasmatic representations of society. It amounts to the cut of dislocation threatening all symbolisations of the social, to the ultimate subversion of any sedimentation of political reality. It is the moment in which the ontological impossibility of the real affects socio-political reality. It is also a moment located prior to all attempts and promises to cover over this lack, to reconstitute the fantasmatic coherence of the dislocated reality. Although it is internal to the development of such a desire, although it constitutes its condition of possibility, it evaporates as soon as the play of construction begins: it is what makes possible the articulation of new political projects and new social fantasies but is not compatible with them; their constitution demands the repression of the political. The political is associated thus with the moment of contingency and undecidability marking the gap between the dislocation of one socio-political identification and the creation of the desire for a new one.[3]

Exploring political reality

Stressing the constitutivity of the political is not, however, diminishing the importance of politics: 'the references to the political do not entail a dissolution of the formal sphere of politics. It merely calls for a distinction between the two registers that do not cease to intertwine with each other, to contaminate one another' (Arditi, 1993: 15). If Lacanian theory can provide the impetus behind a political theory exploring the connections between the political and the real or rather focusing on the moment of the political as an encounter with the Lacanian real, this is not equivalent to saying that Lacan has nothing to offer to a study of the ways in which political reality is constructed. As every reality, political reality, the world of politics, is constructed on the symbolic level (through the intervention of metonymic and metaphoric mechanisms as well as *points de capiton* and empty signifiers) and supported by fantasmatic frames providing its imaginary coherence by promising it an anchor in the real. Let me illustrate this point *vis à vis* political reality by presenting a series of concrete political examples:

Metaphor and metonymy or equivalence and difference? What is the relevance of metaphoric and metonymic production of meaning for the analysis of political reality? An answer to this question may be found in Laclau's and Mouffe's *Hegemony and Socialist Strategy*, where the construction of political spaces is revealed as governed by the principles of equivalence and difference. These two deeply political discursive principles are not alien to the linguistic and semiotic idea of the two poles of language (syntagmatic and paradigmatic) which, as mentioned in the previous chapter, Lacan connects directly to the logics of metaphor and metonymy:

> we could say that the logic of difference tends to expand the syntagmatic pole of language, the number of positions that can enter into a relation of combination and hence of continuity with each other; while the logic of equivalence expands the paradigmatic pole – that is, the elements that can be substituted for one another – thereby reducing the number of positions which can possibly be combined.
>
> (Laclau and Mouffe, 1985: 130)

But what is the exact nature of the logics of equivalence and difference? An extreme example of the way the logic of equivalence works is given in the logic of the revolutionary millenarianism of the Middle Ages. In the millenarian universe the world is divided into two paratactical chains of equivalences: the peasant world is conceived as standing against urban culture which is presented as the incarnation of evil. The second chain is constructed as the negative reverse of the first. It is the religious imagery of the bible which, when applied to political mobilisation, easily leads to such formations: 'Men coming to the bible with no historical sense but with the highest expectations found in it a message of direct contemporary relevance' (Hill, 1984: 93). In revolutionary millenarianism social struggle is not a struggle for specific objectives (something associated with a differential schema) but acquires a cataclysmic dimension; it becomes the showdown between two opposed camps (this is the principle of an equivalential organisation of political spaces). Social and political struggle is symbolised in terms of the division between hell and heaven, damnation and salvation, fall and redemption. In that sense, the logic of equivalence entails the simplification of political spaces and the expansion of the paradigmatic pole of meaning. Here, the logic of metaphor seems to be dominant.

An example of how the logic of difference plays itself out is the political project of Disraeli in the nineteenth century. Disraeli starts from acknowledging the existence of the two worlds (poverty and wealth) in order to eventually overcome this paratactical (equivalential) division. His main concern thus is the unification of a divided society (Vincent, 1990: 80–5). This aspiration is epitomised in his slogan: 'One Nation':

> Disraeli's rhetoric of national identity and the mutual interest and interdependence of classes effectively dissolved the problem of social cleavage which he had dramatised in *Sybil*, by treating it as an aberration from the norm of social relations. He saw it as caused mainly by the excesses of liberal individualism, and by an inattentiveness on the part of property to its social duties which could be compensated if its representatives showed, by the passing of social legislation such as that which distinguished Disraeli's second ministry, that the national institutions were responsive to the people's needs.
>
> (Smith, 1996: 218)

Simply put, Disraeli's project is based on the absorption of all social divisions into an ever-expanding system supported by the illusion of a society encompassing all differences and demands. The fantasmatic prototype of his ideal is that of a happy family: ' "One nation" was the celebration of shared experience within a happy family' (Vincent, 1990: 15). This is a logic of expansion of the syntagmatic pole of meaning, of the number of positions entering into a relation of combination (Laclau and Mouffe, 1985: 130) – a deeply metonymic political logic.

The difference between these two ways governing the organisation of political spaces and ideological frontiers is also evident in more recent examples, such as the comparison of Thatcherite and Blairite ideological strategies. There is no doubt that both these projects hegemonised the political field for a certain period of time as a result of a fierce ideological and electoral struggle. The Thatcherite right, for example, has to be understood 'in direct relation to alternative political formations attempting to occupy and command the same space. It is engaged in a struggle for hegemony, within the dominant bloc, against both social democracy and the moderate wing of its own party' (Hall, 1988: 44). The same applies, *ceteris paribus*, for the rise of Blairism. 'New Labour' is different (or presented as different) both from Old Labour and from the right. However, the way each of these political hegemonic projects represents the political space within which it operates (both before and after their electoral victory) seems completely opposite. The kernel of this opposition is the difference between the signifying domination of difference and the signifying domination of equivalence, between the logics of metaphor and metonymy:

77

Thatcherism was exclusionary; New Labour is inclusionary. Margaret Thatcher was a warrior; Tony Blair is a healer. Where she divided, he unites. Where she spoke of 'enemies within', he speaks of the 'people'. The Thatcherites saw themselves as a beleaguered minority, surrounded by insidious, relentless and powerful enemies. There were always new battles to fight, new obstacles to uproot, new heresies to stamp out. New Labour, with the same, not particularly impressive, proportion of the popular vote behind it, speaks and acts as though it embodies a national consensus – a consensus of all the well-intentioned, embracing rich and poor, young and old, suburbs and inner cities, black and white, hunters and animal rights campaigners, successful and unsuccessful. In place of the cold shower, it offers a warm bath, administered by a hegemonic people's party appealing equally to every part of the nation.

(Marquand, 1998: 19)

Points de capiton and empty signifiers We have already explained in some detail the function of the *point de capiton* in Chapter 2. A very good example of the importance of the *point de capiton* in the construction and coherence of a socio-political collectivity/objectivity is the Freudian description of the bonds holding a mass together as they are developed in *Group Psychology*. In Freud's view, what can unite thousands or millions of people is the relation – and the libidinal investment of this relation – of each one of them to a leader (political, religious or military) or an idea occupying the position of a *point de capiton*, a common point of reference. When the leader disappears (when for example the general is killed in battle) the mass disintegrates. It is the *point de capiton* then which creates unity. This is very well illustrated in a joke concerning 3,000 people who are taking part in a mass rally. Suddenly they realise that their leader has disappeared. The question which is immediately asked is the following: 'Where are we going, 3,000 people alone?'. What creates the feeling of unity and collectivity is not reduced to the physical presence of 3,000 people. When the identificatory link with the leader is cut the illusory character of collective identity and group power is uncovered. Without the intervention of a *point de capiton* (the leader in this case), instead of constituting a collectivity they are reduced just to 3,000 isolated individuals.

Given the importance of the *point de capiton* in creating a sense of unity, it is no surprise that the logic of the *point de capiton* has been central for the development of a Lacanian analysis of ideology, ideology being an important part of what we have called political reality. The crucial question here is the one formulated by Slavoj Žižek: 'What creates and sustains the identity of a given ideological field beyond all possible variations of its positive content?' And he answers: 'the multitude of floating signifiers, of

78

proto-ideological elements, is structured into a unified field through the intervention of a certain nodal point (the Lacanian *point de capiton*) which quilts them, stops their sliding and fixes their meaning' (Žižek, 1989: 87). In the vocabulary of discourse theory, which is used by Žižek in the preceding quotation, the Lacanian *'points de capiton'* become 'nodal points' – one more affinity between Lacanian theory and the work of Laclau and Mouffe:

> If the social does not manage to fix itself in the intelligible and insti-
> tuted forms of a society, the social only exists, however, as an effort
> to construct that impossible object. Any discourse is constituted as
> an attempt to dominate the field of discursivity, to arrest the flow
> of difference, to construct a centre. We will call the privileged dis-
> cursive points of this partial fixation, nodal points. (Lacan has in-
> sisted on these partial fixations through his concept of *points de
> capiton*, that is, of privileged signifiers that fix the meaning of a sig-
> nifying chain).
>
> (Laclau and Mouffe, 1985: 112)

In that sense ideological discourse should be conceived as an articulation (a chain) of ideological elements around a nodal point, a *point de capiton* (or a family of nodal points) 'such that their identity is modified as a result of the articulatory practice' (Laclau and Mouffe, 1985: 112). The structured totality resulting from the articulation is exactly what ideological discourse is. As Lefort has pointed out, ideological discourse is constituted as such 'by subjecting all spheres of society to the imperative of organisation' (Lefort, 1986: 218). The differential positions appearing articulated in a discourse, that is, appearing in the chain of signifiers of ideological discourse, are the *moments* of the discourse while *elements* (remember Žižek's proto-ideological elements) are called by Laclau and Mouffe all those differences that are not yet discursively articulated (Laclau and Mouffe, 1985: 105). The *point de capiton*, the signifier fixing the meaning and transforming the free-floating elements to moments of an ideological discourse, is present in Lefort in the metaphor of a centre which is always implied in ideology and from which 'social life is organised' (Lefort, 1986: 219). Let me illustrate this logic of discursive articulation with an example used by Žižek. In the ideological discourse of communism a series of floating signifiers or proto-ideological elements (previously articulated in other ideological discourses) such as democracy, state, freedom, etc. acquire a certain meaning through their quilting by the signifier 'communism'. Thus they are transformed to internal moments of the communist ideological discourse. Democracy is conceived as real democracy opposing bourgeois democracy, freedom acquires an economic connotation, etc. In other words, they acquire the meaning imposed by the *point de capiton* 'communism'; this is how communism can hegemonise a set of available signifiers. The same, of course, applies to all signifiers that acquire a political role and aspire to hegemonise a given politico-discursive field. It is in this sense that 'the Lacanian concept of the *point de capiton*, the nodal point that fixes meaning, is profoundly relevant for a theory of hegemony' (Laclau, 1988: 255).

It is evident that what is at stake in the function of the *point de capiton* is the fixation of a given discursive construct, the inclusion of a number of especially decontested signifiers in its signifying chain. Such an inclusion presupposes a certain exclusion, that is to say a signification of the limits of political reality. Social groups, for example, tend to define themselves through exclusion, by comparing themselves to 'strangers'. But how are these strangers defined? One crucial element is the lack of communication. What adds the uncanny flavour to the encounter with the stranger is the lack of a common language, the failure of communication. This is because it is impossible to represent linguistically, to communicate, what is beyond language. A number of names are employed to encircle this unrepresentable terrain: 'Terms like "gogim", "barbaroi", and "nemtsi" all imply such perception of the human incompleteness of persons who could not communicate with the in-group, which constituted the only "real men" ' (Armstrong, 1982: 5–6). It is because reality is constructed in discursive terms that the encounter with a non-member of a given linguistic community poses the problem of the limits of language and reality; it is the encounter with a real beyond our construction of reality. Only the exclusion of this real can guarantee the stability of our reality. Our reality can be real only if the real outside reality is negated, attributed to the Other who somehow stole it from us.[4] Benveniste has shown that anthropological historians were correct in perceiving this close relation between linguistic exclusion and the construction of an ethnic or other identity. It is possible to locate particular signifiers that function as 'traffic lights warning a group member when he is approaching a barrier separating his group from another [his reality from a real beyond his control]' (Armstrong, 1982: 5–6).

Both the *point de capiton* (for example the signifier 'communism', to return to our previous example) and the signifier marking the limit of political reality, the signifier representing, within our fantasmatic scenario, the excluded real ('capitalism' could be one from the point of view of a communist discourse) are empty signifiers. The *point de capiton*, on the one hand, can function as a point of reference only if posited as an incarnation of the universality of a certain group or collectivity, as a representative of the pure being or the systematicity of the system. In the *point de capiton* a particular signifier is called to incarnate a function beyond its concreteness, it is 'emptied' from its particular signification in order to represent fullness in general and be able to articulate a large number of heterogeneous signifiers. The nation is clearly such an empty signifier that serves as a *point de capiton* uniting a whole community (Demertzis, 1996). The signifier of exclusion, on the other hand, is also an empty signifier, but one that represents the opposite of the *point de capiton*: pure negativity; what has to be negated and excluded in order for reality to signify its limits. Reagan's characterisation of the USSR as the evil empire is a good case in point. Here again a particular signifier is 'emptied' from its concrete content in order to represent a negative universal, to stigmatise the always escaping real. We should not forget, however, that the symbolic construct articulated around the *point de capiton* and founded on the signification of the exclusion of the real can function properly only within a certain fantasmatic frame; the empty signifier can only function as an *objet petit a*. It has been argued that our linguistically constructed reality (an ethnic or nationalist ideology for example) depends on the incorporation of all 'individual symbols, verbal and non-verbal, in a mythic structure' (Armstrong, 1982: 6). It is necessary then to move from the consideration of the symbolic structure of political reality to its fantasmatic support. This movement is inscribed in the structure of the empty signifier itself insofar as the empty signifier is emptied of particular contents; the illusion is that it can become completely empty so that it can contain everything; within a certain transferential illusion, it is supposed that anything can be inscribed into it. The other side of semiotic emptiness is fantasmatic fullness.[5]

The fantasmatic support If political reality is a symbolic construction produced through metaphoric and metonymic processes and articulated around *points de capiton* and empty signifiers, it nevertheless depends on fantasy in order to constitute itself. This dimension must have become evident from our argumentation so far. It is useful however to present one more example in which this dimension is illustrated with clarity.

Fantasies of mastery, especially mastery of knowledge, have direct political significance. Thomas Richards, in his book *The Imperial Archive: Knowledge and the Fantasy of the Empire*, explores the importance of fantasy in the construction of the British empire. There is no doubt that no nation can close its hand around the whole of the world. In that sense an empire is always, at least partly, a fiction. Absolute political control is impossible due to a variety of reasons, such as the lack of information and control in distant parts of the imperial territory. This gap in knowledge (in the symbolic constitution of the empire) and control, was covered over by the fantasy construction of the imperial archive, 'a fantasy of knowledge collected and united in the service of state and empire'. In that sense 'the myth of imperial archive brought together in fantasy what was breaking apart in fact' and was thus shared widely; it even had an impact in policy-making (Richards, 1993: 6). This imperial archive was not a real museum or a real library, it was not a building or a collection of texts, but a fantasy of projected total knowledge: it constituted a 'collectively imagined junction of all that was known or knowable, a fantastic representation of an epistemological master pattern, a virtual focal point for the heterogeneous local knowledge of metropolis and empire' (Richards, 1993: 11). In this utopian space, disorder was transformed to order, heterogeneity to homogeneity and lack of political control and information to an imaginary empire of knowledge and power.

Such a fantasmatic support is, however, discernible in all the examples we have already presented. This is because all ideological formations, all constructions of political reality, although not in the same degree or in the same way, aspire to eliminate anxiety and loss, to defeat dislocation, in order to achieve a state of fullness. Thus 'what Thatcherism as an ideology does, is to address the fears, the anxieties, the lost identities, of a people....It is addressed to our collective fantasies, to Britain as an imagined community, to the social imaginary' (Hall, 1988: 167). The same applies to nationalism, to millenarian redemption, as well as to Disraeli's 'One Nation' and to Blairism. This fantasmatic element is crucial for the desirability of all these discourses, in other words for their hegemonic appeal. All political projects to reconstitute society as a well-ordered and harmonious ensemble aim at this impossible object which reduces utopia to a fantasmatic screen. If, according to Laclau's Lacanian dictum, 'society does not exist' (as a harmonious ensemble), this impossible existence is all the time constructed and reconstructed through the symbolic production of discourse and its fantasmatic investment, through the reduction of the political to politics.

Some difficulties in Lacanian political theory

The epistemology of the real

There are at least two objections that could be raised against such a political reading of Lacanian theory. The first one is of an epistemological and theoretical nature; it questions the 'epistemological' plausibility and operationality of Lacanian discourse. The second is of an ethico-political nature; it concerns the political relevance of this discourse as well as its effectivity and ethical grounding. Let's approach the first one through a point raised by Judith Butler in connection to the *status* of the real and our symbolic use of it in theoretical discourse. Butler argues that

> to claim that the real resists symbolisation is still to symbolise the real as a kind of resistance. The former claim (the real resists symbolisation) can only be true if the latter claim ('the real resists symbolisation' is a symbolisation) is true, but if the second claim is true, the first is necessarily false.
>
> (Butler, 1993: 207)

What Butler is in fact reiterating here is the well-known paradox of Epimenides who, as a Cretan himself, claimed that 'All Cretans are liars'. If this statement is true then he is also a liar but if he is a liar then his statement cannot be true. In both cases the paradox is irresolvable. Yet, what these paradoxes point to is exactly the real lack in our symbolic media, the real limits of any process of symbolic signification and resolution. And although we can never symbolise the real in itself, it is possible to encircle (even in a metaphorical way) the limits it poses to signification and representation. Although it is impossible to touch the real, it is possible to encircle its impossibility, exactly because this impossibility is always emerging within a symbolisation. Hence Lacan's position: 'I always speak the truth. Not the whole truth, because there's no way to say it all. Saying it all is literally impossible: words fail. Yet it's through this very impossibility that the truth holds onto the real' (1987: 7). Beyond the imaginary ideal of absolute knowledge, 'Truth is nothing other than that which knowledge can apprehend as knowledge only by setting its ignorance to work' (E: 296).[6] In that sense, Butler's claim is misleading because the statement 'the real resists symbolisation' is not a symbolisation of the real *per se*[7] but a symbolic expression of the limits it poses, a recognition of its structural causality as it is revealed in its relation to the world of symbolisation.[8] In the second case we have a symbolic gesture which has no positive-representational content. Underlying this view is the idea that psychoanalytic practice ultimately subverts – but cannot eliminate – the philosophical distinctions between the discursive and the extra-discursive, the linguistic and the extra-linguistic, the real and knowledge. What is shown sometimes in clinical experience (an analyst or an analysand may know something about that) is that analytic discourse is capable of effecting changes in the real *jouissance* of the subject, without reducing it (or its impossibility) to a positive representation (as in the case of a fantasmatic scenario).

It was Foucault who posed this crucial question back in the early 1960s, in *The Order of Things*, by formulating the following phrase: 'How can one think what he does not think [and the real in Lacan is something beyond whatever we can think about it] , inhabit as though by a mute occupation something that eludes him, animate with a kind of frozen movement that figure of himself that takes the form of a stubborn exteriority?' (Foucault, 1989: 323). And although his position was altered later in his work, his answer at that time was that psychoanalysis, instead of turning its back to this dark continent of the unthought, points directly to it, to the limits of representation, unmaking the positivity of man created by the human sciences (Foucault, 1989: 374–9). Psychoanalysis belongs to a form of reflection which involves 'for the first time, man's being in that dimension where thought addresses the unthought and articulates itself upon it' (Foucault, 1989: 325). This attitude is inscribed in the Freudian notion of the unconscious. The unconscious is a psychical agency whose existence 'we are obliged to assume', to infer it from its effects, 'but of which we know nothing' (Freud in Roazen, 1969: 49). Freud affirms that the unconscious –

and this is the real dimension of the unconscious – is unknowable as such and thus unsymbolisable in itself. Psychoanalysis aims at formulating a logic of relations and connections that 'attempt to encircle this unknowability', to represent the limit of the symbolic (of language and knowledge) and traverse the closure of fantasy, a move which becomes possible exactly because this limit is surfacing within the symbolic order of language and knowledge; this limit is an internal limit, an internal exteriority (Samuels, 1993: 144).

In this light, if the question is 'How do we know that the real resists symbolisation in the first place?' the answer must be 'Exactly because this resistance, this limit of symbolisation, is shown within the level of representation'. Psychoanalysis is based on the idea that the real is shown in certain effects persisting in discourse[9] – although it lacks representation *per se* – and that it is possible to enact the symbolic gestures which can encircle these moments of 'showing'; 'something true can still be said [and 'we have to show' how this can be done] about what cannot be demonstrated' (XX: 119). The question which remains open is what is the nature of these symbolic gestures. It is not so much a question of 'if' but a question of 'how': 'How can we know the real, if everything that can be categorised and explained within the framework of a scientific theory belongs to reality? How can any discourse reflect an authentic knowledge of the real?' (Lee, 1990: 137). Thurston is asking a similar question: 'How can an instance of language escape the semiotic conditions of representation?' (Thurston, 1998: 158); a question posed in the following terms by Badiou: 'How can a truth come to knowledge, whose own being, or relationship to being, is not able to be known?' (Badiou, 1996: 24). First of all it is impossible to do it by articulating some kind of pure meta-language; for Lacan, there is no meta-language except for a failed one, precisely because every meta-linguistic function has to be articulated in language (XX: 122). Whatever we can show about that which escapes language has to be shown in and through language, especially through the points where meaning is disrupted. The meta-linguistic aspiration to articulate an impossible knowledge of the real has to work

> between the words, between the lines. We have to *expose* the kind of real to which it grants us access. We have to show where the shaping (*mise en forme*) of that metalanguage – which is not, and which I make ex-sist – is going.
>
> (XX: 119)

One then has to locate the exact points within linguistic or discursive representation in which the real is surfacing. What is at stake here is our ability to inscribe, without neutralising it, to recognise using a symbolic strategy, the ultimate impossibility of the real as it is revealed in our traumatic encounters with it (traumatic in the sense that they disrupt the ordinary forms of symbolisation); what is at stake is our 'memory' of the political beyond the 'forgetting' orchestrated by political reality. It is clear that Lacan believes that it is possible to escape from the illusion of closure and approach the real by means of a study of paradox and bizarre representational structures such as topology (the Borromean knot, for example, is capable of showing a certain real; it 'represents' the real – XX: 133). In his 1972–3 seminar *Encore*, he makes it clear that the real can only be inscribed on the basis of an impasse of formalisation (XX: 93). It is through the failures of symbolisation – the play of paradox, the areas of inconsistency and incompleteness – that it becomes possible to grasp 'the limits, the points of impasse, of dead-end, which show the real yielding to the symbolic' (Lacan in Lee, 1990: 171). It is no coincidence that these moments are usually accompanied by anxiety.

Encircling the real can be also achieved through art. It does not need to be abstract art. In fact, artistic expression which uses the most naive realism – the representation of a pipe by Magritte pointing to the absolute mastery of the real by reality (Magritte's pipe purports to be not a representation of a pipe but the pipe itself) – is most successful in subverting it from within – the inscription 'this is not a pipe' subverts this fantasy by revealing in the most unexpected place the failure of representation to capture the real, 'showing' the real by revealing the distance between representation and the real. This failure is all the more evident because Magritte uses the most literal way of artistic expression; he uses 'literalism to undermine itself' (Harkness, 1983: 9). He allows the old field of representation to rule, but only temporarily, only on the surface; beneath there is nothing: the most literal representation is transformed to a gravestone of realist representation itself (Foucault, 1983: 41). What remains as a trace of the real is an absence inscribed within the field of representation (Foucault, 1983: 54).[10] But it is not only art; it is also philosophy and even politics. As we shall try to show in our discussion of Lacanian ethics in Chapter 5, it might be possible to inscribe a recognition of the real, to institute the moment of the political within the space of politics.[11]

However, Butler's point entails one more misunderstanding. It seems to imply that Lacanian discourse elevates the real to the status of a *Taboo*. Here Žižek's following formulation *à propos* of historical analysis is very important:

> Lacan is as far as it is possible to be from any 'tabooing' of the real, from elevating it into an untouchable entity exempted from historical analysis – his point, rather, is that the only true ethical stance is to assume fully the impossible task of symbolising the real, inclusive of its necessary failure.
>
> (Žižek, 1994a: 199–200)

In the face of the irreducibility of the real we have no other option but to symbolise; but such a symbolisation can take at least two forms: first, a fantasmatic one which will attempt to repress the real and to eliminate once and for all its structural causality. Psychoanalysis favours the second and more complex one: the articulation of symbolic constructs that will include a recognition of the real limits of the symbolic and will attempt to symbolically 'institutionalise' real lack.

Let me illustrate this point by returning to one of the examples I used earlier, that of nature. The crucial question regarding our access to the natural world becomes now: how can we then, if in fact we can, approach nature before it becomes Nature, the real before it becomes reality, before its symbolisation? This is the question posed by Evernden: how can we return to things 'before they were captured and explained, in which transaction they ceased to be themselves and became instead functionaries in the world of social discourse [?]' (Evernden, 1992: 110). How can we encounter the pre-symbolic Other in its radical otherness, an otherness escaping all our representations, if he is always 'beyond'? (ibid.: 118). Well, in fact we can't; what we can do, however, is acknowledge this failure, this constitutive impossibility, within our symbolisations. Trapped as we are within the world of social meaning, all our representations of reality are doomed to fail due to their symbolic character. Every attempt to construct what is impossible to be constructed fails due to our entrapment within the world of construction. The only moment in which we come face to face with the irreducible real beyond representation is when our constructions are dislocated. It is only when Nature, our construction of external reality, meets a stumbling block, something which cannot be symbolically integrated, that we come close to the real of nature. Nature, constructed Nature, is nothing but 'a mode of concealment, a cloak of abstractions which obscures that discomforting wildness that defies our paranoid urge to delineate the boundaries of Being' (Evernden, 1992: 132). Only when these boundaries collapse, in that minute intermission before we draw new ones, can we sense the *unheimlich* of real nature. It is in that sense that – as argued in Chapter 2 – Lacanian theory opens the road to a realist constructionism or a constructionist realism; it does so by accepting the priority of a real which is, however, unrepresentable, but, nevertheless, can be encountered in the failure of every construction. One final point before concluding this section: when applied to our own discourse isn't this recognition introducing a certain ethical principle? Recognising at the same time the impossibility of mastering the real and our obligation to recognise this impossibility through the failure of our attempts to symbolise it, indeed seems to introduce a certain principle which cannot be by-passed. Of necessity this is a principle affecting the structure of knowledge and science in late modern societies.

What is, in fact, at stake here is our attitude towards the element of negativity and uncertainty inherent in human experience. The unpredictability and severity of natural forces, for example, have prompted people, from time immemorial, to attempt to understand and master them through processes of imaginary representation and symbolic integration. This usually entails a symbolisation of the real of nature. The product of this symbolisation has frequently been described as a 'story' or a 'paradigm' about how the world works. We can trace such a story, or many competing stories, in any civilisation or cultural ensemble. Primal people often understood planetary forces and natural disastrous events as acts of god. As Mircea Eliade has pointed out, in *The Myth of the Eternal Return*, for traditional societies, historic profane events such as natural catastrophes, disasters, and misfortunes, that is to say, every encounter with the real of nature, denote the 'void', the non-existent, the unreal *par excellence*. Thus, they can only produce unbearable terror. They can only be tolerated if conceived as produced by the breaking of a taboo, by a magical action of an enemy or by the divine will; only if integrated, for example, in a schema of indefinite repetition of archetypes revealed *ab origine* by gods and heroes and repeated by men in cosmogonic recreative rituals and myths. As soon as the cause is pinpointed, the suffering of the encounter with the real of nature becomes tolerable, we have the symbolisation of the real. The suffering now has 'a [fantasmatic] meaning and a cause, hence it can be fitted into a system and explained' (Eliade, 1989: 98). It is symbolically integrated into a 'story' or a 'paradigm'. What is crucial here is not the exact form of this construction but its ability to provide a meaning capable of alleviating the uncanny character of experience.

Modernity is primarily associated with the dislocation of traditional constructions of this sort. The unexpected, and doubt, resurface on the horizon and are inscribed, perhaps for the first time with such force, in scientific and philosophical discourse and political imagination. Descartes' example is revealing since his whole enterprise is based on the recognition of the constitutive nature of doubt. But this position is not eliminating the traumatic character of negativity. It was understandable for people who were used to seek absolute constructions to continue to need them within the modern universe of meaning. This is why modern science 'reoccupied' the field of pre-modern certainties. One should not forget that even in Descartes' argument the constitutivity of doubt is acknowledged only to be eliminated, in a second move, by the emergence of absolute certainty. Thus, the recognition of doubt causes new anti-modern outbreaks that attempt to eliminate doubt anew and create new certainties that would put an end to the continuous questioning entailed by modernity in its critical dimension (Beck, 1997).

Although modern science is founded on the critique of pre-modern certainties, of 'objective' reason in Horkheimer's vocabulary, it did not manage to

> abandon the idea of a harmony between thought and the world, but just replaced the medieval idea that this harmony was preordained with the notion that thought and world could be brought into harmony with the use of a 'neutral' and 'objective' scientific discourse.
>
> (Szerszynski, 1996: 107–8)

In both cases the aim was to eliminate the distance between the real and reality, to articulate privileged representations of the world with universal validity independent of any social, cultural or discursive context (ibid.). Thus, modernity identified itself with the emergence of absolute certainties in the place of their dislocated pre-modern equivalents. The problem here is that seeking final and objective answers and failing to recognise that every answer of this kind is finite, articulated within a particular historical and social context, signals a return to the pre-modern world (Douglas and Wildavsky, 1982: 30). Negating its own founding moment, the moment of doubt and critique, Enlightenment becomes trapped in the pre-modern urge to master the totality of the real, to reach absolute certainty. This is the project of a royal science:

> The project of a knowledge that would unify this multiplicity of 'things to be known' into a homogeneous representable structure, the idea of a possible *science of the structure* of the real, capable of making it explicit, outside of any false semblance, and of assuring the control over this real without the risks of interpretation (therefore a scientific self-reading of the real, without faults or lack) – this project obviously corresponds to an urgency so vivid, so universally 'human', tied (knotted) so well (around the same stake of domination/resistance) to the interests of successive masters of this world, as well as to those of the wretched of the earth, that the phantasm of such an effective, manageable, and transmissible knowledge could not fail historically to use any means to make itself materialize.
>
> The promise of a royal science as conceptually rigorous as mathematics, as concretely effective as material technologies, as omnipresent as philosophy and politics – how could humanity resist such a godsend?
>
> (Pêcheux, 1988: 640)

In this regard, Lacan is extremely clear. Through this fantasy modern society returns to a state of myth:

How is one to return, if not on the basis of a peculiar (special) discourse, to a prediscursive reality? That is the dream – the dream behind every conception (idea) of knowledge. But it is also what must be considered mythical. There's no such thing as a prediscursive reality. Every reality is founded and defined by a discourse.

(XX: 32)

In opposition to such a 'regressive' attitude, Lacanian theory promotes a return to the founding moment of modernity. Recognising the irreducible character of impossibility, the constitutivity of the real as expressed primarily in the failure of our discursive world and its continuous rearticulation through acts of identification, far from being a postmodern move, reveals the truly modern character of the Lacanian project; instead of a postmodern mysticism it leads to a reorientation of science and knowledge. Recognising the constitutivity of the real does not entail that we stop symbolising; it means that we start trying to incorporate this recognition within the symbolic itself, in fact it means that since the symbolic entails lack as such, we abstain from covering it over with fantasmatic constructs – or, if one accepts that we are always trapped within the field of fantasy, that we never stop traversing it. The guiding principle in this kind of approach is to move beyond fantasy towards a self-critical symbolic gesture recognising the contingent and transient character of every symbolic construct. This is a scientific discourse different from the reified science of standard modernity.

I take my lead, in this regard, from Lacan's text 'Science and Truth' (it is the opening lecture of his 1965–6 seminar on *The Object of Psychoanalysis*). In this particular text, Jacques Lacan stages a critique of modern science as it has been articulated up to now, that is as a discourse constantly identifying the knowledge it produces with the truth of the real. If the constitutive, non-reducible character of the real introduces a lack into human reality, to our scientific constructions of reality for example, science usually attempts to suture and eliminate this gap. Lacan, for his part, stresses the importance of that which puts in danger this self-fulfilling nature of scientific axioms: the importance of the real, of the element which is not developing according to what we think about it. In that sense, science *à la* Lacan entails the recognition of the structural causality of the real as the element which interrupts the smooth flow of our fantasmatic and symbolic representations of reality. Within such a context, this real, the obstacle encountered by standard science, is not bypassed discretely but introduced within the theory it can destabilise. The point here is that truth as the encounter with the real is 'encountered' face to face (Fink, 1995a: 140–1). It is in this sense that psychoanalysis can be described as a science of the impossible, a science that does not repress the impossible real. For Lacan, what is involved in the structuration of the discourse of science is a certain *Verwerfung* of the Thing which is presupposed by the ideal of absolute knowledge, an ideal which 'as everybody knows...was historically proved in the end to be a failure' (VII: 131). In other words, we cannot be certain that definite knowledge is attainable. In fact, for Lacan, certainty is not something we should attribute to our knowledge of things. Certainty is a defining characteristic of psychosis. In Lacan's view, it constitutes its elementary phenomenon, the basis of delusional belief (III: 75). Opening up our symbolic resources to uncertainty is, on the other hand, the only prudent move we have left. What we can know has to be expressed within the structure of language but this structure has to incorporate a recognition of its own limits. This is not a development which should cause unease; as Nancy has put it

> What will become of our world is something we cannot know, and we can no longer believe in being able to predict or command it. But we can act in such a way that this world is a world able to open itself up to its own uncertainty as such....Invention is always without a model and without warranty. But indeed that implies facing up to turmoil, anxiety, even disarray. Where certainties come apart, there too gathers the strength that no certainty can match.
> (Nancy in Lacoue-Labarthe and Nancy, 1997: 157–8)

On The Title of the Letter

Given the stage our discussion of the Lacanian negotiation between the real and the symbolic has reached, a short detour might be pertinent. This is because in their work *The Title of the Letter*, Jean-Luc Nancy and Philipe Lacoue-Labarthe are primarily engaged with this crucial part of Lacan's work. In *Encore*, Lacan has praised the book, saying that he had never been read that well, although he objected to the concluding part of Nancy and Lacoue-Labarthe's deconstructive argumentation and his comments are sometimes quite ironic. Nevertheless, the points made by the authors are very successful in summarising Lacan's position in a variety of questions. Initially in relation to Saussurean linguistics, they recognise that Lacan is rigorously challenging traditional linguistic theory, enacting a certain 'diversion' of linguistics. They go on, however, to argue that, in a second moment, Lacan is reintroducing some of the themes this diversion attempts to subvert, and thus his project remains for them a paradoxical one, not that radically differentiated from classical forms of philosophical foundationalism and systematicity. Let us examine these two arguments one by one.[12]

First, Lacan, by introducing the algorithm of signification dislocates the unity of the Saussurean sign; the sign and its representational function are subjected to a treatment with destructing, or rather, disruptive effects: the bar between signifier and signified now represents their radical disjunction. The substanceless signifier becomes effectively autonomous since there can be no access to the signified which is thus lost. The sign is accordingly discarded as the nodal point of linguistic reflection. Lacanian linguistics, his *linguistérie*, centres around the gap, the hole located at the centre of meaning and represented by the bar: 'What is primordial (and foundational) is in fact the bar' (Lacoue-Labarthe and Nancy, 1992: 36). Meaning depends on the logic of the signifier, a logic 'paradoxically "centered" on a hole or lack' (Lacoue-Labarthe and Nancy, 1992: 49).

Second, Lacoue-Labarthe and Nancy, though, argue that this diversion of linguistics is followed, in Lacan's discourse, by a reintroduction of a unitary, centred philosophical system in which the point of the bar, the hole in meaning, serves as the centre around which a certain systematic unity, with an *arche* and *telos*, are emerging: 'the bar is foundational or originary. It is the *arche* of a system which, while systematizing the division, the lack, or the hole in the places of origin, has nevertheless maintained its own "archaic" value of systematicity – that is, of origin and centre – without questioning it further' (Lacoue-Labarthe and Nancy, 1992: 112). This argument is reiterated in relation to a variety of levels: for example, at the level of the subject, although Lacan's linguistics reveal the split and alienating character of the lacking subject, subjectivity as such is never put into question: what subverts the subject is, at the same time, its ultimate foundation. The lack in the subject creates a metonymic sliding of desire – a desire conditioned by the quest for a mastery of meaning equalling the emergence of a substantial full subjectivity – which acquires the form of a teleology (albeit a teleology without ever reaching its telos, except in Lacan's discourse itself where the telos of metonymy '*is* in fact achieved') (Lacoue-Labarthe and Nancy, 1992: 75, 113). Lacanian theory is revealed thus as a 'negative' theory, but nevertheless a theory unable to escape the traps of sublation and ontology, able only to displace but not to subvert metaphysics. The principle of its movement remains 'mediation and, thus, *Aufhebung*' (Lacoue-Labarthe and Nancy, 1992: 124). Lacan is presented as ultimately adopting the aims of the philosophical in its Cartesian and Hegelian mutations, including the appropriation of a knowledge of truth (as the Heideggerian *aletheia*), systematicity and the mastery of foundation (Lacoue-Labarthe and Nancy, 1992: xxix). This is Lacan's paradox: 'Is it somewhat paradoxical that this text, a text devoted to the subversion of the "classical" authority of discourse, should itself reconstruct another classical discourse?' (Lacoue-Labarthe and Nancy, 1992: 11). Is it then the case that the whole Lacanian strategy undermines itself?

Let us examine Lacoue-Labarthe and Nancy's points one by one. On a fairly simple level one may argue that, as already mentioned above, *Aufhebung* and sublation are definitely not the goals of Lacan's project. For Lacan there is no *Aufhebung*. We know from Freud that psychoanalysis can only promise the transformation of hysterical misery to common unhappiness, and we also know that, for Lacan, psychoanalysis promises no harmony whatsoever. Its end cannot be reduced to any miraculous accomplishments. It does not attempt to cover over the constitutive lack marking the human condition and making impossible any final resolution in terms of social and subjective completeness. As Miller has put it: 'Psychoanalysis promises no harmony, no achievements, no success, and no fulfilment of any lack, which is, on the contrary, structural' (Miller, 1997: 98). To counter this substantive objection Lacoue-Labarthe and Nancy can, of course, claim that their main argument is that although this may be true in terms of the concrete content of Lacan's discourse, it is not the case with the structure of his argumentation which aspires to a certain systematicity and closure. This point is crucial because it relates to our previous discussion: is the Lacanian strategy to recognise the causality of the real within the symbolic located beyond the closure of its fantasmatic domestication (a position dominant in everyday life and philosophical reflection) or is it a mere reoccupation of this same strategy?

In Lacoue-Labarthe and Nancy's discourse, Lacan is presented as someone who, attempting to avoid orthopaedics, cannot prevent his project from becoming orthopaedic; his only achievement is the articulation of an '*antiorthopedic* orthopedics' (Lacoue-Labarthe and Nancy, 1992: 90). His negative ontology, an ontology 'that opens onto – and is founded (that is, closed) on – a gaping hole whose bottom is hidden but whose outline can be discerned', resembles the metaphysical tradition of negative theology. Lacanian theory is reduced to a repetition – a rigorous one, for that matter – of negative theology (Lacoue-Labarthe and Nancy, 1992: 127). Beyond philosophical uneasiness, such a standpoint can also create political uneasiness. Judith Butler seems to be perplexed by the structural centrality of lack and failure in Laclau's (and even her own) political theory when she wonders

> whether failure...does not become a kind of universal condition...to what extent are we also bound together through this 'failure'? How does the limitation on subject constitution become, oddly [sic], a new source of community or collectivity or a presumed condition of universality?
>
> (Butler, 1997: 10)

Although this argument is not developed with direct reference to Lacanian theory it is extremely relevant to our discussion. The fear behind all these philosophical and politico-theoretical objections is clear; it is that Lacan's strategy *vis à vis* the symbolic encircling of the real reproduces the metaphysical and theoretical problems it attempts to supersede. Thus, although it constitutes a certain subversion or negation of traditional theorisation, it nevertheless remains inscribed within the same discursive frame. Is this, however, a plausible criticism of Lacan?

It is true that for Lacan there is a need for a minimum of systematicity and formalisation. Rather, it is impossible to avoid this minimum of systematicity; as human beings we are doomed to symbolise. If Lacan's discourse is articulated around a nodal point this is exactly because it is impossible to articulate an argument without one (unless we move into the territory of psychosis, a 'Lawless' territory). The paradoxical nature of his project is due to the fact that he is consciously trying to de-essentialise this point of reference; in the place of the cornerstones of metaphysics and philosophy he locates a hole as the site in which truth hits the real. For Lacan the crucial question is how can we preserve within our symbolisations a space for the recognition of the impossibility of their closure? As I have tried to show up to now, Lacan employs a series of strategies to this effect. For example, he introduces a set of concepts and categories, such as the real (and his iconoclastic radicalism is evident in the choice of this word; his choice to use the cornerstone of realist objectivism as a signpost of an always escaping and unrepresentable impossibility), and structures his argument in such a way that traverses the fantasy of closure. The Lacanian system is perhaps the closest we can get to a discourse opening itself up to what exceeds its limits. In order to miss this dimension of Lacan's teaching one has to prioritise his writing at one particular point, reducing Lacan's indeterminate discourse to one static picture, and, furthermore, avoid any reference to concepts such as the real. Not surprisingly, this is exactly what Lacoue-Labarthe and Nancy do. It is worthwhile noting, for example, that their critique is articulated on the basis of reading only one Lacanian text.

Besides, if this Lacanian strategy is something that has to be exposed, it is difficult to see from which point of view this critique issues forth. As if it is possible to move beyond this point, as if it is possible to articulate some sort of pure meta-language that would solve once and for all this problem. Well, for Lacan such a meta-language is lacking. If what exceeds representation is surfacing in the limits of representation and if in order to speak about it – or about anything else for that matter – we need a minimum of systematicity, then it is difficult to see what other possibilities remain open: either the invention of a pure meta-language capable of representing the unrepresentable outside common language (a philosophical theology), or total silence. Since neither of these two options seems to be akin to Lacoue-Labarthe and Nancy's position (although written in a period of militant deconstructionism it is hard to see how such a standpoint can support philosophical theology or absolute silence, especially since deconstruction itself always works 'systematically' within a text or a tradition, by borrowing the resources that can lead to its subversion – besides, they themselves articulate a philosophical reading of Lacan) what is wrong then with Lacan's strategy? It is at this point that a certain indeterminacy surfaces in their argumentation. While in the beginning they object to Lacan's supposed reoccupation of the ground of traditional metaphysics, they are gradually led to stigmatise his ambiguity – as if it would be possible to subvert these rigid metaphysics without recourse to ambiguity and paradox. In any case, this is where something goes wrong in their account. It is impossible to have it both ways (*Aufhebung* cannot be paradoxical).

This unresolved confusion expands as their argument progresses to the point of threatening the coherence of their exposition. After 120 pages one is led to ask: is Lacan's project a repetition of negative theology, as they initially argue, or a 'negative atheology', as they argue later on? (Lacoue-Labarthe and Nancy, 1992: 127). Once again, it seems to me that it cannot be both at the same time. It is illegitimate to equate these two positions, since beyond philosophical theology and silence, negative theology and negative atheology (its difference from negative theology being that it aims at no ineffable union with god) seem to be two preferable but distinct alternatives. And although Lacan flirts with the first one – for Lacan, mystical jaculations (including negative theology) provide 'some of the best reading one can find' (XX: 76) – Lacanian theory, together with deconstruction, seems to be located at the atheological side. What is wrong, after all, with a negative atheology? It is this negative atheological character which accounts for Lacan's undecidability, for the radical character of his text, which is constantly resurfacing and cannot be silenced. Even Lacoue-Labarthe and Nancy are eventually led to acknowledge:

> But if Lacan's discourse indeed lends itself to this interpretation, it nevertheless exceeds it, and our whole reading attempts to make the resources of this ambivalence evident...he attempts to bring something to light that 'works' and disrupts philosophy from its very closure.
>
> (Lacoue-Labarthe and Nancy, 1992: xxix)

Later on they ask themselves: 'does diversion go as far as diverting the system which seems to be (re)constituted in Lacanian discourse? Or, on the contrary, does such a (re)constitution turn the diversion itself into a system? Unless, of course, this alternative itself proves undecidable' (Lacoue-Labarthe and Nancy, 1992: 106). If this is the case, then Lacan's epistemology of the real is proved successfully balanced, even from a deconstructionist perspective. No doubt this is a dynamic balance that can be negatively described as a paradox. It is precisely this paradox or tension, however, that makes Lacan's work original, interesting and important for political theory.

Politics and ethics: an outline

Thus we are brought to the second difficulty. If the first difficulty was of an epistemological and theoretical nature the second is of an ethico-political nature. It is not concerned with the possibility of showing and encircling the real within the symbolic, but with the political desirability of such a move; is it desirable to encircle the political within politics? What changes in our political reality would such an attempt inspire? Are these changes ethically justified? This whole discussion has to do, first of all, with the supposedly reactionary nature of Lacan's views. This criticism, reminiscent of Deleuze and Guattari's critique of the reactionary character of psychoanalysis (both Lacanian and non-Lacanian) (Elliott, 1994: 31), and staged, to give only a first example, by Anthony Elliott in his *Social Theory and Psychoanalysis in Transition*, is based on the fact that Lacan posits 'an inevitable human condition which is the no-exit of lack and antagonism' (Elliott, 1992: 191). Hence, to move to another example from contemporary critical theorisation, due to his 'pessimist' account of the human condition Lacan has been accused of the 'obscuring of political choices and the authoritarianism implicit in his anti-humanist stance' (Frosh, 1987: 271). Well, it is true; for Lacan there is no *Aufhebung*, there is no utopian solution to human suffering: 'when one gives rise to two (*quand un fait deux*), there is never a return. They don't revert to making one again, even if it is a new one. The *Aufhebung* is one of philosophy's pretty little dreams' (XX: 86). The elimination of lack through a definite symbolisation of the real is impossible. Yet this is the condition of possibility of our freedom because it means that no order, no matter how repressive it might be, can acquire a stable character: 'Lacan's formulation of what might be termed a circular causality between the symbolic and the real makes it possible to account for the fact that individual subjects are produced by discourse and yet manage to retain some capacity for resistance' (Bracher, 1994: 1). Besides, the ethics of psychoanalysis, as formulated in the Lacanian tradition, point to the possibility and the ethical superiority of a symbolic recognition and institutionalisation of the political moment of real lack and this opens a huge field of creation of which the democratic revolution constitutes only one example – perhaps the most important.

Why then have attempts to demonstrate the centrality of the Lacanian problematic in the construction of an ethico-political project for our times – and I am mainly thinking of the work of Žižek and Laclau and Mouffe – generated so much criticism? Take the example of Bellamy, Butler and Lane. Bellamy's concern is articulated at the subjective level: 'Can certain forms of political compromise (a collective "we" that must be formed out of diversity and conflict) be usefully characterised as the overcoming of psychic conflict?' (Bellamy, 1993: 35). Butler's concern is articulated at the social level. Her fear is that stressing the irreducibility and constitutivity of 'antagonism' (or, more properly, political 'dislocation' *qua* encounter with the real) may 'preclude the very possibility of a future rearticulation of that boundary which is central to the democratic project that Žižek, Laclau and Mouffe promote' (Butler, 1994: 206–7). In a similar vein, Lane asks why does the left continue to advance contingency and alienation as if both were not simply a psychic condition *par excellence* but also a reason for celebration? Why does the argument that society is radically incomplete and now alarmingly fraying generate a certain optimism[?].

(Lane, 1996: 115)

According to my reading, Bellamy, Butler and Lane are questioning the value of recognising the effects and the structural causality of the real in society; instead of the political they prioritise politics, in fact traditional fantasmatic politics. This seems to be the kernel of their argument: Even if this move is possible – encircling the unavoidable political modality of the real – is it really desirable, is it ethically and politically satisfactory?

The fear behind all these statements is common; it is that the stress on the political *qua* encounter with the real precludes the possibility of presenting a more or less stable (present or future) ground for ethics and democracy, that it undermines their universal character and the possibility of any final reconciliation at either the subjective or the social level. Frosh is summarising this fear *à propos* of the issue of human rights: 'if humanism is a fraud [as Lacan insists] and there is no fundamental human entity that is to be valued in each person [an essence of the psyche maybe?], one is left with no way of defending the "basic rights" of the individual' (Frosh, 1987: 137). In the two final chapters of this book I shall argue that the reason behind all these fears is the continuing hegemony of an ethics of harmony. Against such a position the ethics of the real entails a recognition of the irreducibility of the real and an attempt to institutionalise social lack. Thus it might be possible to achieve an ethically and politically satisfactory institution of the social field beyond the fantasy of closure which has proved so problematic, if not catastrophic. In other words, the best way to organise the social might be one which recognises the ultimate impossibility around which it is always structured.

What could be some of the parameters of this new organisation of the social in our late modern terrain? Ulrich Beck's theory seems to be relevant in this respect. According to our reading of Beck's schema, contemporary societies are faced with the return of uncertainty, a return of the repressed without doubt, and the inability of mastering the totality of the real. We are forced thus to recognise the ambiguity of our experience and to articulate an auto-critical position towards our ability to master the real. It is now revealed that although repressing doubt and uncertainty can provide a temporary safety of meaning, it is nevertheless a dangerous strategy, a strategy that depends on a fantasmatic illusion. This realisation, contrary to any nihilistic reaction, is nothing but the starting point for a new form of society which is emerging around us, together of course with the reactionary attempts to reinstate an ageing modernity:

Perhaps the decline of the lodestars of primary Enlightenment, the individual, identity, truth, reality, science, technology, and so on, is the prerequisite for the start of an alternative Enlightenment, one which does not fear doubt, but instead makes it the element of its life and survival.

(Beck, 1997: 161)

Is it not striking that Lacanian theory stands at the forefront of the struggle to make us change our minds about all these grandiose fantasies? Beck argues that such an openness towards doubt can be learned from Socrates, Montaigne, and others; it might be possible to add Lacan to this list. In other words, doubt, which threatens our false certainties, can become the nodal point for another modernity that will respect the right to err. Scepticism

contrary to a widespread error, makes everything possible again: questions and dialogue of course, as well as faith, science, knowledge, criticism, morality, society, only differently...things unsuspected and incongruous, with the tolerance based and rooted in the ultimate certainty of error.

(Beck, 1997: 163)

In that sense, what is at stake in our current theoretico-political terrain is not the central categories or projects of modernity *per se* (the idea of critique, science, democracy, etc.), but their ontological *status*, their foundation. The crisis of their current foundations, weakens their absolutist character and creates the opportunity to ground them in much more appropriate foundations (Laclau, 1988a). Doubts liberate; they make things possible. First of all the possibility of a new vision for society. An anti-utopian vision founded on the principle '*Dubio ergo sum*' (Beck, 1997: 162) closer to the subversive doubtfulness of Montaigne than to the deceptive scepticism of Descartes. Although Lacan thought that in Montaigne scepticism had not acquired the form of an ethic, he nevertheless pointed out that

Montaigne is truly the one who has centred himself, not around scepticism but around the living moment of the *aphanisis* of the subject. And it is in this that he is fruitful, that he is an eternal guide, who goes beyond whatever may be represented of the moment to be defined as a historical turning-point.

(XI: 223–4)

This is a standpoint which is both critical and self-critical: there is no foundation 'of such a scope and elasticity for a critical theory of society (which would then automatically be a self-critical theory) as doubt' (Beck, 1997: 173). Doubt, the invigorating champagne of thinking, points to a new modernity 'more modern than the old, industrial modernity that we know. The latter after all, is based on certainty, on repelling and suppressing doubt' (ibid.: 173). Beck asks us to fight for 'a modernity which is beginning to doubt itself, which, if things go well, will make doubt the measure and architect of its self-limitation and self-modification' (ibid.: 163). He asks us, to use Paul Celan's phrase, to 'build on inconsistencies'. This will be a modernity instituting a new politics, a politics recognising the uncertainty of the moment of the political. It will be a modernity recognising the constitutivity of the real in the social. A truly political modernity (ibid.: 5). In the next two chapters I will try to show the way in which Lacanian political theory can act as a catalyst for this change. The current crisis of utopian politics, instead of generating pessimism, can become the starting point for a renewal of democratic politics within a radically transformed ethical framework.

4

BEYOND THE FANTASY OF UTOPIA

The aporia of politics and the challenge of democracy

Utopia or dystopia?

Our age is clearly an age of social fragmentation, political disenchantment and open cynicism characterised by the decline of the political mutations of modern universalism – a universalism that, by replacing God with Reason, reoccupied the ground of a pre-modern aspiration to fully represent and master the essence and the totality of the real. On the political level this universalist fantasy took the form of a series of utopian constructions of a reconciled future society. The fragmentation of our present social terrain and cultural *milieu* entails the collapse of such grandiose fantasies.[1] Today, talk about utopia is usually characterised by a certain ambiguity. For some, of course, utopian constructions are still seen as positive results of human creativity in the socio-political sphere: 'utopia is the expression of a desire for a better way of being' (Levitas, 1990: 8). Other, more suspicious views, such as the one expressed in Marie Berneri's book *Journey through Utopia*, warn – taking into account experiences like the Second World War – of the dangers entailed in trusting the idea of a perfect, ordered and regimented world. For some, instead of being 'how can we realise our utopias?', the crucial question has become 'how can we prevent their final realisation?....[How can] we return to a non-utopian society, less perfect and more free' (Berdiaev in Berneri, 1971: 309).[2] It is particularly the political experience of these last decades that led to the dislocation of utopian sensibilities and brought to the fore a novel appreciation of human finitude, together with a growing suspicion of all grandiose political projects and the meta-narratives traditionally associated with them (Whitebook, 1995: 75). All these developments, that is to say the crisis of the utopian imaginary, seem however to leave politics without its prime motivating force: the politics of today is a politics of aporia. In our current political terrain, hope seems to be replaced by pessimism or even resignation. This is a result of the crisis in the dominant modality of our political imagination (meaning utopianism in its various forms) and of our inability to resolve this crisis in a productive way.[3] In this chapter, I will try to show that Lacanian theory provides new angles through which we can reflect on our historical experience of utopia and reorient our political imagination beyond its suffocating strait-jacket. Let's start our exploration with the most elementary of questions: what is the meaning of the current crisis of utopia? And is this crisis a development to be regretted or cherished?

In order to answer these questions it is crucial to enumerate the conditions of possibility and the basic characteristics of utopian thinking. First of all it seems that the need for utopian meaning arises in periods of increased uncertainty, social instability and conflict, when the element of the political subverts the fantasmatic stability of our political reality. Utopias are generated by the surfacing of grave antagonisms and dislocations in the social field. As Tillich has put it 'all utopias strive to negate the negative...in human existence; it is the negative in that existence which makes the idea of utopia necessary' (Tillich in Levitas, 1990: 103). Utopia then is one of the possible responses to the ever-present negativity, to the real antagonism which is constitutive of human experience. Furthermore, from the time of More's *Utopia* (1516) it is conceived as an answer to the negativity inherent in concrete political antagonism. What is, however, the exact nature of this response? Utopias are images of future human communities in which these antagonisms and the dislocations fuelling them (the element of the political) will be forever resolved, leading to a reconciled and harmonious world – it is not a coincidence that, among others, Fourier names his utopian community 'Harmony' and that the name of the Owenite utopian community in the New World was 'New Harmony'. As Marin has put it, utopia sets in view an imaginary resolution to social contradiction; it is a simulacrum of synthesis which dissimulates social antagonism by projecting it onto a screen representing a harmonious and immobile equilibrium (Marin, 1984: 61). This final resolution is the essence of the utopian promise.

What I will try to do in this chapter is, first of all, to demonstrate the deeply problematic nature of utopian politics. Simply put, my argument will be that every utopian fantasy construction needs a 'scapegoat' in order to constitute itself – the Nazi utopian fantasy and the production of the 'Jew' is a good example, especially as pointed out in Žižek's analysis.[4] Every utopian fantasy produces its reverse and calls for its elimination. Put another way, the beatific side of fantasy is coupled in utopian constructions with a horrific side, a paranoid need for a stigmatised scapegoat. The naivety – and also the danger – of utopian structures is revealed when the realisation of this fantasy is attempted. It is then that we are brought close to the frightening kernel of the real: stigmatisation is followed by extermination. This is not an accident. It is inscribed in the structure of utopian constructions; it seems to be the way all fantasy constructions work. If in almost all utopian visions, violence and antagonism are eliminated, if utopia is based on the expulsion and repression of violence (this is its beatific side) this is only because it owes its own creation to violence; it is sustained and fed by violence (this is its horrific side). This repressed moment of violence resurfaces, as Marin points out, in the difference inscribed in the name utopia itself (Marin, 1984: 110). What we shall argue is that it also resurfaces in the production of the figure of an enemy. To use a phrase enunciated by the utopianist Fourier, what is 'driven out through the door comes back through the window' (is not this a 'precursor' of Lacan's *dictum* that 'what is foreclosed in the symbolic reappears in the real'? – VII: 131).[5] The work of Norman Cohn and other historians permits the articulation of a genealogy of this manichean, equivalential way of understanding the world, from the great witch-hunt up to modern anti-Semitism, and Lacanian theory can provide valuable insights into any attempt to understand the logic behind this utopian operation – here the approach to fantasy developed in Chapter 2 will further demonstrate its potential in analysing our political experience. In fact, from the time of his unpublished seminar on *The Formations of the Unconscious*, Lacan identified the utopian dream of a perfectly functioning society as a highly problematic area (seminar of 18 June 1958).

The historical argument

In order to realise the problematic character of the utopian operation it is necessary to articulate a genealogy of this way of representing and making sense of the world. The work of Norman Cohn seems especially designed to serve this purpose. What is most important is that in Cohn's schema we can encounter the three basic characteristics of utopian fantasies that we have already singled out: first, their link to instances of disorder, to the element of negativity. Since human experience is a continuous battle with the unexpected there is always a need to represent and master this unexpected, to transform disorder to order. Second, this representation is usually articulated as a total and universal representation, a promise of absolute mastery of the totality of the real, a vision of the end of history. A future utopian state is envisaged in which disorder will be totally eliminated. Third, this symbolisation produces its own remainder; there is always a certain particularity remaining outside the universal schema. It is to the existence of this evil agent, which can be easily localised, that all persisting disorder is attributed. The elimination of disorder depends then on the elimination of this group. The result is always horrible: persecution, massacres, holocausts. Needless to say, no utopian fantasy is ever realised as a result of all these 'crimes' – as mentioned in Chapter 2, the purpose of fantasy is not to satisfy an (impossible) desire but to constitute it as such. What is of great interest for our approach is the way in which Cohn himself articulates a genealogy of the pair utopia/demonisation in his books *The Pursuit of the Millennium* and *Europe's Inner Demons* (Cohn, 1993b, 1993c). The same applies to his book *Warrant for Genocide* (Cohn, 1996) which will also be implicated at a certain stage in our analysis. These books are concerned with the same social phenomenon, the idea of purifying humanity through the extermination of some category of human beings which are conceived as agents of corruption, disorder and evil. The contexts are, of course, different, but the urge remains the same (Cohn, 1993b: xi). All these works then, at least according to my reading, are concerned with the production of an arch-enemy which goes together with the utopian mentality.

It could be argued that the roots of both demonisation and utopian thinking can be traced back to the shift from a cyclical to a unilinear representation of history (Cohn, 1993a: 227).[6] However, we will start our reading of Cohn's work by going back to Roman civilisation. As Cohn claims, a profound demonising tendency is discernible in Ancient Rome: within the imperium, the Romans accused the Christians of cannibalism and the Jews were accused by Greeks of ritual murder and cannibalism. Yet in the ancient Roman world, although Judaism was regarded as a bizarre religion, it was nevertheless a *religio licita*, a religion that was officially recognised. Things were different with the newly formed Christian sect. In fact the Christian Eucharist could easily be interpreted as cannibalistic (Cohn, 1993b: 8). In almost all their ways Christians ignored or even negated the fundamental convictions by which the pagan Graeco-Roman world lived. It is not at all surprising then that to the Romans they looked like a bunch of conspirators plotting to destroy society. Towards the end of the second century, according to Tertullian, it was taken as a given that

the Christians are the cause of every public catastrophe, every disaster that hits the populace. If the Tiber floods or the Nile fails to, if there is a drought or an earthquake, a famine or a plague, the cry goes up at once: 'Throw the Christians to the Lions!'.

(Tertullian in Cohn, 1993b: 14)

This defamation of Christians that led to their exclusion from the boundaries of humanity and to their relentless persecution is a pattern that was repeated many times in later centuries, when both the persecutors and the persecuted were Christians (Cohn, 1993b: 15). Bogomiles, Waldensians, the Fraticelli movement and the Cathars – all the groups appearing in Umberto Eco's fascinating books, especially in *The Name of the Rose* – were later on persecuted within a similar discursive context. The same happened with the demonisation of Christians, the fantasy that led to the great witch-hunt. Again, the conditions of possibility for this demonisation can be accurately defined. First, some kind of misfortune or catastrophe had to occur, and second, there had to be someone who could be singled out as the cause of this misfortune (Cohn, 1993b: 226).

In Cohn's view then, social dislocation and unrest, on the one hand, and millenarian exaltation, on the other, do overlap. When segments of the poor population were mesmerised by a prophet, their understandable desire to improve their living conditions became transfused with fantasies of a future community reborn into innocence through

> a final, apocalyptic massacre. The evil ones – variously identified with the Jews, the clergy or the rich – were to be exterminated; after which the Saints – i.e. the poor in question – would set up their kingdom, a realm without suffering or sin.
>
> (Cohn, 1993c: 14–15)

It was at times of acute dislocation and disorientation that this demonising tendency was more present. When people were faced with a situation totally alien to their experience of normality, when they were faced with unfamiliar hazards dislocating their constructions of reality – when they encountered the real – the collective flight into the world of demonology could occur more easily (ibid.: 87). The same applies to the emergence of millenarian fantasies. The vast majority of revolutionary millenarian outbreaks takes place against a background of disaster. Cohn refers to the plagues that generated the first Crusade and the flagellant movements of 1260, 1348–9, 1391 and 1400, the famines that preluded the first and second Crusade, the pseudo-Baldwin movement and other millenarian outbreaks and, of course, the Black Death that precipitated a whole wave of millenarian excitement (ibid.: 282).[7]

It is perhaps striking that all the characteristics we have encountered up to now are also marking modern phenomena such as Nazi anti-Semitic utopianism. In fact, in the modern anti-Semitic fantasy the remnants of past demonological terrors are blended with anxieties and resentments emerging for the first time with modernity (Cohn, 1996: 27). In structural terms the situation remains pretty much the same. The first condition of possibility for its emergence is the dislocation of traditional forms of organising and making sense of society, a dislocation inflicted by the increased hegemony of secularism, liberalism, socialism, industrialisation, etc. Faced with such disorientating developments, people can very easily resort to a promise for the re-establishment of a lost harmony. Within such a context Hitler proved successful in persuading the Germans that he was their only hope. Heartfield's genius collages exposing the dark kernel of National Socialism didn't prove very effective against Nazi propaganda. It was mass unemployment, misery and anxiety (especially of the middle classes) that led to Hitler's hegemony, to the hegemony of the Nazi utopian promise. At the very time when German society was turning into one of the great industrial powers of Europe, a land of factories and cities, technology and bureaucracy, many Germans were dreaming of an archaic world of Germanic peasants, organically linked by bonds of blood in a 'natural' community. Yet, as Cohn very successfully points out, 'such a view of the world requires an anti-figure, and this was supplied partly by the liberal West but also, and more effectively, by the Jews' (Cohn, 1996: 188). The emergence of the Jew as a modern antichrist follows directly from this structural necessity for an anti-figure. Rosenberg, Goebbels and other (virtually all) Nazi ideologues

> used the phantom of the Jewish race as a lynch-pin binding the fears of the past and prospective victims of modernisation, which they articulated, and the ideal *volkish* society of the future which they proposed to create in order to forestall further advances of modernity.
>
> (Bauman, 1989: 61)

No doubt the idea of a Jewish world conspiracy is a revival, in a secularised form, of certain apocalyptic beliefs. There is clearly a connection between the famous forgery known as *The Protocols of the Elders of Zion* and the antichrist prophecy (Cohn, 1996: 48). The *Protocols* were first published by Nilus as part of his book *The Great in the Small: Antichrist Considered as an Imminent Political Possibility* and were published in 1917 with the title *He is Near, At the Door...Here comes Antichrist and the Reign of the Devil on Earth*. As the famous Nazi propagandist Rosenberg points out 'One of the advance signs of the coming struggle for the new organisation of the world is this understanding of the very nature of the demon which has caused our present downfall. Then the way will be open for a new age' (Rosenberg in Cohn, 1996: 217). Within this schema the elimination of the antichrist, that is the Jews, is considered as the remedy for all dislocations, the key to a new harmonious world. Jews

> were seen as deserving death (and resented for that reason) because they stood between this one imperfect and tension-ridden reality and the hoped-for world of tranquil happiness...the disappearance of the Jews was instrumental in bringing about the world of perfection.
>
> (Bauman, 1989: 76)

As Sartre claims, for the anti-Semite the Good itself is reduced to the destruction of Evil. Underneath the bitterness of the anti-Semite one can only reveal the optimistic belief that harmony will be reconstituted of itself, once Evil is destroyed. When the mission of the anti-Semite as holy destroyer is fulfilled, the lost paradise will be re-established (Sartre, 1995: 43–5).[8] In Adorno's words, 'charging the Jews with all existing evils seems to penetrate the darkness of reality like a searchlight and to allow for quick and all-comprising orientation....It is the great Panacea...the *key* to everything' (Adorno, 1993: 311, my emphasis).

Simply put, the elimination of the Jew is posited as the only thing that can transform the Nazi dream to reality, the only thing that can realise utopia.[9] As it is pointed out by an American Nazi propagandist, 'our problem is very simple. Get rid of the Jews and we'd be on the way to *Utopia* tomorrow. The Jews are the root of all our trouble' (True in Cohn, 1996: 264, my emphasis). The same is, of course, true of Stalinism. Zygmunt Bauman brings the two cases together: Hitler's and Stalin's victims

> were not killed in order to capture and colonise the territory they occupied....They were killed because they did not fit, for one reason or another, the scheme of a perfect society. Their killing was not the work of destruction but creation. They were eliminated, so that an objectively better human world – more efficient, more moral, more beautiful – could be established. A Communist world. Or a racially pure, Aryan world. In both cases, a harmonious world, conflict free, docile in the hands of their rulers, orderly, controlled.
>
> (Bauman, 1989: 93)

In any case, one should not forget that the fact that the anti-figure in Nazi ideology came to be the Jew is not an essential but a contingent development. In principle, it could have been anyone. Any of us can be a substitute for the Jew. And this is not a mere theoretical possibility. In their classical study of the authoritarian personality Theodor Adorno and his colleagues point out that 'subjects in our sample find numerous other substitutes for the Jew, such as the Mexicans and the Greeks' (Adorno, 1993: 303). Although the need for the structural position of the anti-figure remains constant the identity of the 'subject' occupying that position is never given *a priori*. This does not mean that within a certain historical configuration with a particular social sedimentation and hegemonic structure all the possibilities are open to the same extent; it means though that in principle nobody is excluded from being stigmatised. Of course, the decision on who will eventually be stigmatised depends largely on the *availability* within a particular social configuration of groups that can perform this role in social fantasy, and this availability is socially constructed out of the existing materials. As Lacan points out in *Anxiety*, although a lack or a void can be filled in several ways (in principle), experience – and, in fact, analytic experience – shows that it is never actually filled in 99 different ways (seminar of 21 November 1962).

What we have here is basically a play of incarnation. This play of incarnation is marking both the pole of the utopian fantasies and the pole of the evil powers that stand between us and them. As Cohn concludes, Middle Ages prophecies had a deep effect on the political attitudes of the times. For people in the Middle Ages, the drama of the Last Days was not a distant and hazy but an infallible prophecy which at any given moment was felt to be on the point of fulfilment:

> In even the most unlikely reigns chroniclers tried to perceive that harmony among Christians, that triumph over misbelievers, that unparalleled plenty and prosperity which were going to be the marks of the new Golden Age....When each time experience brought the inevitable disillusionment people merely imagined the glorious consummation postponed to the next reign.
>
> (Cohn, 1993c: 35)

But this fantasy cannot be separated by the coming of the antichrist which was even more tensely awaited. Generation after generation of medieval people lived in continuous expectation of signs of the antichrist, and since these signs, as presented in the prophecies, included comets, plague, bad rulers, famine, etc. a similar play of incarnation was played out in terms of determining the true face of the antichrist (ibid.).

This play of incarnation is very well documented in Christopher Hill's study of the representation of antichrist in seventeenth-century England. What is astonishing in Hill's text is the immense richness of the different incarnations/localisations of antichrist. As Hill points out, even Francis Bacon in his *De Augmentis* went so far as to compare Aristotle with the antichrist. For others, Pope was the antichrist as Jesus Christ was the son of God; the first statement was no less true than the second. In 1635, Robert Shelford, in his *A Treatise Showing the Antichrist not to be Yet Come* argued, following an older idea, that the antichrist would be a Jew (Hill, 1990: 38). Even the English Church itself was accused as being the yoke of antichrist. In fact, the political significance of the use of the myth of the antichrist was so immense that we can locate it both in statements that support the dominant configuration of power ('all deniers that the Pope is the Antichrist are secret enemies to the King's supremacy' – quoted by Hill, 1990: 66) and in oppositional statements (for Milton censorship was popish, deriving from 'the most antichristian council' – quoted by Hill, 1990: 94). Antichrist was even extended to cover the civil government. The parliament, for example, was named antichristian and the Mayor of London a limb of antichrist. Even universities, especially Oxford and Cambridge, were called schools or lieutenants of antichrist (Hill, 1990: 141–2): 'Antichrist thus ceased to be an exclusively ecclesiastical power and could be a symbol for any kind of political power – monarchy, the Lord Mayor of London, Parliament, the rule of gentry, the protectorate of Oliver Cromwell' (Hill, 1990: 131). Cromwell himself had once said to John Rogers that 'you fix the name of antichristian upon anything' (Cromwell in Hill, 1990: 132). One can find innumerable examples of this play of incarnation which is in no way limited to the incarnations of the antichrist. As an illustration of this instability let me refer to one more example, that of anti-Semitism. It is the unbridgeable distance between the universalised structural position of the enemy or the demon (of the negation of society) and the particular agents chosen to incarnate this function within utopian discourse which accounts for this instability. During the First World War many anti-Semites in England believed that Jews were allied to Bolsheviks and Germany. In Germany, on the other hand, the Jews were considered as allies of the Bolsheviks and the forces of the *Entente*. The paranoid nature of such beliefs is shown by the fact that Hitler had admitted in private that he believed that even Christianity was part of the Jewish plot. Furthermore, Eichmann, in his trial, maintained that Hitler himself was a pawn and a marionette in the hands of 'the Satanic international high-finance of the western world', that is to say, of the Jews (Eichmann in Cohn, 1996: 230–1).[10]

Up to now we have documented, using a multitude of historical examples, the structure and function of the utopian operation:

1 We have located as a condition of its possibility the irreducible negativity of human experience.
2 Utopian fantasies promise to eliminate for ever this negativity.
3 The essential and constant 'by-product' of this operation is the production of an arch-enemy to be eliminated at all cost.
4 Although the structural triangle of this schema (negativity/utopian future society/arch-enemy) remains the same, the occupiers of each of the three structural positions can vary immensely.[11]

How can we make sense of this whole discursive operation and its historical repetitiveness? Here, Lacanian theory can be of some help. To Marin's question 'How can a text carry with it a figure, an almost iconic representation [of harmony]?' (Marin, 1984: 61) the only answer can be that this figure is produced as 'a fantasy or fantasm' (Marin, 1984: 196). The Lacanian notion of fantasy is all the more useful here because it can account successfully for the dialectic between fantasy and the production of the enemy.

The psychoanalytic argument

In the light of our theoretical framework, fantasy can only exist as the negation of real dislocation, as a negation of the generalised lack, the antagonism that crosses the field of the social. Fantasy negates the real by promising to 'realise' it, by promising to close the gap between the real and reality, by repressing the discursive nature of reality's production. Yet any promise of absolute positivity – the construction of an imaginarised false real – is founded on a violent/negative origin; it is sustained by the exclusion of a real – a non-domesticated real – which always returns to its place. Sustaining a promise of full positivity leads to a proliferation of negativity. As we have already pointed out, the fantasy of a utopian harmonious social order can only be sustained if all the persisting disorders can be attributed to an alien intruder. Since the realisation of the utopian fantasy is impossible, utopian discourse can remain hegemonically appealing only if it attributes this impossibility – that is to say, its own ultimate impossibility – to an alien intruder. As Sartre has put it 'the anti-Semite is in the unhappy position of having a vital need for the very enemy he wishes to destroy' (Sartre, 1995: 28). The impossibility of the Nazi utopia cannot be incorporated within utopian discourse. This truth is not easy to admit; it is easier to attribute all negativity to the Jew:

> All that is bad in society (crises, wars, famines, upheavals, and re-volts) is directly or indirectly imputable to him. The anti-Semite is afraid of discovering that the world is ill-contrived, for then it would be necessary for him to invent and modify, with the result that man would be found to be the master of his own destinies, burdened with an agonising and infinite responsibility. Thus he lo-calises all the evil of the universe in the Jews.
>
> (Sartre, 1995: 40)[12]

As Jerrold Post has pointed out, we are always bound to those we hate: 'We need enemies to keep our treasured – and idealised – selves intact' (Post, 1996: 28–9). And this for 'fear of being free' (Sartre, 1995: 27). The fantasy of attaining a perfect harmonious world, of realising the universal, can only be sustained through the construction/localisation of a certain particularity which cannot be assimilated but, instead, has to be eliminated. There exists then a crucial dialectic between the universal fantasy of utopia and the particularity of the – always local – enemy who is posited as negating it. The result of this dialectic is always the same:

> The tragic paradox of utopianism has been that instead of bringing about, as it promised, a system of final and permanent stability, it gave rise to utter restlessness, and in place of a reconciliation be-tween human freedom and social cohesion, it brought totalitarian coercion.
>
> (Talmon, 1971: 95)

In that sense, as it was implicitly argued in Chapter 2, the notion of fantasy constitutes an exemplary case of a dialectical *coincidentia opositorum*.[13] On the one hand, fantasy has a beatific side, a stabilising dimension, it is identical to 'the dream of a state without disturbances, out of reach of human depravity'; on the other hand, we have fantasy as something profoundly 'destabilising': 'And does the fundamental lesson of so-called totalitarianism not concern the co-dependence of these two aspects of the notion of fantasy?' asks Žižek. All those who aspire fully to realise its first harmonious side have recourse to its other dark dimension in order to explain their failure:

> the foreclosed obverse of the Nazi harmonious *Volksgemeinschaft* returned in their paranoiac obsession with 'the Jewish plot'. Similarly, the Stalinist's compulsive discovery of ever-new enemies of socialism was the inescapable obverse of their pretending to realise the idea of the 'New Socialist Man'.
>
> (Žižek, 1996a: 116)

For Žižek, these two dimensions 'are like front and back of the same coin: insofar as a community experiences its reality as regulated, structured, by fantasy^1, it has to disavow its inherent impossibility, the antagonism in its very heart – and fantasy^2 (the figure of the 'conceptual Jew' for example) gives body to this disavowal. In short, the effectiveness of fantasy^2 is the condition for fantasy^1 to maintain its hold' (ibid.). Utopia is not that far from dystopia.

What is at stake in the Lacanian conception of fantasy is, as we have already pointed out, enjoyment (*jouissance*). If the effects of the normative idealist or Enlightenment-style critique of racism are severely limited, if this critique is not enough (Lipowatz, 1995a: 213), this is because, to use one of Sloterdijk's formulations, it 'has remained more naive than the consciousness it wanted to expose' (Sloterdijk, 1988: 3). In its rationality it has exhausted itself. In other words, it didn't take into account that what is at stake here is not rational argumentation but the organisation and administration of enjoyment:

> The impotence of the attitude of traditional Enlightenment is best exemplified by the anti-racist who, at the level of rational argumentation, produces a series of convincing reasons against the racist Other, but is nonetheless clearly fascinated by the object of his critique – and consequently, all his defence disintegrates in the moment of real crisis (when 'the fatherland is in danger' for example).
>
> (Sloterdijk, 1988: 3)

Thus, the question of *la traversée du fantasme*, that is to say 'of how to gain the minimum of distance from the fantasmatic frame that organises our enjoyment, of how to suspend its efficiency, is crucial not only for the concept of the psychoanalytic cure and its conclusion: today, in our era of renewed racist tensions, of universalised anti-Semitism, it is perhaps the foremost political question' (Žižek, 1996a: 117–18).

In light of this, traversing the fantasy of utopian thought seems to be one of the most important political tasks of our age. The current crisis of utopia is not cause for concern but for celebration. But then why is the politics of today a politics of aporia? There can be only one plausible explanation: just because, in the ethical sphere, the fantasmatic ideal of harmony is still dominant. If we are situated today in a terrain of aporia and frustration it is because we still fantasise something that is increasingly revealed as impossible and catastrophic. Accepting this ultimate impossibility seems to be the only way out of this troubling state.

Utopia and hope: a necessary relation?

Does not, however, this acceptance of the impossibility of utopia entail the danger of a *de facto* legitimisation of the existing socio-ideological order? This seems to be Paul Ricoeur's fear since for him 'the judgement of ideology is always the judgement from a utopia' (Ricoeur, 1986: 172–3). Ricoeur, although critical of Mannheim's inability to solve the problem of the contrast to a, more or less, objectively perceived reality, albeit a changing and relational one, builds on his idea to contrast utopia to ideology, and particularly on his idea that ideology serves a certain social order while utopia shatters it (Mannheim, 1991). According to this point of view, if the central function of ideology is integration, the preservation of the established status quo, the central function of utopia is exploring the possible. Utopian constructions question the present social order; utopia is an imaginative variation on

> the nature of power, the family, religion, and so on. We are forced to experience the contingency of the social order....The intention of utopia is to change – to shatter – the present order....Here Ricoeur builds on a sentiment of Mannheim's that the latter was not able to incorporate into his theory, that the death of utopia would be the death of society. A society without utopia would be dead, because it would no longer have any project, any prospective goals.
>
> (Taylor, 1986: xxi)

With utopia, then, we experience the contingency of order. This is, for Ricoeur, the main value of utopias. At a certain historical period, when everything is blocked by systems which although failed seem unbeatable – this is his appreciation of the present – he sees utopia as our only recourse. For him, it is not only an escape, but also, and most importantly, an arm of critique (Ricoeur, 1986: 300). In that sense, Ricoeur's solution to the aporia of contemporary politics is the reinvigoration of the utopian operation. But such a reinvigoration entails the danger of producing new arch-enemies,

110

new 'Jews'. This seems to be a structural risk inscribed in the kernel of the utopian operation. In other words, what Ricoeur does not see is that utopia constitutes an ideological critique of ideology (Marin, 1984: 196), providing no solution whatsoever to the misery and injustice entailed in our social arrangements and political orders.

What should not be neglected however in Ricoeur's standpoint is the centrality of the element of hope. No doubt, a society without hope is a dead society. Yet, in reality, to eliminate the element of hope from human life is not only undesirable but also impossible. As Jacques Derrida has put it:

> There is no language without the performative dimension of the promise, the minute I open my mouth I am in the promise. Even if I say 'I don't believe in truth' or whatever, the minute I open my mouth there is a 'believe me' at work. Even when I lie, and perhaps especially when I lie, there is a 'believe me' in play. And this 'I promise you that I am speaking the truth' is a messianic a priori, a promise which, even if it is not kept, even if one knows it cannot be kept, takes place and *qua* promise is messianic.
>
> (Derrida, 1996: 82–3)

In addition, for Derrida, this element of hope is not necessarily utopian: 'I would not call this attitude utopian. The messianic experience of which I spoke takes place here and now; that is the fact of promising and speaking is an event that takes place here and now and is not utopian' (ibid.).

Is it then possible to retain this element of hope without incorporating it into a utopian vision? Can we have passion in politics without holocausts? Furthermore, is it possible to have a politics of hope, a politics of change without utopia? The experience of the democratic revolution permits a certain optimism. Democratisation is certainly a political project of hope. But democratic discourse is not (or should not be) based on the vision of a utopian harmonious society. It is based on the recognition of the impossibility and the catastrophic consequences of such a dream. What differentiates democracy from other political forms of society is the legitimisation of conflict and the refusal to eliminate it through the establishment of an authoritarian harmonious order. Within this framework the antagonistic diversity between different conceptions of the good is not seen as something negative that should be eliminated, but as something to be

> valued and celebrated. This requires the presence of institutions that establish a specific dynamic between consensus and dissent...this is why democratic politics cannot aim towards harmony and reconciliation. To believe that a final resolution of conflict is eventually possible, even when it is envisaged as asymptotic approaching to

the regulative idea of a free unconstrained communication, as in Habermas, is to put the pluralist democratic project at risk.

(Mouffe, 1996b: 8)[14]

Democratic politics – and politics in general – can never eliminate conflict and dislocation, antagonism and division. The aim is rather to establish unity within an environment of conflict and diversity; to create a thoroughly doubtful society, beset by productive self-doubt, a society that traverses its utopian mirror image by identifying with its supposed enemy (Beck, 1997: 169). In that sense, understanding and accepting the nature of democratic politics requires accepting the anti-utopian dimension of antagonism and dislocation, the constitutivity of the political *qua* encounter with the real. Today, the hegemonic appeal of this democratic anti-utopian hope depends on the creation of a democratic ethos: 'the real issue is not to find arguments to justify the rationality and universality of liberal democracy...what is needed is the creation of a democratic *ethos*'.[15] The emergence and maintenance of democratic forms of identity is a matter of *identification* with this democratic ethos, an ethos associated with the mobilisation of passions and sentiments, the multiplication of practices, institutions and language games providing the conditions of possibility for the radicalisation of democracy (Mouffe, 1996b: 5–8).[16] But this is not an identification with a utopian image, it is an identification entailing the acceptance of the impossibility of attaining such a goal, it is an identification with the symptom in the Lacanian sense of the word. Isn't it something worth fighting for? Yet, before answering this question, before developing our argument for this psychoanalytic grounding of modern democracy, we have to deal with the argumentation put forward against this kind of confluence between Lacan and the political (democracy being an order based on the recognition and institutionalisation of the political *par excellence*).

Does the politics of impossibility entail the impossibility of politics?

A crucial problem which still remains open is the hegemonic efficacy of a political project based on this anti-utopian recognition of the very impossibility of society. It is necessary to tackle this problem before engaging in a detailed way with our Lacanian account of democracy. The idea of the impossibility of society, for example, as Sean Homer argues, 'may make for good theory but...does it make for good politics?' (Homer, 1996: 101). In other words, Homer's fear is that Lacanian political theory, although successful as a theoretical enterprise, leads to a dangerous no-way-out in terms of political praxis (Homer, 1996: 102).

This is because, in Homer's view, the recognition of the impossibility of society leads to the impossibility of politics: 'what is occluded in the elision between *object a* and the social as an impossible object is the possibility of politics itself' (Homer, 1996: 102). Psychoanalytic political theory is presented by Homer as politically impotent since it does not articulate itself as an ideological discourse. And, of course, although psychoanalysis and theorists such as Laclau criticise and even unmask the gap between our symbolic fictions and the real, this gap will always be filled by new ideological discourses, and so on and so forth:

> Marx recognized this in what I have termed his prophetic discourse, a discourse that is, according to Laclau, radically inconsistent with both Marxism's and psychoanalysis's critical impulse but is, I suggest *politically necessary*. For if psychoanalysis cannot articulate or envisage a move beyond the impasse I have delineated, that is to say, if it cannot function as an ideological discourse, then there are plenty of other, more often than not stridently anti-psychoanalytic, theories and ideologies waiting to fill the vacuum.
>
> (Homer, 1996: 108, my emphasis)

This becomes all the more necessary because 'to dwell on the impossibility of the subject or society is also to facilitate the possibility of potentially more conservative and reactionary positions' (ibid.: 109). For Žižek, lack and antagonism are constitutive and thus all utopian constructions, including Marx's prophetic discourse in the *Communist Manifesto* and elsewhere, that is to say his utopian impulse, are missing the point. Nevertheless, Homer is determined to 'repeat that error today' (Homer, 1996: 107). Not that he is in a position to fully envisage utopia. This, as he recognises, is, in Lacanian terms, 'structurally impossible' (ibid.) – it is well known that Lacan considered *Aufhebung* as a sweet dream of philosophy. But it seems to him as the only way 'to go beyond the impasse of the impossible, and to link theory back to practice' (ibid.).

Homer's position seems extremely interesting in its simplifying clarity. Let me extract the basic moments in his argumentation as I understand them:

1 Psychoanalytic political theory, by concentrating on the irreducible lack in the Other, on the impossibility of society, does not permit itself to engage in an ideological – utopian is the correct word here – attempt to cover over that lack.

2 If psychoanalytic political theory does not engage in ideological construction, in trying to fill the gap in the social, other ideologies and discourses do and will continue to do so.

3   Thus, by being politically impotent, since politics is identified with constructing ideological utopias or quasi-utopian 'heuristic devices', Lacanian political theory leaves the road open for other (conservative) political ideologies.

4   What becomes necessary is the articulation of a psychoanalytic ideology or maybe a Lacanian quasi-utopia. This is the only way, according to Homer, to move beyond the current impasse of psychoanalytic political theory and to articulate a truly psychoanalytic politics. In other words 'utopia strikes back'.

Needless to say, Homer's argument is only the most recent in a long series of voices on the left that resist abandoning the legacy of the 1960s – epitomised by Marcuse – and want 'to insist very strongly on the necessity of the reinvention of the utopian vision in any contemporary politics' (Jameson, 1991: 159).

Now it is possible to examine the plausibility of these points one by one. First of all it is of course true that Lacanian political theory is a discourse on impossibility. But it could be also argued that impossibility constitutes the nodal point of the most interesting part of Lacanian theory in general, insofar as the real is understood as the impossible *par excellence*, that is to say, impossible to represent in the imaginary or the symbolic plane. The examples are countless. Does not the phrase 'there is no sexual relationship' mean that every relationship between the sexes only takes place against the background of a fundamental real impossibility? (Žižek, 1994a: 155). It is clearly no accident that this recognition is something denied in utopian writing. In Campanella's utopia for example, fat girls are matched with thin men in order for a harmony between the sexes to be restored. To provide a more contemporary illustration, this close relation between the political promise of utopia and the relationship between the sexes is clearly shown in the grandiose sculpture of V. Mukhina installed in the Soviet pavilion at the 1937 Paris International Exhibition; a sculpture representing the harmonious union between an industrial worker (the male stereotype according to socialist realism, depicted holding the hammer) and a collective farm girl (the female equivalent, depicted holding the sickle and thus supplementing a kind of harmonious yin and yang representation of the sexual relationship) in their march towards Stalin's utopia. Against this utopian fantasy of the sexual relationship Lacanian theory stresses the constitutive impossibility of a harmonious sexual relationship. In the film *Sesso Matto* by the Italian director Dino Risi, Giancarlo Gianini falls in love with a married transvestite prostitute who is revealed to be his long lost brother. His position is perhaps the only reflection on sexual harmony that can be accepted within a Lacanian perspective:

Except for the fact that you're married; except for the fact that you are a whore and not a nice girl; and except for the fact that you're my brother and not...for example...my cousin...we' re perfect for each other, and our love would be ideal.

(Benvenuto, 1996: 126)

We can also approach this constitutive play between possibility and impossibility through the example of communication. What Lacan argues, and here his difference from Habermas is most forcefully demonstrated, is that it is exactly because total communication is impossible, because it is exposed as an impossible fantasy, that communication itself becomes possible. Lacan

starts from the assumption that communication is always a failure: moreover, *that it has to be a failure*, and that's the reason we keep on talking. If we understood each other, we would all remain silent. Luckily enough, we don't understand each other, so we keep on talking.

(Verhaeghe, 1995: 81)

The utopian fantasy of a perfect universal language, a language common to all humanity, was designed to remedy this lack in communication insofar as it is caused by the different idioms and languages in use (Eco, 1995: 19). The perfect language was conceived as the final solution to this linguistic confusion, the *confusio linguarum*, which inscribed an irreducible lack at the heart of our symbolic universe, showing its inability to represent the real. It entailed a fantasmatic return to a pre-confusion state in which a perfect language existed between Adam and God. This was a language that mirrored reality, an isomorphic language which had direct and unmediated access to the essence of things: 'In its original form...language was an absolutely certain and transparent sign for things, because it resembled them. The names of things were lodged in the things they designated....This transparency was destroyed at Babel as a punishment for men' (Foucault, 1989: 36). Human imagination never stopped longing for that lost/impossible state when language, instead of the agency of castration, was the field of a perfect harmony; hence all the attempts to construct a perfect language, to realise fantasy: Umberto Eco in his *Search for the Perfect Language* recounts the history of all these attempts within European culture, from St. Augustine's fantasy, in which the distance between object and symbol is annulled,[17] up to Dante, *a priori* philosophical languages and Esperanto. This history is, of course, a genealogy of failures, the history of the insistence on the realisation of an impossible dream, a dream, however, that was designed as a perfect solution to the inherent division of the social. As Eco points out, linguistic confusion is conceived as standing at the root of religious and political division, even of difficulties in economic exchange (Eco, 1995: 42–3). In that sense, the achievement of perfect communication is articulated as the perfect solution to all these problems. This is clearly a utopian problematic. Alas, as Antonio Gramsci points out in his text 'Universal Language and Esperanto', no advent of a universal language can be planned in advance:

> the present attempts at such a language belong only in the realm of Utopia: they are the product of the same mentality that wanted Falangists and happy colonies. In history and social life nothing is fixed, rigid and final. There never will be...this flow of molten volcanic matter, burns and annihilates the Utopias built on arbitrary acts and vain delusions such as those of a universal language and of Esperanto.
>
> (Gramsci, 1975: 33)

The main point here is that society and history are all the time constituted and reconstituted through this unending play between possibility and impossibility, order and disorder: 'society is nothing but a web of social relations that is constantly being spun, broken, and spun again, invariably (unlike a spider's web) in slightly different form' (Wrong, 1994: 45). As we have already seen in Chapter 2, our encounters with the real, the moments of failure and dislocation of our discursive constructions, have both a destructive and a productive dimension. Baudrillard even argues that catastrophes, crises and dislocations might be a certain strategy of our species. By bringing to the fore the possibility or the idea of a total catastrophe they stimulate a series of processes – in the economy as well as in politics, art and history – that attempt to patch things up (Baudrillard, 1996: 81). Homer is correct and consistent with his psychoanalytic framework when he argues that the filling of the gap in the social field will always be the aim of numerous discourses and ideologies; this is the way things generally work. It is also true that if no psychoanalytic ideology emerges to (try to) suture that gap, other discourses and ideologies will.

Since, however, Lacanian political theory aims at bringing to the fore, again and again, the lack in the Other, the same lack that utopian fantasy attempts to mask, it would be self-defeating, if not absurd, to engage itself in utopian or quasi-utopian fantasy construction. Is it really possible and consistent to point to the lack in the Other and, at the same time, to attempt to fill it in a quasi-utopian move? Such a question can also be posed in ethical or even strategic terms. It could be argued of course that Homer's vision of a psychoanalytic politics does not foreclose the recognition of the impossibility of the social but that in his schema this recognition, and the promise to eliminate it (as part of a quasi-utopian regulative principle) go side by side;

that in fact this political promise is legitimised by the conclusions of psychoanalytic political theory. But this coexistence is nothing new. This recognition of the 'impossibility of society', of an antagonism that cross-cuts the social field, constitutes the starting point for almost every political ideology. Only if presented against the background of this 'disorder' the final harmonious 'order' promised by a utopian fantasy acquires hegemonic force. The problem is that all this schema is based on the elimination of the first moment, of the recognition of impossibility. The centrality of political dislocation is always repressed in favour of the second moment, the utopian promise. Utopian fantasy can sound appealing only if presented as the final solution to the problem that constitutes its starting point. In that sense, the moment of impossibility is only acknowledged in order to be eliminated. In Marx, for instance, the constitutivity of class struggle is recognised only to be eliminated in the future communist society. Thus, when Homer says that he wants to repeat Marx's error today he is simply acknowledging that his psychoanalytic politics is nothing but traditional fantasmatic politics articulated with the use of a psychoanalytic vocabulary.

The danger of reoccupation

Homer's psychoanalytic politics are nothing but 'politics as such' – this is his own phrase – and what is 'politics as such' if not the return of something very old, the 'reoccupation' of traditional radical politics. I use here the term 'reoccupation' as it is introduced by Hans Blumenberg in his book *The Legitimacy of the Modern Age* (Blumenberg, 1983). The term is introduced in connection with the relation between pre-modernity and modernity and has to do with the way modernity reproduces the mistakes or problems of pre-modernity.[18] As the translator of Blumemberg's book argues:

Christianity, he [Blumenberg] says, through its claim to be able to account for the overall pattern of world history in terms of the poles of creation and eschatology, had put in place a new question, one that had been (as Löwith so forcefully insists) unknown to the Greeks: the question of the meaning and pattern of world history as a whole. When modern thinkers abandoned the Christian 'answers' they still felt an obligation to answer the questions that went with them – to show that modern thought was equal to any challenge, as it were. It was this compulsion to 'reoccupy' the 'position' of the medieval Christian schema of creation and eschatology – rather than leave it empty, as a rationality that was aware of its own limits might have done – that led to the grandiose constructions of the philosophy of history.

(Wallace, 1985: xx–xxi)

As Ernesto Laclau has put it, by 'reoccupation' we mean a process by which certain notions, linked to the advent of a new vision and new problems, 'have the function of replacing ancient notions that had been formed on the ground of a different set of issues, with the result that the latter end up imposing their demands on the new notions and inevitably deforming them' (Laclau, 1990: 74). What I want to suggest is that in Homer's schema psychoanalytic politics 'reoccupies' the ground of traditional fantasmatic politics. The result is that this fantasmatic conception of politics ends up imposing its demands on the psychoanalytic part of the argumentation. Thus, this latter part is necessarily deformed: if it is not recognised in its radical constitutivity, the impossibility of society, the irreducibility of the real within the social, loses all its power. In that sense, the ultimate consequence of Homer's argumentation is the following: the absorption of Lacanian political theory by radical quasi-utopianism will offer left-wing radicalism the hegemonic appeal entailed in the articulation of one more signifier ('psychoanalysis') in its signifying chain, but psychoanalytic political theory has nothing to gain beyond its own deformation. Well, it doesn't sound like a very good deal.

In fact, articulating Lacanian theory with fantasmatic politics is equivalent to affirming the irrelevance of Lacanian theory for radical politics since this articulation presupposes the repression of all the political insights implicit in Lacan's reading and highlighted in this book. The alleged irrelevance of Lacan for radical politics is also the argument put forward by Collier in a recent article in *Radical Philosophy*. Collier's argument is that since it is capitalism that shatters our wholeness and disempowers us (as if without capitalism we would be on the road to utopia; obviously, capitalism occupies the structural position of the antichrist in this sort of leftist preaching), then Lacan's theory is, in fact, normalising capitalist damage, precisely because alienation is so deep for Lacan that nothing can be done to eliminate it ('Lacan is deeply pessimistic, rejecting cure or *happiness* as possible goals', my emphasis).[19] Thus Lacan has nothing to offer radical politics. Something not entirely surprising since, according to Collier, psychological theory in general has no political implications whatsoever. The conclusion is predictable: 'Let us go to Freud and Klein for our psychotherapy [Lacan is of course excluded] and to Marx and the environmental sciences for our politics, and not get our lines crossed' (Collier, 1998: 41–3). Surprisingly enough this is almost identical with Homer's conclusion: Lacanian theory is OK as an analytical tool but let us go back to Marx for our ideological seminar and our utopian catechism!

It is clear that from a Lacanian point of view it is necessary to resist all such 'reoccupations' of traditional fantasmatic politics. At least this is the strategy that Lacan follows on similar occasions. Faced with the alienating dimension of every identification, Lacan locates the end of analysis beyond identification. Since utopian or quasi-utopian constructions function through identification it is legitimate, I think, to draw the analogies with the social field. If analysis resists the 'reoccupation' of the traditional strategy of identification – although it recognises its crucial, but alienating, role in the formation of subjectivity – why should psychoanalytic politics, after unmasking the crucial but alienating character of traditional, fantasmatic, identificatory politics, 'reoccupy' their ground? This rationale underlying the Lacanian position is not far away from what Beardsworth articulates as a political reading of Derrida. For Beardsworth, deconstruction also refuses to implicate itself in traditional politics, in the 'local sense of politics' in Beardsworth's terminology:

> In its affirmative refusal to advocate a politics, deconstruction forms, firstly, an account of why all political projects fail. Since the projection of any decision has ethical implications, deconstruction in fact generalizes what is meant by the political well beyond the local sense of politics. In this sense it becomes a radical 'critique' of institutions.
>
> (Beardsworth, 1996: 19)

Similarly, the radicality and political importance of the Lacanian critique depends on its ability to keep its distance from fantasmatic politics, from politics in the traditional sense; which is not the same as saying that psychoanalysis is apolitical: in fact, it becomes political precisely by being critical of traditional politics, exactly because, as argued in the previous chapter, the political is located beyond the utopian or quasi-utopian sedimentations of political reality.

One final point before concluding our argumentation in this chapter. There is a question which seems to remains open. It is the following: if we resist the 'reoccupation' put forward by Homer and others does that mean that we accept the supposed political impotence of psychoanalytic political theory? Assuming that psychoanalytically inspired political theory is based on the recognition of the political as an encounter with the real (although he doesn't formulate it in exactly these terms), Rustin argues that 'it seems likely that a politics constructed largely on this principle will generate paranoid-schizoid states of mind as its normal psychic condition'. If we prioritise the 'negative' 'what kind of progressive political or social project can be built if the "positive" – that is concepts, theories, norms and consistent techniques – is to be refused as innately inauthentic?' (Rustin, 1995: 241–3). Political impotence seems to be the logical outcome. Homer's argument seems finally vindicated. Yet this conclusion is accurate only if we identify progressive political action with traditional fantasmatic utopian politics. This is, however, a reductionist move *par excellence*. This idea, and Homer's whole argumentative construction, is based on the foreclosure of another political possibility which is clearly situated beyond any 'reoccupations' and is consistent with psychoanalytic theory instead of deforming it. This is the possibility of a post-fantasmatic or less-fantasmatic politics. The best example is democratic politics.

It is true that democracy is an essentially contested term and that the struggle for a 'final' decontestation of its meaning constitutes a fundamental characteristic of modern societies. It is also true that in the past these attempts at decontestation were articulated within an essentialist, foundationalist framework, that is to say, democracy was conceived as a natural law, a natural right, or even as something guaranteed by divine providence. Today, in our postmodern terrain, these foundations are no longer valid. Yet democracy did not share the fate of its various foundations. This is because democracy cannot be reduced to any of these fantasmatic positive contents. As John Keane, among others, has put it, democracy is not based on or guided by a certain positive, foundational, normative principle (Keane, 1995: 167). On the contrary, democracy is based on the recognition of the fact that no such principle can claim to be truly universal, on the fact that no symbolic social construct can ever claim to master the impossible real. Democracy entails the acceptance of antagonism, in other words, the recognition of the fact that the social will always be structured around a real impossibility which cannot be sutured. Instead of attempting this impossible suture of the social entailed in every utopian or quasi-utopian discourse, democracy envisages a social field which is unified by the recognition of its own constitutive impossibility. As Chaitin points out, democracy provides a concrete example of what we would call a post-fantasmatic or less-fantasmatic politics:

> most significant [in terms of Lacan's importance for literary, ethical and cultural theory and political praxis], perhaps, is the new light his analysis of the interaction of the universal and the particular has begun to shed on the question of maintaining a democratic social order which can safeguard universal human rights while protecting the difference of competing political and ethnic groups.
>
> (Chaitin, 1996: 11)

Thus, a whole political project, the project of radical democracy, is based not on the futile fantasmatic suture of the lack in the Other but on the recognition of its own irreducibility.[20] And this is a political possibility totally neglected by Homer.[21]

Today, it seems that we have the chance to overcome or limit the consequences of traditional fantasmatic politics. In that sense, the collapse of utopian politics should not be the source of resentment, disappointment or even nostalgia for a supposedly lost harmony. On the contrary, it is a development that enhances the prospects for radicalising modern democracy. But this cannot be done for as long as the ethics of harmony are still hegemonic. What we need is a new ethical framework. This cannot be an ethics of harmony aspiring to realise a fantasy construction; it can only be an ethics that is articulated around the recognition of the ultimate impossibility of such an idea and follows this recognition up to its political – and, in fact, democratic – consequences. In the next chapter I will try to show that Lacanian theory is absolutely crucial in such an undertaking. Not only because some Lacanian societies tend to be more democratic than other psychoanalytic institutions (the École Freudienne de Paris was, in certain of its aspects, an extremely democratic society) nor because psychoanalysis is stigmatised or banned in almost all anti-democratic regimes. Beyond these superfluous approaches, Lacanian ethics can offer a non-fantasmatic grounding for radical democracy.

5

AMBIGUOUS DEMOCRACY
AND THE ETHICS OF
PSYCHOANALYSIS

The ambiguities of modern democracy: beyond the politics of harmony

My aim in this chapter will be to forge a perspective on the radicalisation and institutionalisation of democracy as one possible way of conceiving what it might mean to enable the crossing of fantasy and thus the avoidance of extreme utopianism with all its catastrophic consequences, discussed and exposed in the previous chapter. Such a perspective can only be an ethico-political one. The ethical dimension is crucial here; this is what our current experience shows. It is certainly one of the dimensions through which aporia surfaces within our current political and theoretical setting. Consider, for example, the contemporary crisis of democracy: the increasing hegemony of the dominant democratic model – both in theory and in practice – instead of generating optimism has reinforced the disappointment produced by the experience of democracy. In fact, it is one of the paradoxes of our age that the 'success' of democracy in Eastern Europe and South Africa is coupled by grave disappointment in Western Europe, the 'birthplace' of modern democracies. It is true, of course, that modern democracy is based on a constitutive tension, it has an ambiguous character. For example, as William Connolly has pointed out, both individualists and communalists are disappointed because democratic theory and practice entails the ambiguity of simultaneously differentiating and 'harmonising' individuality and commonality. This disappointment, however, stems from the belief of both sides that 'this is an ambiguity to be resolved rather than acknowledged and expressed in the institutional life' (Connolly, 1987: 5–6). John Dunn has also pointed out the intersection of 'two incompatible rationalities' that reveal another facet of the ambiguity of democracy: the need for a least badly controlled mode of government and the principle of human fulfilment and liberty (Dunn, 1979). It seems that democracy entails, of necessity, the attempt to combine apparently contradictory demands: the rule of law with the representation of particular interests – ensuring respect for human freedom and at the same time organising society in a way the majority considers just (Touraine, 1994: 2–5).

For Dunn, though, unlike Connolly, this ambiguity is the source of grave disappointment: 'if we are all democrats today, it is not a very cheerful fate to share. Today, in politics, democracy is the name for what we cannot have – yet cannot cease to want' (Dunn, 1979: 28). We can speculate that Dunn belongs to those political philosophers who would like to see this ambiguity resolved and the democratic 'chaos' transformed into a new harmony. But, as Connolly argues, this ambiguity is democracy itself; to cover up the ambiguity in democracy is to *de-democratise* democracy. This is the effect of what Connolly calls the ontologies of concord and harmony starting from Hobbes, Locke and Kant up to Marx and Habermas. In *Identity/Difference* it becomes clear that these ontologies project a conception of harmony in order to eliminate the threat of contingency, or in Laclau's vocabulary the increasing centrality of dislocation characterising modernity, late modernity in particular. This ontology of concord and harmony, and may I add, a whole ethics of harmony, is also inherent in a variety of contemporary theories of politics – and theories of democracy – that attempt to reduce the threat of contingency: individualists, collectivists and communitarians belong to this group (Connolly, 1991: 28). Hence the source of the disappointment with democracy is revealed as the antithesis between an ontology and an ethics of concord and harmony, and the ambiguity of democracy, that is to say, the inherent and institutionalised disharmony of democratic arrangements. My aim in this concluding part of *Lacan and the Political* is to show that the aspiration to eliminate the ambiguity of democracy ignores the historical specificity and the innovative logic of democratic politics. If the ethics of harmony lead to a de-democratisation of democracy I shall argue that what a radical democratic project needs today is an ethical basis of a totally different nature. Here, the ethics of psycho-analysis as formulated in the Lacanian tradition can be of great help.

First of all, however, let me briefly expand on the idea that democracy entails a constitutive tension, a central ambiguity, the recognition and institutionalisation of a disharmony. In this regard, Claude Lefort has very well shown that democracy connotes the ambiguity in question. This idea is already evident in Alexis de Tocqueville's intuitive vision of democracy as a form of society in which a general contradiction comes to the fore, a contradiction that arises when the social order no longer has a basis, meaning that it can no longer rest on the theologico-political conception of the prince (Lefort, 1988: 15). If before the democratic revolution the prince is the embodiment, the incarnate of power, the unprecedented result of the democratic revolution is that 'the *locus* of power becomes an empty place' (Lefort, 1988: 17). The fact that democracy destroys the organic unity of the *ancien régime* does not mean that there is no unity any more. It only means that this unity is not given *a priori* but it can only be the result of political hegemonic struggle. Unity and power cannot be cosubstantial with a certain limited political force or person. The institutional apparatus of democracy prevents this cosubstantiality by institutionalising political antagonism: In democracy

> the exercise of power is subject to procedures of periodical redistribution. It represents the outcome of a controlled contest with permanent rules. This phenomenon implies an institutionalisation of conflict. The *locus* of power is an empty place, it cannot be occupied – it is such that no individual and no group can be cosubstantial with it – and cannot be represented.
>
> (Lefort, 1988: 17)

Now unity depends on the erection of a stage of political competition. Thus unity is constituted on the basis of recognising division (Lefort, 1988: 18).[1] It is the recognition of division and antagonism and the dissolution of 'predemocratic' unconditional points of reference that institute a deep ambiguity in the heart of democracy; but this is not an accident, it is the *differentia specifica* of democracy:

> Democracy is instituted and sustained by the dissolution of the markers of certainty. It inaugurates a history in which people experience a fundamental indeterminacy...at every level where division and especially the division between those who held power and those who were subject to them, could once be articulated as a result of a belief in the nature of things or in a supernatural principle.
>
> (Lefort, 1988: 19)

Understanding this radical character of the democratic invention presupposes accepting the fact that 'society does not exist', in the sense that its unity – and consequently its existence in any particular form – is not guaranteed in advance. The dislocation of traditional societies clearly shows that there is no essential organic unity that can define society once and for all. This is also shown by the historical, cultural relativity of different forms of social unity, different forms (constructions) of society. Consequently, any discussion on democracy cannot proceed from identifying a privileged essentialist point of reference (an ideal that would guarantee unity) to erecting it in the heart of society in order to resolve its ambiguity. Following from this, democracy should not be viewed as a form of institutional arrangements that are applied in a given society in order to meet its essential needs. Modern democracies are constructed when it is realised that there are no essential needs and no unity founded on an *a priori* positive point of reference. The primary terrain on which democracy emerges is the terrain of social dislocation. The great innovation of democracy is that it recognises this fact and attempts to build a new sense of unity on this recognition. As Laclau and Zac have pointed out, with the emergence of democratic discourse in modernity 'what is at stake is more than mere procedures: it is the institution of signifiers of a social lack resulting from the absence of God as fullness of being' (Laclau and Zac, 1994: 36). But that means that the ambiguity of democracy is not an ambiguity caused by democracy. Obviously, ambiguity and division, the dislocation of organic social unity, precede the democratic invention. Democracy does not produce the ambiguity and the lack characterising the human condition; it does not produce the irreducible division and disharmony characterising every social form. It only attempts to come to terms with them by recognising them in their irreducibility, thus producing a new post-fantasmatic form of social unity.

The uniqueness of democracy will be more clearly shown in its opposition to two trends that threaten it. These trends are defined by Touraine as the true external threats to democracy: democracy can be destroyed either from above, by authoritarian power, or from below, 'through chaos, violence and civil war' (Touraine, 1994: 2). The rise and electoral success today of neo-fascist parties and movements makes imperative the comparison between democracy and totalitarianism. Totalitarianism emerges when a particular party or political movement claims by its own nature to be different from all the other parties and forces. It destroys all opposition since it claims to represent the whole of society 'and to possess a legitimacy that places it above the law' (Lefort, 1988: 13). If democracy recognises and institutional-ises the division of the social, totalitarianism in contrast claims to under-stand the universal law of societal organisation and development which, applied to the social, can bring back the lost organic unity and eliminate any division and disharmony; with totalitarianism the dawn of 'utopia' is never too far away.[2] Democracy, however, is not threatened only by universalist totalitarian tendencies attempting to reinstate a universal organic unity: 'There is also a symmetrically opposite danger of a lack of all reference to this unity' (Laclau and Mouffe, 1985: 188). This is the danger of particular-ism and of the fragmentation of the social fabric into segments that deny the possibility of any meaningful articulation between them.

One cannot but be struck by the fact that these two threats to democracy constitute a vicious cycle. The dislocation of traditional unities and the threat of fragmentation cause a resentment that is fuelling the propagation of universalist and totalitarian tendencies; in fact, what usually happens is that the success of totalitarianism follows a period of social fragmentation and chaos. On the other hand, the same dislocation opens the road for a wave of particularism opposing any unifying tendency, including certain democratic attempts to articulate some sort of democratic unity; here again particularism is most successful when fighting a strong totalitarian or quasi-totalitarian force. But the most important point here is that both tendencies despise democracy for exactly the opposite reasons. Totalitarianism because it 'dissolves' social unity and leads to chaos and fragmentation, to particularism; and particularism because it attempts to articulate a unity and every unity is thought of as synonymous with totalitarianism. What is ignored or foreclosed here is the existence of a third possibility: if the existence of both these opposite tendencies is coextensive with the constitution of the social as such the ambiguity on which democracy is based is irreducible and, in fact, democracy provides the best possibility for a mediation between the two:

> Between the logic of complete identity and that of pure difference, the experience of democracy should consist of the recognition of the multiplicity of social logics along with the necessity of their articulation. But this articulation should be constantly re-created and renegotiated, and there is no final point at which a balance will be definitely achieved.
>
> (Laclau and Mouffe, 1985: 188)

As Alain Touraine has put it, democracy can only be based on the dual concern of having a government that ensures social integration – that achieves a sense of unity and creates an awareness of citizenship – and of respecting the multiplicity of the social forces, the interests and opinions that operate in the social. *E Pluribus unum* (Touraine, 1991: 261).

Simply put, modern societies are faced with an irreducible unbridgeable gap between a universal pole – the need for a force which acts in the name of the whole community – and the particularism of all social forces (Laclau, 1991: 59). This gap is not produced by democracy; it precedes democracy. As a matter of fact it is exactly what makes democracy possible: 'The recognition of the constitutive nature of this gap and its political institutionalisation is the starting point of modern democracy' (Laclau, 1994: 8). In that sense the irreducibility of this gap should not be viewed as a source of disappointment or resentment, feelings fuelling an aporia that can clearly lead to totalitarian or particularist identifications, the results of which can only be catastrophic. On the contrary, this gap should be viewed as opening the optimistic possibility of democracy as opposed to totalitarianism or radical fragmentation;[3] a possibility that rests on the recognition of the constitutive character of this gap, this division, the inherent disharmony between universalism and particularism, community and individual, the government and the governed, etc. Democracy depends on an originary disharmony or disorder. The demos is at the same time the name of a community and of its division (Ranciere, 1992: 3).

Up to now in this chapter I have tried to show that the historical specificity and uniqueness of modern democracy, its difference from totalitarianism and fragmentation and its potential efficacy in mediating between these two opposed tendencies that characterise modern societies, depends on the recognition and preservation of the emptiness in the *locus* of power, on the recognition of a gap – a constitutive division – at the heart of society and on the institutionalisation of this division. No one, however, can deny that such an understanding of democracy raises an important ethical issue. The goals of traditional ethical discourse are radically overturned; instead of a utopian harmony we are meant to legitimise disharmony and recognise division. Thus the disappointment with democracy is revealed as a deeply ethical problem. Democracy has to show that recognising division and institutionalising social lack, far from being detrimental and intolerable both at the subjective and the collective/objective level – this is a common misperception – is, in fact, opening an ethically satisfactory way beyond the barrier of traditional ethics. It is in that sense that Connolly asserts that what democracy needs is an ethics of disharmony – an ethics compatible with the anti-utopian ambiguities of democracy. Connolly seems to be in agreement here with Mouffe's call for a democratic ethos. They are both also close to Touraine's idea of the need for a new democratic culture beyond all 'semi-modern' (if we want to use Ulrich Beck's vocabulary) or even anti-modern reoccupations of fantasmatic politics. It is this democratic ethos or culture that is associated with modernity because 'real' modernity is based on the disappearance of the One, on the elimination of all utopian principles used to define a unitary harmonious society (Touraine, 1997: 147). In the rest of this chapter, I will argue that the ethics of psychoanalysis, Lacanian ethics, seem to be the most likely candidate for the job.

Lacanian ethics: beyond the ethics of harmony

In the first place Lacan's suggestion that the *status* of the Freudian conception of the unconscious is ethical (XI: 33) and that Freud's initial central intuition is ethical in kind might seem strange. However, his seminar of 1959–60 devoted to *The Ethics of Psychoanalysis* proves the importance he attributed to the question of ethics. Moreover, he was to return again and again to the problematic of the *Ethics* seminar, starting from the seminar of the following year (*Transference*) up to *Encore* (1972–3) which starts with a reference to the seminar on *The Ethics of Psychoanalysis*. In fact, it is in *Encore* where Lacan states that his *Ethics* seminar was the only one he wanted to rewrite and publish as a written text (XX: 53) – for someone accused of logocentrism this is a very important statement. However, it is not the place here to embark on an analysis or even a presentation of Lacan's seminar; instead I will use some of the insights developed there as a starting point in order to articulate an ethical position relevant to the discussion on democracy articulated in the previous section of this chapter.

Psychoanalytic ethics is clearly not an ethics of the ideal or the good as is the case with traditional ethics. The ideal, as master signifier, belongs to the field of the ideological or even the utopian: 'A sensitive subject such as ethics is not nowadays separable from what is called ideology' (VII: 182). For Lacan, the 'ethics of the good' or the ideal is no more a real philosophical possibility (Rajchman, 1991: 46). This is clearly shown in his seminar on *The Ethics of Psychoanalysis* where the good is definitely the most important issue in question. But Lacan makes clear from the beginning that he is going to speak about the good from a bizarre point of view: 'I will speak then about the *good*, and perhaps what I have to say will be *bad* in the sense that I don't have all the goodness required to speak well of it' (VII: 218, my emphasis). In Lacan's view, 'the good as such – something that has been the eternal object of the philosopher's quest in the sphere of ethics, the philosopher's stone of all the moralities' is radically denied by Freud (VII: 96). This is because 'the Sovereign good, which is *das Ding*, which is the mother, is also the object of incest, is a forbidden good, and [because]...there is no other good. Such is the foundation of the moral law as turned on its head by Freud' (VII: 70). Generalising from his analysis one can argue that almost the whole of the history of Western philosophy and ethical thought is an unending but always doomed quest for harmony based on successive conceptions of the good:

> I have emphasized this since the beginning of the year: from the origin of moral philosophy, from the moment when the term ethics acquired the meaning of man's reflection on his condition and calculation of the proper paths to follow, all mediation on man's good has taken place as a function of the index of pleasure. And I mean all, since Plato, certainly since Aristotle, and down through the Stoics, the Epicureans, and even through Christian thought itself in St Thomas Aquinas. As far as the determination of different goods is concerned, things have clearly developed along the paths of an essentially hedonist problematic. It is only too evident that all that has involved the greatest of difficulties, and that these difficulties are those of experience. And in order to resolve them, all the philosophers have been led to discern not true pleasures from false, for such a distinction is impossible to make, but the true and false goods that pleasure points to.
>
> (VII: 221)

This is also the case with the majority of ethical standpoints in everyday life. The clear aim of all these attempts is to reinstate the big Other, the symbolic system, the field of social construction, as a harmonious unified whole by referring it to a single positive principle; the same applies to the subject – maybe primarily to the subject which, according to traditional ethics, can be harmonised by being subjected to the ethical law. It is evident that an ethical view based on the fantasy of harmony applied both to the subject and to the social is not compatible with democracy, rather it can only reinforce 'totalitarianism' or 'fragmentation'. Instead of a harmonious society democracy recognises a social field inherently divided; in a sense it is founded on the recognition of the lack in the Other. Instead of harmonising subjectivities democracy recognises the division of the citizens' identities and the fluidity of their political persuasions. In fact it points to the lack in the subject, to a conception of subjectivity which is not unified by reference to a single positive principle. Thus the intervention of psychoanalysis in the field of this antithesis between traditional ethics and democracy is of the utmost importance.

In the course of history the search for the proper ideal, for the 'real' good, has led to numerous distinctions between true and false goods. This enterprise of ethical thought aims at the fantasmatic reduction of all impossibility, at the elimination of the intervention of $\tau \acute{\upsilon} \chi \eta$ in human life. A certain idea of the good is instituted at the place of the constitutive aporia of the human life. But this is a dead end; the successive failures of all these attempts not only put into question the particular ideas of the good that have been dislocated but this whole strategy:

> the question of the Sovereign Good is one that man has asked himself since time immemorial, but the analyst knows that that is a question that is closed. Not only doesn't he have that Sovereign Good that is asked of him, but he also knows there isn't any.
>
> (VII: 300)

In Lacan's view, 'the sphere of the good erects a strong wall across the path of our desire...the first barrier that we have to deal with' (VII: 230). Lacan's central question is: what lies beyond this barrier, beyond the historical frontier of the good? This is the central question that guides the argumentation in *The Ethics of Psychoanalysis*. What lies beyond the successive conceptions of the good, beyond the ways of traditional ethical thinking, is their ultimate failure, their inability to master the central impossibility, the constitutive lack around which human experience is organised. In fact, this impossibility exercises a structural causality over the history of ethical thought. Its intolerable character causes the attempts of ethical thought to eliminate it. But this elimination entails the danger of turning good to evil, utopia to dystopia: 'the world of the good is historically revealed to be the world of evil – as epitomized not only by the famous reversibility of "Kant with Sade" but also by the unending murders under the reign of the politics of happiness' (Lacoue-Labarthe, 1997: 58). On the other hand, the irreducible character of this impossibility shows the limits of all these attempts. The name of this impossibility in Lacan is, of course, the real.

The real stands at the heart of the Lacanian ethics of psychoanalysis:

As odd as it may seem to that superficial opinion which assures any inquiry into ethics must concern the field of the ideal, if not of the unreal, I, on the contrary, will proceed instead from the other direction by going deeply into the notion of the real. The question of ethics is to be articulated from the point of view of the location of man in relation to the real.

(VII: 11)

As we have repeatedly mentioned in this book, the real here is the impossible, that is to say, impossible to represent in any imaginary way or inscribe in any symbolic system. It is the impossible *jouissance* – an enjoyment beyond any limit, any barrier – the link between death and the libido. It is this same Thing that escapes from the mediation of discourse; it escapes its representation and symbolisation and returns always to its place to show their limits. It is the constitutivity of the real that reveals the subject as a subject of lack. It is the constitutivity of the real that creates the lack in the Other; it is the constitutivity and irreducibility of the impossible real that splits the social field. The erection of the good or the ideal of traditional ethics aimed at mastering this structural impossibility of the real. Its failure opens the road to a different strategy, that of recognising its centrality and irreducibility.

The ethics of psychoanalysis is an ethics without an ideal (Miller, 1987: 9). The possibility of such a discourse is based on the psychoanalytic idea that there can be an ethically satisfactory (though not necessarily 'satisfying') position to be achieved in encircling the real, the lack, the *béance* as such (Lee, 1990: 98). Although the real in itself cannot be touched there are two strategies in confronting its structural causality. The first one is to defensively by-pass it – as traditional ethical discourse does – while the second is to encircle it (Lipowatz, 1995b: 139). This later strategy entails a symbolic recognition of the irreducibility of the real and an attempt to institutionalise social lack.[4] This attitude is what Žižek has called the ethics of the real. The ethics of the real calls us to remember the past dislocation, the past trauma: 'All we have to do is to mark repeatedly the trauma as such, in its very "impossibility", in its non-integrated horror, by means of some "empty" symbolic gesture' (Žižek, 1991b: 272). Of course we cannot touch the real but we can encircle it again and again, we can touch the tombstone which just marks the site of the dead. Žižek calls us not to give way: We 'must preserve the traces of all historical traumas, dreams and catastrophes which the ruling ideology...would prefer to obliterate'. We ourselves must become the marks of these traumas. 'Such an attitude...is the only possibility for attaining a distance on the [ideological] present, a distance which will enable us to discern signs of the New' (Žižek, 1991b:

273). The ethics of the real breaks the vicious cycle of traditional 'ideological' or utopian ethics. The ultimate failure of the successive conceptions of the good cannot be resolved by identifying with a new conception of the good. Our focus must be on the dislocation of these conceptions itself. This is the moment when the real (through its political modality) makes its presence felt and we have to recognise the ethical *status* of this presence.

Two axes of Lacanian ethics: sublimation and identification with the symptom

In analytic theory there are at least two axes in which it is attempted to move beyond traditional ethical identification with certain conceptions of the good. The first one is the axis of sublimation which is not only an aesthetic but also an ethical category (Rajchman, 1991: 71). Sublimation is 'quite different' from idealisation in the traditional ethical sense (VII: 111). We know from Freud that sublimation implies a change in the direction of the drive towards an aim other than sexual satisfaction. For Lacan, sublimation is defined as that which

> provides the *Trieb* (drive) with a satisfaction different from its aim – an aim that is still defined as its natural aim – is precisely that which reveals the true nature of the *Trieb* insofar as...[it] has a relationship to *das Ding* as such, to the Thing, insofar as it is different from the object.
>
> (VII: 111)[5]

In that sense, although sublimation does not involve a change in the drive's object it involves a new relation between the drive and something in addition to the object, something separate but also related to it; it involves the dimension of the Thing (Lee, 1990: 163). Sublimation raises an object to the dignity of the Thing, it is thus directly related to the real. This is because here the Thing is the lost/impossible real whose place is reoccupied by imaginary or symbolic objects – the ethical ideal being just one of them – without, however, any of them being able to compensate us or cover over this loss which is a product of this same symbolisation. What I want to suggest is that sublimation moves beyond traditional ethical identification by taking into account the dimension of the impossible real. But what is most important in sublimation and relates to our discussion on democracy is that sublimation creates a public space. Although it can only be individual it nevertheless creates a public space – a certain unifying field.

This paradox is very well exemplified in the valuation and overvaluation of art within civilisation, art being sublimation *par excellence*. The work of art is, on the one hand, strictly individual, tied to the libido of a particular

131

body, that of the artist. But the artist's work is also addressed to the public; it entails the creation of a public space without ever abolishing its singularity: 'the public of sublimation is not, in this sense, a public of common denominator, of communality. Sublimation is rather the public space in which our singular perverse bodies may make contact with one another through the creation of beautiful objects that stand for them' (Rajchman, 1991: 73). This is not then a public space created by identification with a common purpose or good as in traditional ethics: 'Sublimation involves another sort of "bond" among us' (Rajchman, 1991: 73). One that mediates between the individual and the common, the particular and the universal. Sublimation does not provide a total representation of the lost Thing, the impossible real; it only 'recreates' 'the *vide* left by this loss, which is structurally unrepresentable for us' (Rajchman, 1991: 74). Sublimation recognises lack and the centrality of the real instead of attempting its 'impossible' elimination as identification with an ideal does. Lack is the organising principle of the public, common space created by sublimation. Needless to say, sublimation is not mere intellectual gymnastics either. Sublimation involves the possibility of constructing a 'material' edifice around the recognition of the real, the recognition of the lack that cross-cuts the subject and the social field. This is illustrated in Lacan's argument about the vase in *The Ethics of Psychoanalysis* already mentioned in Chapter 2:

> Now if you consider the vase from the point of view I first proposed, as an object made to represent the existence of the emptiness at the centre of the real that is called the Thing, this emptiness as represented in the representation presents itself as a nihil, as nothing. And that is why the potter, just like you to whom I am speaking, creates the vase with his hand around the emptiness.
>
> (VII: 121)

Isn't that what democracy attempts to do, that is to say, to create a unity founded on emptiness, on lack and division?

On the one hand, then, sublimation is closely related to an attempt to encircle the real, to create a space for the unrepresentable within representation. Art – sublime art that is – is thus revealed as articulating, as 'showing' an impossibility. In this regard democracy can be sublime, revealing politics as an 'art of the impossible', a perpetual attempt to institutionalise within political reality, within the field of political institution, the moment of the impossible, the political modality of the real. Artistic creation is not limited within fantasy and political invention is not limited within utopian politics. On the other hand, one should not neglect Lacan's comments on the ultimately imaginary nature of sublimation. For all his intelligent negotiation of sublimation, Lacan's position remains ambiguous. Sublimation never stops providing an ultimately fantasmatic answer to the subject of the Thing; fantasy seems to contaminate the field of sublimation:

> At the level of sublimation the object is inseparable from imaginary and especially cultural elaborations. It is not just that the collectivity recognizes in them useful objects; it finds rather a space of relaxation where it may in a way delude itself on the subject of *das Ding*, colonize the field of *das Ding* with imaginary schemes. That is how collective, socially accepted sublimations operate.
>
> Society takes some comfort from the mirages that moralists, artists, artisans, designers of dresses and hats, and the creators of imaginary forms in general supply it with. But it is not simply in the approval that society gladly accords it that we must seek the power of sublimation. It is rather in an imaginary function, and, in particular, that for which we will use the symbolization of the fantasm ($ \mathcal{S} \lozenge a$), which is the form on which depends the subject's desire.
>
> (VII: 99)

It becomes necessary then to move to the second axis. This second axis entails an identification with the symptom as *sinthome*. This axis is founded on the final Lacanian definition of analysis as, paradoxically, an identification; identification with the symptom, a recognition, in other words, in the real of our symptom of the only support of our being (Žižek, 1989: 75). This is also how Freud's ethical dictum *Wo es war soll Ich werden* should be read: the subject must identify with the place where the symptom already was: 'In its pathological particularity [it]...must recognise the element which gives consistency to [its]...being' (Žižek, 1989: 75). In that sense, beyond identification with the ideal, beyond this barrier, stands identification with the symptom. In social analysis the symptom would be that which is ideologically thought to introduce disharmony in a society that would otherwise be harmoniously unified under a certain utopian ideal. In an anti-Semitic discourse the symptom would be the Jew, in an anti-democratic totalitarian discourse the symptom would be democracy itself. The problem with such discourses is that, as I have already pointed out, the disharmony is not due to the symptom itself; for instance it is not due to democracy. It is constitutive of the social. In order to acknowledge that, one has to place in the position of the harmonious – fantasmatic – ideal the 'supposed source of disharmony' itself, that is to say, the symptom. In this sense identification with the symptom goes through the utopian fantasy articulated around a certain conception of the good.

By saying 'We are all Jews!', 'We all live in Chernobyl!' or 'We are all boat people!' – all paradigms used by Žižek in *Looking Awry* (Žižek, 1991b: 140) – we elevate the symptom, the excluded truth of the social field (which has been stigmatised as an alien particularity) to the place of the universal –

to the point of our common identification which was, up to now, sustained by its exclusion or elimination. The same happens when we say 'We are all gypsies!' – the central slogan in a recent anti-racist protest in Athens – or when it is argued that we will be in a stronger position to fight anti-Semitism only when the Holocaust is recognised as a true part of all and not only of Jewish history, this localisation silencing its significance; only when 'on finding out what happened, everyone, and not just the Jews, thinks: "it could have been me – the victim that is" ' (Monchi, 1997: 80). What is promoted here is an attitude consistent with identifying with the symptom of the social and traversing social fantasy. It is only by accepting such an impossible representation, by making this declaration of impossibility, that it is possible to 'represent' the impossible or rather to identify with the impossibility of its representation. Identification with the symptom is thus related to the traversing of fantasy. Going through fantasy entails the realisation of the lack or inconsistency in the Other which is masked by fantasy, the separation between *objet petit a* and the Other, a separation which is not only ethically sound but also 'liberating' for our political imagination:

> it is precisely this lack in the Other which enables the subject to achieve a kind of 'de-alienation' called by Lacan *séparation*...[in the sense that it is realised] that the Other itself 'hasn't got it', hasn't got the final answer....This lack in the Other gives the subject – so to speak – a breathing space, it enables him to avoid the total aliena-tion in the signifier not by filling out his lack but by allowing him to identify himself, his own lack, with the lack in the Other.
>
> (Žižek, 1989: 122)

What is clearly at stake here is the possibility of enacting symbolic gestures that institutionalise social lack, that is to say incorporate the ethical recognition of the impossibility of social closure. We know that this does not entail silence. It is closer to the Socratic attitude of radical but productive ignorance or to the anti-utopian science of a Gödel or a Heisenberg[6] (a whole scientific construction aiming at acknowledging the ultimate impossibility of scientific representation) or to statements like the one made by Luis Buñuel, the great surrealist film director whom Lacan admired: 'Thank God I'm an atheist!'.[7] What is common in all these cases is that we come face to face with the linguistic representation of an unrepresentable impossibility (or of the impossibility of representation).[8] And what is most important is that this impossibility can be expressed through representation itself, through a particular set of language games which can proliferate around us. What would be the political and, in fact, democratic equivalent of such an attitude?

In place of a conclusion: psychoanalysis, ethics and politics

Slavoj Žižek starts *Tarrying with the Negative* by presenting the most striking and sublime expression of a political attempt to encircle the lack of the real, to show the political within a space of political representation: the flag of the rebels in the violent overthrow of Ceausescu in Romania. In this flag, the red star, the communist symbol constituting the nodal point of the flag and of a whole political order, the 'symbol standing for the organising principle of the national life' is cut out; what remains in its place is only a hole. It is in this brief moment, after the collapse of an order and before the articulation of another one, that it becomes possible to attest to the visibility of the hole in the big Other, to sense the presence of the political. If there is a duty for critical intellectuals today it is to occupy all the time the space of this hole, especially when a new order (a new reoccupation of traditional politics) is stabilised and attempts to make invisible this lack in the Other (Žižek, 1993: 1–2). As far as political praxis is concerned our ethical duty can only be to attempt the institutionalisation of this lack within political reality. This duty is a truly and radically democratic one. It is also an ethical duty that marks the philosophical dimension of democracy. As Bernasconi and Critchley point out, if democracy is an ethically grounded form of political life which does not cease to call itself into question by asking of its legitimacy, if legitimate communities are those that call themselves into question, then these communities are philosophical (Critchley, 1992: 239).

In this light, what becomes fundamental in democracy is that it makes visible the political institution, the limit of all political forces. By instituting antagonism it points to the distance between every utopian symbolisation and the real it attempts to master. But how exactly is this distance marked and made visible?

> This visibility is only obtained in so far as opposite forms of institution (of the social) are possible, and this possibility is revealed when those forms are actually postulated and fought for in the historical arena. For it is only in their antagonistic relation to other projects that the contingency of particular acts of institution is shown, and it is this contingency that gives them their political character.
>
> (Laclau, 1994: 4)

In other words, the conditions for maintaining the visibility of the constitutive lack and the contingent nature of a structure are, according to Laclau's schema, the following: first, to make visible the (external) conflict between the different political projects, the different contents that purport to fill this lack (none of which is pre-determined to perform this task); and second, to make visible the (internal) split marking each of these projects, a split between their function as representatives of (universal) fullness and their concrete (particular) content (Laclau, 1993: 285). Democracy attempts to maintain this visibility, to institutionalise this lack by including 'as a part of its "normal", "regular" reproduction' the moment of the suspension/dissolution of political reality. This particular moment of the eruption of the real is, as Žižek points out, the moment of elections:

> At the moment of elections, the whole hierarchic network of social relations is in a way suspended, put in parentheses; 'society' as an organic unity ceases to exist, it changes into a contingent collection of atomized individuals, of abstract units, and the result depends on a purely quantitative mechanism of counting, ultimately on a stochastic process: some wholly unforeseeable (or manipulated) event – a scandal which erupts a few days before an election, for example – can add that 'half per cent' one way or the other that determines the general orientation of the country's politics over the next few years....In vain do we conceal this thoroughly 'irrational' character of what we call 'formal democracy'....Only the acceptance of such a risk, only such a readiness to hand over one's fate to 'irrational' hazard, renders 'democracy' possible.
>
> (Žižek, 1989: 147)

This suspension of sedimented political reality, this opening to the moment of the political, presupposes the institutionalisation both of the external antagonism between competing political forces and, most importantly, of the internal split marking the identity of all these forces (Žižek's pure antagonism), since the repetition of the moment of elections inscribes deep in our political culture the recognition that none of these forces can sublate its internal split; if we need elections every once in a while it is because we accept that the hegemonic link between a concrete content and its incarnation of fullness has to be continuously re-established and renegotiated. This is one of the ways in which democracy identifies with the symptom (the constitutive antagonism of the social which is usually presented as a mere epiphenomenon) and traverses the fantasy of a harmonious social order: by instituting lack at the place of the principle of societal organisation.[9]

To recapitulate, the starting point of this chapter was the disappointment and resentment caused by the ambiguity constitutive of democracy. We have pointed out that, contrary to what anti-democratic discourses argue, this ambiguity, the existence of an original lack at the heart of the social field, is not due to democracy. Division and disharmony are constitutive of the human condition. The experience of modernity, the Death of God, in other words the dislocation of external universal markers of certainty, brought to the fore a sense of history with no guaranteed eschatological or other meaning and made visible the contingency of existence in its naked horror. The place of power is no longer cosubstantial with the prince under the guarantee of God. In front of this development one can act in two opposite directions. The lack of meaning that this process makes visible can lead to an attempted return to a pre-modern simulation of certainly; thus modernity is reoccupying (in the Blumenbergian sense of the word) the place of pre-modernity. Totalitarianism and particularism move in such a direction. On the other hand, democracy attempts to come to terms with that lack of meaning in a radically different way. It recognises in that lack the only possibility of mediating between universalism and particularism in achieving a non-totalitarian sense of social unity. The virtue of democracy is that it is not blind in front of the constitutivity of division, disharmony, lack; their recognition and institutionalisation is the only way of coming to terms with the human condition after Auschwitz and the Gulags. Democracy is the political form of historical society where history as punctuated by contingency, τύχη, lack, is no longer referred to as an external unifying principle of meaning. This fact alone which is stressed by Lefort shows that the virtue of democracy, its resolve to face history, disharmony, lack and to attempt to institutionalise them also constitutes the greatest danger for democracy. As Mircea Eliade has very clearly shown in *The Myth of the Eternal Return*, up to now, facing history in such a way was thought of as intolerable (Eliade, 1989). This is then the task of modern democracy: to persuade us that what was thought of as intolerable has an ethical *status*.[10] This is also the reason why democracy can cause a generalised resentment or frustration and reinforce aporetic inactivity or even reactive politics. These developments are due to the fact that in the field of ethics (and ontology) the ideal of harmony is still hegemonic; an ideal which is incompatible with democracy. What constantly emerges from this exposition is that for democracy to flourish 'the politics of generalised resentment must be subdued' (Connolly, 1991: 211), and for that to be done the ethics of harmony must be replaced by an ethics compatible with democracy. It is here that the ethics of psychoanalysis becomes crucial for democratic theory.

As I have tried to show the ethics of psychoanalysis moves beyond traditional ethics of the good, moves beyond the barrier of the fantasmatic ethics of harmony to come to terms with the impossible real, by recognising its ultimate irreducibility and its structural causality. As argued earlier in this chapter, the Lacanian real and lack have a thoroughly ethical dimension and both sublimation and identification with the symptom, by moving beyond traditional ethical identification with a certain imaginary conception of the good, attest to the ethicality of recognising and institutionalising them. In that sense, with the help of psychoanalysis, democracy can promote an ethical hegemony which is essential for its political survival and effectiveness[11] while Lacanian theory and Lacanian ethics can find in democracy the field of an affinity which signals their relevance for socio-political analysis and political praxis. In that sense, achieving a better (but not a perfect) society, a more democratic and just society, is possible but such a project cannot depend on the 'visions of the psychic imaginary' as Whitebook insists. Only the fracture of imaginary utopian visions can create the chance of pursuing a democratic course, a course which is profoundly self-critical: 'The just polity is one that actively maintains its own interruption or ironization as that which sustains it' (Critchley, 1992: 238). Such a standpoint seems to be at the antipodes of Whitebook's view, according to which 'without the input of the imaginary, any such debate [on achieving a better society]...is in danger of being empty' (Whitebook, 1995: 89). What Whitebook cannot realise is that it is exactly the emptiness of the Lacanian lack in the Other, the emptiness in the *locus* of democratic power in Lefort, that becomes the point of reference for the articulation of such a new political vision, a vision beyond imaginary lures.[12]

To avoid any possible confusion, it must be stressed, however, that democracy cannot be reduced to anarchy or chaos; it is a form of 'order'. A principle of societal organisation exists. A society without a principle of organisation would be a meaningless society; it would not be able to constitute itself as such. It would amount to a state of pure anxiety insofar as, according to Lacan's comments in *Anxiety*, the appearance of anxiety is the sign of the temporary collapse of all points of identificatory reference (seminar of 2 May 1962). As I have pointed out, the importance of the democratic invention is that, in a double movement, it provides a point of reference, a *point de capiton* for the institution of society, without reducing society to a positive content pertaining to this point of reference.[13] This is achieved because the positive content of democracy is the acceptance of the constitutive lack and antagonism (and consequently hegemony) that splits every total representation of the social field. And the *status* of this lack, as an encounter with the real, is ethical. If democracy entails, as Niklas Luhmann argues, the principle of allowing opposition as a value-concept this means exactly that the lack acquires a certain ethical dimension. This is an ethics without ideals; the place of the ideal is occupied by the dividing line of opposition and by the undecidable moment of elections; in other words by the recognition of the real of our symptom, of the antagonistic nature of society. For Luhmann the place of the ideal is occupied by a pure difference; that between government and opposition. Thus 'politics loses the possibility of [total] representation. It cannot presume to be – or even to represent – the whole within the whole' (Luhmann, 1990: 233). In the democratic vision the whole of society is lacking, it is crossed, *barré* by the impossible real.

There are two more very brief points I would like to mention in bringing this chapter to a close. The first one concerns similar attempts to the one presented here, based on the ethics of deconstruction (Critchley, 1992) or more simply on an ethics of difference (Connolly, 1991). The second one focuses on the political consequences of my argument.

First, it is certain that this text shares with both Connolly and Critchley the aspiration to articulate an ethics of 'disharmony' in order to enhance the prospects of democracy. Our difference is that they both think that an ethics founded on a recognition of Otherness and difference is enough. Connolly's argumentation is developed along the polarity identity/difference with the ethical sting being a recognition of Otherness. For Critchley also, what seems to be at stake in deconstruction is the relation with 'The Other' – although this Other is not understood in exactly the same terms as the Lacanian Other (Critchley, 1992: 197). Drawing on Levinasian ethics where the ethical is related to the disruption of totalising politics, he contends that: 'any attempt to bring closure to the social is continually denied by the non-totalisable relation to the Other' (Critchley, 1992: 238). Thus, the possibility of democracy rests on the recognition of the Other: 'The community remains an open community in so far as it is based on the recognition of difference, of the difference of the Other' (Critchley, 1992: 219). Moreover, political responsibility in democracy has 'its horizon in responsibility for the Other' (ibid.: 239). This is also Touraine's position: democracy entails the 'recognition of the other' (Touraine, 1997: 192). The problem with such an analysis is that it presupposes the Other as a unified totality or, even if this is not always the case, it seems to be offering a positive point of identification remaining thus within the limits of traditional ethical strategies or, in any case, not undermining them in a radical way. What has to be highlighted is that it is precisely this relation – the identification with the Other – that attempts to bring closure to the social. In order to have a non-totalisable relation to the Other we must relate – identify – with the lack in the Other and not with the Other *per se*. This is the radical innovation of Lacanian ethics. And this is what democracy needs today.

Second, the preceding argumentation does not mean that actually existing democracies constitute total embodiments of the Lacanian ethical standpoint. Such a view would be totally alien to almost everything that has been articulated in this chapter: 'one must not restrict oneself to conceiving of democracy as an existent political form (and, once again, certainly not as an apologetics for Western liberal democracy)' (Critchley, 1992: 240). From that point of view Derrida's conception of a *démocratie à venir* seems absolutely relevant. In doing so, however, one must be very careful not to idealise democracy by relapsing into traditional ethical discourse or utopian politics.[14] Furthermore, in articulating a critique of present democratic institutions one must also keep in mind what Žižek has so successfully formulated:

It is true that democracy makes possible all sorts of manipulation, corruption, the rule of demagogy, and so on, but as soon as we eliminate the possibility of such deformations, we lose democracy itself; if we want to remove these deformations and to grasp the

Universal in its intact purity, we obtain its very opposite. So-called
'real democracy' is just another name for non-democracy.

(Žižek, 1989: 148)

In that sense, from a Lacanian point of view, one is entitled to conclude that
a real and pure democracy 'does not exist'. The radicalisation of democracy
can only be the result of a continuous *ascesis*, it depends on our ability to
move beyond the Scylla of conformity and the Charybdis of utopianism and
maintain, in the fullness of time, our distance from both of them.[15]

NOTES

INTRODUCTION

1 The naivety of Wilhelm Reich and of some versions of Freudo-Marxism are obviously not innocent in this respect. Lacanian theory, however, has also been accused of entailing the danger of such a reductionism. Consider, for example, Stuart Hall's following statement: 'I think that Lacanianism is in danger of substituting a psychoanalytic essentialism for a class essentialism' (Hall, 1988: 68). Although Hall is speaking about essentialism, the problem is clearly the reduction of the social to a class or a psychoanalytic essence. However, insofar as every analysis presupposes the elucidation of a particular problem or field by reference to an element which is usually external to it, and thus articulates a certain meta-discourse (if we are studying a linguistic phenomenon this would be a meta-linguistic discourse; if it is a psychological phenomenon one can speak of a meta-psychology) every analysis becomes, to a certain extent, reductionist. Even the most 'objective' (casual) reading of a text, the most simple analysis of an issue, is contaminated by a certain reductionism. In that sense, reductionism is unavoidable (the same seems to apply to essentialism; our reference to Hall's statement was not that innocent) – although the crude reductionism criticised by Wrong is certainly avoidable (as Lacan points out 'we must, with the utmost rigor, distinguish from psychoanalytic theory the constant fallacious attempts to base on analytic theory notions such as those of a model personality, a national character, or a collective superego' – 1996a: 16). On the other hand, this unavoidability does not mean that it is possible to articulate a closed successful reduction, a closed successful meta-language. According to Lacan, the meta-linguistic position is something necessary (all language is a meta-language – III: 226) but ultimately impossible (no meta-language is possible – E: 311 – not least because every meta-linguistic formalisation of language has to use language itself and thus its pure character is undermined – XX: 119). No doubt Lacan's strategy is to show that there is no meta-language; but this revelation can only take place through the recognition of the impossibility entailed in every meta-linguistic operation. For this to be shown, one has to locate oneself within the terrain of meta-language. If meta-language was to be negated from the outside then the fantasy of avoiding it altogether would be sustained and with it the whole meta-linguistic position would remain intact. In this sense, Lacan articulates a meta-linguistic negation of meta-language; the meta-linguistic operation is presupposed but only as a failed operation. Similarly, moving beyond or rather creating a distance from reductionism, presupposes a certain risk of reductionism. When dealing with reductionism, essentialism and other such

categories and positions from a Lacanian point of view, it is necessary to avoid absolute positions – 'absolutism' presupposes repression – and introduce a set of language games which permit a more subtle but effective handling of the problem. The important question is not 'reduction or no-reduction' but 'what kind of reduction?'. In order to create a distance from crude reduction it is necessary to operate within the field of reduction; it is necessary to *reduce reduction* to its own *impossibility*.

2 On the other hand, however, it could be argued that in an age of interdisciplinarity and (undistorted?) communication between different scientific fields and theoretical currents, that is to say, in an age of openness (though this is not the whole picture but rather the one in which the Western intellectual likes to identify himself) it would be absurd to remain stuck within some *a priori* drawn boundaries. This argument, though, should not be understood as entailing an 'anything goes' logic – an impossible position in itself: it should lead to the re-evaluation and redrawing rather than to a 'post-modern' abolition of all kinds of boundaries and limits. It is such a redrawing that is always at stake, even when one is fantasising that an abolition is possible.

3 This seems to be especially the case with Freud's book on President Wilson. This book, a psychological biography of the president, which was the result of the collaboration between Freud and his ex-patient, the American Ambassador to Paris, W. C. Bullitt, was only published in 1967 (Freud and Bullitt, 1967). Although Freud's exact involvement in writing this book is not clear, its originality is not disputed. Instead of being a model of a study crossing the boundaries between psychoanalysis and politics, it should rather be read as an index of what has to be avoided in such undertakings. As Roazen concludes 'there are some specific points in the Wilson book which can teach us what to avoid' (Roazen, 1969: 319).

4 As we shall see, it could also be argued that it is exactly because of his non-reductionist conception of subjectivity that Lacan is able to reach a new conception of the socio-symbolic order of the Other: 'the advent of the split subject signals a corresponding division or breakdown of the Other' (Fink, 1995a: 46).

5 See especially Roustang, 1982 and 1990. Critique of Lacan, either as a theorist or as a clinician, very often takes the form of a personal and vitriolic attack. Lacan is invariably presented as a harmful agent, an evil figure compared to Sade, as the founder of a monstrous theoretical and institutional edifice returning psychoanalysis to the 1920s (Castoriadis, 1991: 81–95) or even, and more recently, as simply 'the shrink from hell', a 'physically attractive psychopath' guilty of damaging 'patients, colleagues, mistresses, wives, children, publishers, editors and opponents' – it is indeed a miracle that the author of that article survived, despite obviously being an opponent. Maybe his article is proof of the damage inflicted on him by encountering extremely little of Lacan's 'lunatic legacy' that he seems to understand – the success of Lacan can only be attributed to 'the aura which surrounded him' – well, after all he was a 'handsome dandy' (Tallis, 1997: 20).

6 It is true that Lacan's work constitutes a complex entity from which it is impossible to extract some bits while ignoring all the others, without arriving at grotesque conclusions (Verhaeghe, 1997: 91). This is evident in Alan Sokal's recent critique of the use of mathematical formulations by Lacan. Not surprisingly, isolated from their wider context they make no sense at all.

7 Yet it should not be forgotten that during these last 10 years some extremely interesting and challenging works on the relation between Lacan, philosophy and the political have appeared due to the path-breaking interventions of theorists such as Slavoj Žižek, Ernesto Laclau, Thanos Lipowatz and others.

Without these works this book might not be possible and certainly would not be the same.

8 Furthermore, even when a tripartite schema is prioritised, the signposts dividing the three phases are not always identical. For example, although it is generally accepted that the third phase starts roughly with the eleventh seminar, it has also been argued that this phase begins in 1960 – with the first phase extending from the publication of Lacan's thesis until 1953, and the second from 1953 up to the late 1950s (Benvenuto and Kennedy, 1986).

9 The radical development of Lacan's theory is coupled with a parallel insistence in the use of an original set of core concepts which remain central although continuously redefined. For example, Lacan devotes one of his last seminars to the concepts of the Real, the Symbolic and the Imaginary (RSI – 1974–5) a title almost identical to his 1953 talk on the Symbolic, the Imaginary and the Real.

10 Here one cannot miss the similarities between Lacan's position and the position of other thinkers such as Saussure and Wittgenstein.

11 This biographical sketch is mainly based on Elisabeth Roudinesco's historical study *Jacques Lacan & Co., A History of Psychoanalysis in France 1925–1985* (Roudinesco, 1990); her recent biography of Lacan, *Jacques Lacan* (Roudinesco, 1997) and Darian Leader's *Lacan for Beginners* (Leader, 1996) as well as on the chronologies included in the introductory books on Lacan by Benvenuto and Kennedy (1986); Bowie (1991) and Lee (1990). Lacan himself never wrote an autobiography and it seems that he was reluctant to recount events of his personal life especially relating to his childhood. As Jacques-Alain Miller, Lacan's son-in-law, points out, during the 1970s a lot of people offered to interview Lacan, including a journalist commissioned by Lacan's publisher, Éditions du Seuil, but he refused without hesitation. His detest for biographies is also revealed in his scornful remarks regarding Freud's biographer, Ernest Jones (Miller, 1996: 4). In that he is definitely following Freud's paradigm since Freud had twice destroyed his manuscripts, correspondence and diaries – in 1885 and 1907. Apparently, Freud's view was that 'as for the biographers, let them worry, we have no desire to make it too easy for them' (Freud in Macey, 1988: 1). Lacan's 'return to Freud' then is also meaningful with respect to their attitudes towards biography, although this attitude was not always identical. In any case this biographical sketch is designed to provide the general background to Lacan's theoretical development and should not be directly implicated in the evaluation of his work which has a life of its own, the life of the letter, independently of its author.

12 This is not to say that Freud was some kind of cynical conservative. In fact, he was rather in favour of greater economic egalitarianism, without however endorsing the view that this egalitarianism would significantly alter human nature (Roazen, 1969: 245). It has been also argued that most of Freud's leading disciples and followers were ardent Social Democrats and that he himself was basically of a socialist inclination, although not of an active type. And although he was sceptical of some of the traditional foundations of democracy, on the other hand many of his followers developed a strong interest in psychoanalysis exactly because of its democratising potential (Kurzweil, 1998: 285–6). On Freud's relation to democracy see Peter Widmer's essay 'Freud und die Demokratie' (Widmer, 1995).

NOTES

1 THE LACANIAN SUBJECT: THE IMPOSSIBILITY OF IDENTITY AND THE CENTRALITY OF IDENTIFICATION

1 Before being baptised a poststructuralist, Lacan had been categorised as a structuralist. Anika Lemmaire, in the first doctoral thesis written on Lacan's work, states with remarkable certainty that 'Jacques Lacan is a structuralist' (Lemaire, 1977: 1). A few pages later she adds: 'Lacan is indeed a structuralist: the unconscious is the structure hidden beneath an apparently conscious and lucid self-disposition' (ibid.: 7). Ten years later Stephen Frosh reaches the final verdict. Not only does Lacan employ structuralist methods but 'he makes psychoanalysis a branch of structuralism, specifically structural linguistics' (Frosh, 1987: 130). Certainly, the whole Lacanian enterprise was influenced by structural linguistics and structural anthropology. However, to reduce Lacanian psychoanalysis to these instances is far from a legitimate move. As Bruce Fink has recently put it 'while structure plays a very important role in Lacan's work, it is not the whole story, nor was it ever at any point in Lacan's development' (Fink, 1995b: 64). The appropriation of Lacanian theory by poststructuralism shows exactly that. If Lacan is attempting a 'reconceptualisation of Freud in the light of poststructuralist theory' (Elliott, 1994: 91), if the influence of the Lacanian school 'has been for "deconstruction" ' (Rustin, 1995: 242) then surely he cannot be a mere structuralist. On the other hand, the poststructuralist reading of Lacan, while attesting to the richness of his theories, is also grossly reductionist. Jonathan Culler is right then when stating that 'the opposition between structuralism and post-structuralism merely complicates the attempt to understand such major figures' (Culler, 1989: 27). What will be shown in the following pages, it is hoped, is that Lacanian theory goes a lot further than both these labels can represent – not least because Lacan is not, strictly speaking, a philosopher; his starting point is always the praxis of psychoanalysis, hence his theory is always articulated as a reflection on the impossibility revealed in our encounter with the real of experience, a real beyond both structuralism and most currents of poststructuralism. On Lacan's relation to poststructuralism, Žižek's 'Why Lacan is not a post-structuralist?' remains indispensable (Žižek, 1987, also incorporated in Žižek, 1989: 153–61). Insisting on the particularity of Lacan's enterprise and its difference from structuralism and poststructuralism (a difference that can be based on a variety of points such as the centrality of the concept of the 'subject', the use of concepts such as *'jouissance'*, the 'real' and 'truth' and the complex language games Lacan articulates with them) does not mean, of course, that exploring the relation between Lacan and poststructuralist theory (especially the work of Jacques Derrida) cannot be a fascinating and fruitful enterprise, and one that has to be undertaken urgently. In fact, it seems that most resistances to such a task are being slowly set aside.

An example of this is the shift in Derrida's position *vis à vis* Lacanian theory. Even though Derrida's 'Purveyor of Truth', published in the early 1970s, is a sometimes unfairly critical essay, attributing to Lacan, among others, a series of transcendental and idealistic truth claims guilty of phonocentrism (the prioritisation of speech and voice over writing, something that Lacan was, in fact, already questioning from his 1961–2 unpublished seminar on *Identification*, that is to say even before the publication of Derrida's critique), in order to contrast them with the deconstructionist position ('here dissemination threatens the law of the signifier and of castration as the contract of truth' Derrida writes – Derrida, 1988: 187), in a recent paper, characteristically entitled 'For the Love of Lacan', Derrida associates himself with a homage to Lacan, a Lacan whose 'sophistication

and competence, his philosophical originality, have no precedent in the psychoanalytic tradition' (Derrida, 1995b: 706). This recent paper, articulated around a
series of personal recollections of Derrida from his relations with Lacan, summa-
rises Derrida's comments as presented in the 'Purveyor of Truth' but only to deny
that they constituted a critique (ibid.: 722) and to note that Lacan had responded
to them in a way bringing him closer to deconstruction: 'Lacan's discourse,
always highly sensitive to all the movements of the theoretical scene – and who
would blame him? – never ceased to readjust, even to revise, and sometimes to
contradict the axioms I have just mentioned [the ones criticised in the 'Purveyor
of Truth']. The emphasis on writing grew constantly stronger after 1968, to the
point of inverting, very "grammatologically", the utterance that I quoted a little
while ago' (ibid.: 720). Irrespective of whether Derrida was right or wrong or
whether Lacan's thought evolved in a 'grammatological' way, Derrida's paper
opens the road to a much needed discussion on the relation between deconstruction and Lacanian theory. We know that Lacan was certainly not dismissive of
such a dialogue, as it is shown in his – not unconditional of course – praise for
Lacoue-Labarthe and Nancy's *The Title of the Letter* (Lacoue-Labarthe and
Nancy 1992 – for a discussion of this book see Chapter 3 of this volume). Derrida
himself is acknowledging that, despite all the difficulties between them, Lacan
always left him 'the greatest freedom of interpretation' (Derrida, 1995b: 710). It is
such a freedom that must guide, in the future, the dialogue between deconstruction and Lacanian theory.

2 Later in his work Lacan was to declare the Cartesian nature of psychoanalysis.
By articulating the constitutivity of the unconscious, itself being shown in the
failure of conscious certainty, Lacan envisages a Cartesian science whose fundamental implication is the dislocation of the Cartesian subject.

3 Lacan refers here to Ego-psychology which he accused of distorting the radical
dimension of the Freudian discoveries. For a recent 'balanced' – that is to say
not polemical – account of Lacan's relation to Ego-psychology see Zeitlin, 1997.
It is also worth reading Smith's *Arguing with Lacan: Ego Psychology and Language*, where the distance between Lacanian theory and Ego-psychology is
minimised (Smith, 1991). In any case, Lacan's justified critique of Ego-
psychology should be seen within the wider context of his rift with the International Psychoanalytic Association (IPA) within which Ego-psychology formed
the dominant current. This was a 'war' that lasted almost 40 years but seems to
be approaching a truce as Lacanians and the IPA are searching for a new *modus
vivendi*. See, in this connection, the recent joint interview given by the President
of the IPA, R. Horacio Etchegoyen and Jacques-Alain Miller (now president of
the Lacanian Association Mondiale de Psychanalyse) in the Argentinean review
Vertex, Revista Argentina de Psiquiatria (Etchegoyen and Miller, 1996). Although it is not certain that Etchegoyen is expressing the views of the majority of
the IPA, and notwithstanding the fact that Miller is not representing the whole
of the Lacanian community (and irrespective of the institutional games behind
this mutual recognition), it cannot be disputed that the conciliatory and open
tone of the discussion, even the fact alone that it breaks 40 years of silence and
distrust, is something impossible to ignore, although the way it will be received
by the sides involved and affected remains largely open.

4 This is a strategy employed by Lacan himself on a variety of occasions. For
example, when in his seminar on *The Ethics of Psychoanalysis* (1959–60), he
approaches the issue of the desire of the analyst he proceeds as follows: 'What
can a desire of this kind, that desire of the analyst be? We can say right away
what it cannot be' (VII: 300). In his recent article 'Lacan with Scholasticism:
Agencies of the Letter' Richard Glejzer argues that Lacanian semiotics are

primarily influenced not by structural linguistics but by Augustine's openings to negative theology – one should not forget that while Augustine is not a negative theologian *par excellence*, such as Pseudo-Dionysius and Meister Eckhart, 'he always haunts certain landscapes of negative theology' (Derrida 1995a: 40). The basis of Glejzer's argumentation is that only negative theology acknowledges the limits of linguistic representation, limits which can be revealed, however, only through our engagement with language: 'learning involves a recognition of ignorance since the divine, for Augustine, is unknowable. What speaking allows for Augustine is the contemplation of the limits of knowledge' (Glejzer 1997: 112). As Derrida affirms, the language of negative theology 'does not cease testing the very limits of language' (Derrida 1995a: 54). In that sense negative theology and its Augustinian use in semiotics share with Lacanian theory a similar epistemological frame.

There remain, though, important differences. Lacan's structuralism, according to Glejzer, is mapping the effects of the real on signification beyond any theological constraint (Glejzer, 1997: 117–18): 'While scholasticism works from sameness as its practice, toward ultimate unification with the ineffable as a way to solving difference, psychoanalysis places the ineffable in being itself, in two bodies existing in language that only seem to be one. This is the ultimate problem with language that Augustine discovered but could not articulate since for him the one did exist' (ibid.: 121). Well, obviously for Lacan this One does not exist: 'Is there a One anterior to discontinuity? I do not think so, and everything I have been taught in recent years has tended to exclude the need for a closed One' (Lacan in Scott, 1989: 76). It is clear, therefore, that Lacanian theory cannot be reduced to an exercise in negative theology. Negative theology, as Derrida has so successfully shown, is only the preparation 'for a silent intuition of God' (Derrida, 1992: 74), for a mystical union with the hyper-essentiality of God, a hyper-essentiality beyond all negation (ibid.: 77–8). The discourse of negative theology is above all articulated as part of a prayer, something alien to both deconstruction and Lacanian theory. Joy points to this gap *a propos* of deconstruction but her statement seems to be also applicable to psychoanalysis: 'But just as the ultimate positive intent of negative theology is disclosed for Derrida by its prayerful framework, so Derrida's own parallel interventions are situated within a (non)teleology of ultimate uncertainty' (Joy 1992: 278). Neither deconstruction nor Lacanian theory then can be reduced to negative theology since they lack the ontological *telos* which informs its whole undertaking (ibid.: 261). For a general introduction to the relation between Lacan and theology I suggest the collective volume *Lacan and Theological Discourse* (Wyschogrod, Crownfield and Raschke, 1989).

5 In fact, as we shall see, from a psychoanalytic point of view, one can speak of an 'irrational' or rather a 'non-rational choice theory' (Wrong, 1994: 116). Rational choice theories presuppose the consistency of the (always rational) agents' actions over their outcomes, highlight the importance of instrumental rationality in attaining these outcomes (Weale, 1992: 39) and, most importantly, reduce the content of these outcomes to the maximisation of benefits and the minimisation of costs for the individuals involved. Curiously enough, what is most alien to psychoanalytic theory in rational choice argumentation is its methodological individualism, the idea that social phenomena are to be explained by recourse to choices and preferences of individual actors and, in fact, choices and preferences that are conscious, transparent and rationally pursued. Obviously, there is no room for the consideration of the unconscious in such a schema (the unconscious, by being beyond the conscious, would blur the transparency of preferences and destabilise any possible stable link between means and ends since both

means and ends are subject to unconscious processes). It is also doubtful whether a rational choice theorist would accept something like the death drive as a source of 'legitimate' preferences within his own framework of analysis. There is a problem, in other words, regarding the importance of non-rational or non-materialist (and not non-material) sources of motivation. Furthermore, as we shall see, psychoanalytic theory – and not only Lacanian theory – is much more sensitive to the socio-symbolic dimension of human desire and preference formation; for Lacan, desire is clearly a social product. In this sense, psycho-analysis, which departs from a seemingly 'individual' clinical experience, is, nonetheless, not in the least individualistic in the way rational choice theories are. Of course, these remarks amount neither to saying that psychoanalytic theory should ignore areas in which instrumental rationality appears dominant nor that recent models in rational choice theory are not becoming sensitive to all these issues. However, their ability to resolve them without getting rid of rational choice theory itself is something not yet very clear.

6 The Lacanian theory of the mirror stage, marking Lacan's first significant contribution to analytic theory (a contribution articulated around the explora-tion of the imaginary *status* of the ego) was first presented at the Fourteenth International Psycho-analytical Congress which was held at Marienbad in 1936, but was rewritten and first published in 1949. The paper is influenced by the work of the famous French psychologist and friend of Lacan, Henri Wallon, who was apparently the first who described in detail the dialectic developed between the human infant and the mirror image.

7 In this respect it could be argued that power stems from the imaginary. All imaginary forms of polarity are characterised by an antagonistic tension; they are zero-sum games between counterparts which can only be resolved through total destruction (Lipowatz, 1986, 1995b: 136). As we shall see, however, power cannot be adequately conceptualised by reference only to the imaginary register.

8 Already in Wallon's schema the mirror image is linked to a certain symbolic element, the infant's name. Wallon makes the following statement in relation to Darwin's relevant observation: 'Darwin's child looks at his mirror-image every time he is called by name. When he hears his name, he no longer applies it, albeit in a passing or intermittent fashioning to his proprioceptive self, but rather to the exteroceptive image of himself that the mirror offers him' (Wallon in Julien, 1994: 30).

9 For a first account of the increasing privileging of the symbolic over the imaginary in the course of Lacan's work and the implications this had for his conception of the mirror stage, see Nobus, 1998. A reading of Lacanian theory which stresses the importance of the imaginary (in its specular and non-specular dimensions) even for the late Lacan, can be found in Julien, 1994.

10 Initially Lacan insisted that alienation belongs to the imaginary, that it is constitutive of the imaginary order (III: 146). Later on, however, – in seminar XI for instance – alienation is also linked to the symbolic and identified with 'the fact that the subject is produced within the language that awaits him or her and is inscribed in the locus of the Other' (Laurent, 1995: 30).

11 Lacan turns his attention to the centrality of language for the first time in his seminal 'Discourse of Rome' which was delivered in Rome in September 1953 during the XVIth conference of Psychoanalysts of the Romance Languages. This discourse is published in the *Écrits* under the title 'Function and Field of Speech and Language in Psychoanalysis', and marks a considerable shift in his interest which was to influence all the subsequent development of his teaching.

12 It is a standard Lacanian move – which, regrettably, is sometimes easily forgotten – to illuminate all the three dimensions or angles characteristic of every

human phenomenon (the imaginary, the symbolic and the real dimension). This is also true of power relations which can be articulated at the imaginary, the symbolic and the real level; some of these dimensions have already been explored or will be explored in the following chapters. The fruitfulness of such an approach will also be shown, for example, in our analysis of signification and the role assigned to the signified in Lacanian theory.

13 In his 1972–3 seminar *Encore*, Lacan points out that 'Mathematical formalism is our goal, our ideal' (XX: 119).

14 This is part of Lacan's general strategy to articulate his own views with readings of Freud's works in a way in which it is not always easy to discern what is an original contribution and what is just the presentation of a Freudian position. This double movement is also characteristic of the philosophical dimension of Lacan's return to Freud: 'it was a highly strategic move that enabled Lacan to sell Freud to the philosophers, while at the same time selling philosophy to psychoanalysts under the same, good-old-Freud label. This strategy proved to be incredibly successful....Which simply means that psychoanalysis, thanks to Lacan, is now the official philosophy of France' (Borch-Jacobsen, 1997: 213).

15 Language can be thought of as the result of a sedimentation, decontestation or even hegemonisation (that is to say of a symbolic domestication) of a primary field of *lalangue*, of the primary chaotic substrate of polysemy and linguistic *jouissance* (Evans, 1996a: 97).

16 Even Hjelmslev, who was keen on excluding any kind of substance from the linguistic domain, promoting a formalism that was crucial in the expansion of the theory of language to other semiotic systems, belatedly sought to reintegrate the referent, a clear substance, to his linguistic model; in his own words he tried to 'semiotize right up to that lump of rebel substance known as the "physical level" ' (Hjelmslev in Gadet, 1986: 126). Gadet's comment is the following and relates directly to our own discussion: 'This [Hjelmslev's] is a strange enterprise, and we may wonder whether linguistics as constituted by Saussure does not get bogged down in it' (Gadet, 1986: 126).

17 'One name stands for one thing, another stands for another thing' as Wittgenstein suggests in *Tractatus* (Wittgenstein, 1988: 22). In his *Philosophical Investigations*, he returns and describes as follows this Augustinian picture of language: 'The individual words name objects – sentences are combinations of such names....Every word has a meaning. This meaning is correlated with the word. It is the object for which the word stands' (Wittgenstein, 1992: 2).

18 Although in the beginning Lacan uses the categories of meaning (*sens*) and signification (*signification*) interchangeably, from the late 1950s onwards he links signification to the imaginary dimension of the signifying process (to the illusory production of the signified) while he uses meaning to refer to the symbolic dimension of this process. Although this distinction is of some clinical importance, it does not influence dramatically our account of Lacan's understanding of the symbolic.

19 As Jacqueline Rose has put it 'the unconscious constantly reveals the "failure" of identity...there is resistance to identity at the very heart of psychic life' (Rose in Butler, 1997: 97).

20 This is the anticipation of an illusory unity, which reveals the imaginary nature of all utopian promises. See, in this respect, the discussion in Chapter 4.

21 In Lacan's conception, which is influenced in this respect by Lévi-Strauss's work, the Law is not understood as a particular piece or positive content of legislation, but as the principle of ordering or structuration which makes possible social existence. Law is the structural condition of possibility for the emergence of the social. And since the social can only be articulated through symbolic exchange,

that is to say within the symbolic order, this Law is, for Lacan, the law of the signifier: 'law, then, is revealed clearly enough as identical with an order of language' (E: 66).

22 For a first introductory exploration of the characteristics of psychosis and of the structural differentiation between the clinical structures of neurosis (obsessional, hysteric and phobic), psychosis and perversion, see, from the bibliography available in English, Miller's short article 'An Introduction to Lacan's Clinical Perspectives' (Miller, 1996b), Bruce Fink's *A Clinical Introduction to Lacanian Psychoanalysis: Theory and Technique* (Fink, 1997) and Joël Dor's *The Clinical Lacan* (Dor, 1997).

23 While the general perception seems to be that Lacan and Foucault, both as persons and as theoretical projects, were alien to each other and largely incompatible, this is not true. Notwithstanding the many important differences, it has to be stressed that at least during his seminars on the *Crucial Problems for Psychoanalysis* (1964–5) and *The Object of Psychoanalysis* (1965–6) Lacan was repeatedly urging his audience to read Foucault's books, and especially praises the affinity of Foucault's work in *The Birth of the Clinic* with his own project (seminar of 31 March 1965). The following year he asked everyone to read *The Order of Things* of 'our friend Michel Foucault' (seminar of 27 April 1966) who attended Lacan's seminar on the 18 May 1966.

24 Recognising the importance of decision is not equivalent to subscribing to a decisionist argumentation. Decisionism is usually founded on a Hobbesian or quasi-Hobbesian conception of subjectivity. While it aspires to eliminate any metaphysical or anthropological foundation in the theory of power by acknowledging the ontological priority of decision, it is usually containing an implicit anthropological kernel. The decisionist presupposes most of the time the constitutivity of a drive of self-preservation which guides decision. In other words, decisionist argumentation is usually replacing the essentialist metaphysical rationalisations of decision with another rationalisation (more heretic but still a rationalisation). What is missed is the radical character of decision which can only be sustained if one views the constitutivity of decision as due to the lack in the subject. In Lacanian terms decision is not primarily functioning according to a pre-existing subjective quality or kernel (a will to power for example), but exactly because any such point of reference is missing. In this sense, decision is symbolically conditioned (it requires the castrating intervention of symbolic Law): what governs decision is the desire for an impossible/prohibited identity.

25 The Lacanian distinction between 'reality' and the 'real' is furher elaborated towards the end of the second chapter.

26 Lacanian psychoanalysis is not reducible to a medical practice. In Lacan, curing effects as such are only by-products of analysis. Here it is necessary to draw a distinction between the results of analysis, meaning its therapeutic results, such as the disappearance of symptoms, the lifting of inhibitions, the increasing of pleasure, etc. and its ends as an experience articulating the truth of the subject, a truth also facilitating the adoption of a different subjective position *vis à vis* the symptomatic formations (Miller, 1991).

27 In fact, Lacan has always been alert to this interaction of the social with the individual. From his doctoral thesis onwards he tried to approach the issue of the relation between the social and the subjective. In his thesis he examines, through a detailed case study, the interaction between personality and the social world. He defines personality as 'the ensemble of specialised functional relations that establishes the originality of man-the-animal, adapting him to the enormous influence exercised by the *milieu* of mankind, or society, on the *milieu* of his life' (Lacan in Muller and Richardson, 1982: 26–7). Not surprisingly, then, his thesis

was favourably received by left-wing publications such as *L' Humanité* and *La Critique Sociale* precisely due to the inclusion of such socio-centric statements.

2 THE LACANIAN OBJECT: DIALECTICS OF SOCIAL IMPOSSIBILITY

1 Lacan was always more than willing to deconstruct the hegemonic bipolarities of Western thought; he introduces, for example, the neologism *extimité* in order to subvert the opposition between the external and the internal.

2 Defining the subjective and the objective, especially in their mutual opposition, is extremely difficult even in mainstream philosophical discourse. This is illustrated, for example, in the opposite and conflicting ways in which they are defined in medieval thought and modern thought (Williams, 1988: 308).

3 Only an empty signifier can represent the promise of this impossible fullness. This is the signifier that both the subject and the Other share: 'What we and the inaccessible Other share is the empty signifier that stands for that X which eludes both positions' (Žižek, 1997a: 51). On the notion of the empty signifier and its political implications see Laclau, 1996, especially pp. 36–46. Also see, in this connection, Chapter 3 of this volume.

4 *Jouissance* is one of the most important but complex terms introduced to the psychoanalytic vocabulary by Lacan. It appears for the first time in Lacan's seminar during the early 1950s but acquires its central location in the Lacanian theoretical edifice towards the late 1960s and 1970s. To simplify things a bit, *jouissance* means enjoyment. Although in the beginning, Lacan links this enjoyment with the pleasures of masturbation and orgasm, later on he opposes pleasure to *jouissance*. *Jouissance* is now posited as the part of the real which is limited by the introduction of the 'pleasure principle', a principle conditioned by symbolic law (Evans, 1996a: 91).

Thus, *jouissance* is clearly located beyond pleasure. It can only be felt through the suffering, the 'painful enjoyment' one extracts from his symptom, insofar as enjoying the symptom is located beyond the barrier of socially sanctioned pleasure. While, however, *jouissance* is denied entrance in the world of 'legitimate' satisfaction, the whole play of desire conditioned by the pleasure principle is articulated around the quest for this ultimately unattainable *jouissance* (if *jouissance* is real then it must be ultimately impossible to attain it). The dialectic of this play will be further examined in this chapter, together with a series of questions raised by the ambiguities in Lacan's use of the category of *jouissance*.

5 The Thing (*das Ding* in Freud's vocabulary) is, according to Lacan, the thing in the real, outside the symbolic network. As such it is posited as lost, as the real object denied by the prohibition of incest, the mother. The Thing acquires its meaning within a context of *jouissance* and is characterised by its affinity to concepts such as the *objet petit a* (Evans, 1996a: 204–5).

6 In his second seminar, Lacan points out that 'the real is absolutely without fissure' (II: 97). It is not very clear if this statement is compatible with his comments during the late 1950s and 1960s (in his unpublished seminar *Desire and its Interpretation*, for example, where he speaks about cuts in the real – seminar of 27 May 1959), to which we have already referred, or if we have to do with a change of opinion. This is a problem which has to do with the general indeterminacy in Lacan's definitions of the real. In this regard, see the discussion in the next section of this chapter.

7 The fantasmatic scenario that attempts to fill the lack in the Other and defend us against castration does not have to be, as far as its particular contents are

concerned, a beatific harmonious picture. This is the most banal case. The real problem with the lack in the Other is that it is as such anxiety producing since it introduces an element of deep – almost ontological – uncertainty. The problem, in other words, is not so much that the Other is lacking, but that we do not know why he is lacking. Fantasy provides a solution to this uncertainty, a solution which is nothing but a compromise. In that sense, it reduces anxiety and creates a semblance of harmony but this harmony may depend on a picture of the Other as demanding something horrible and unpleasant. For the subject – the neurotic subject – even this horrifying picture of the Other is preferable from the state of uncertainty regarding the lack and the desire of the Other: 'The unknown nature of the Other's desire is unbearable here; you prefer to assign it an attribute, any attribute, rather than let it remain an enigma. You prefer to tie it down, give it a name, and put an end to its angst-inducing uncertainty' (Fink, 1997: 60–1). In that sense, fantasy in itself is never a non-lacking entity; if that was true, fantasy would be a part of the real. On the contrary, fantasy entails a domestication of real lack, a certain symbolisation which makes things easier to bear without reducing their lacking character – this is how it conditions or causes our desire. It only gives us a 'constructed' solution as to what we should desire and what prohibits the full realisation of this desire (this is preferable to recognising the impossibility of such a realisation).

Fantasy thus is first of all a scenario that obfuscates the true horror of a situation (castration). In the socio-political level 'for example, instead of a full rendering of the antagonisms that traverse our society, we indulge in the notion of society as an organic Whole, kept together by forces of solidarity and cooperation' (Žižek, 1998: 190). On the other hand, however, the relation between fantasy and the real horror it conceals is never so simple: 'Fantasy conceals that horror, yet at the same time it creates what it purports to conceal, namely its "repressed" point of reference [castration itself is a sort of fantasy and not a real possibility]' (ibid.: 190–1). In fact, as Žižek points out, fantasy stages castration; it is not a transgressive vision but a narrative that gives substance to symbolic castration by staging a particular 'performance' of this impossible 'play'.

In Freud, castration is clearly conceived as a fantasy staging the mutilation of the penis. Lacan links this fantasy with all the other fantasies of dismemberment related to the image of the fragmented body (Evans, 1996a: 21). Consequently, fantasy aims at concealing the fundamental impossibility of covering over the lack in the Other, of encountering an impossible *jouissance*. It does so by assuring us that fullness (the Other's fullness, the encounter with absolute *jouissance*) is not impossible but prohibited, and thus it becomes possible to recapture it sometime in the future (that remains the essence of the fantasmatic promise) if the agency (or rather the agent) of castration is pinpointed and a certain strategy adopted *vis à vis* its function: 'In this precise sense, fantasy is the screen that separates desire from drive. It tells the story that allows the subject to (mis)perceive the void around which drive circulates as the primordial loss constitutive of desire. Or, to put it in yet another way: fantasy provides a *rationale* for the inherent deadlock of desire; it gives a reason to the enigma of "why there is no sexual relationship". Fantasy is thus not simply the fantasy of a successful sexual relationship, but rather the fantasy of why it went wrong. It constructs the scene in which the *jouissance* we are deprived of is concentrated in the Other, who stole it from us. In the anti-Semitic ideological fantasy, social antagonism is explained away via the reference to the Jews as the secret agent who is stealing social *jouissance* from us (by amassing profits, seducing our women, etc.). For that reason also, the notion of fantasy is ambiguous: beatific fantasy (the vision of the state of things "before the Fall") is supported by a disturbing paranoiac fantasy which tells us why things went wrong (why we did not get the girl, why society is antagonistic). Traversing, going through fantasy, means that we accept the vicious circle of revolving around the object and find *jouissance* in it, renouncing the myth that *jouissance* is amassed somewhere else' (Žižek, 1998: 209–10).

To recapitulate, fantasy sustains our desire by staging a state of fullness as lacking, as denied by the castrating Other. This imaginary projection of real fullness is staged as denied by some particular agent; thus its ultimate impossibility is concealed. As we shall see, particularly in Chapter 4, this understanding of fantasy makes it a category crucial for the analysis of politics and especially of the politics of utopia. In Chapter 4 we will stress the dual character of fantasy (beatific and horrific/demonising side) while in this chapter we will also develop a slightly different approach by combining the use of the concept of fantasy in its beatific harmonious sense with that of the Lacanian category of the symptom.

8 In *The Object of Psychoanalysis*, Lacan points out that fantasy is not imaginary and that the *object a*, the object of fantasy, cannot be grasped in the mirror because it constitutes the frame which is emerging when we are opening our eyes (seminar of 18 May 1966). The object cannot be reduced to a specular image and thus is not of a strictly imaginary nature (seminar of 30 March 1966).

9 Let us reflect, for a moment, on the idea of the incompleteness of the symbolic, the lack in the Other. In his *Lacanian Subject*, Bruce Fink develops a crucial angle to this discussion (Fink, 1995a: 29–30). He suggests that it is possible to represent the symbolic as a circle including all available signifiers. Yet, in order to refer to this totality we have to introduce a new signifier, a name for this whole. If we use the name 'Other' we have to accept that this signifier has to be located outside the totality of the Other, outside the circle it names. But then the closed circle is not that closed any more: it does not contain all signifiers (what escapes is its own name, the signifier 'Other'). Even if we start this process anew and introduce a new signifier to name the whole consisting of the Other and its name ('Other'), the signifier 'Complete Other' for example, the problem remains the same since, once more, this new signifier is not part and parcel of the whole it names. Needless to say, this process can be reproduced *ad infinitum*. In that sense, the whole remains always split and incomplete.

Fink's schema seems, however, somewhat abstract. It does not take into account the fact that the signifiers used to name the Other, or the complete Other (and so on and so forth), might not be that alien to the symbolic; in fact, they may be included in the Other. What in reality introduces a certain indeterminacy is that one of the signifiers, one of the equivalent differences within the symbolic, is called to represent the whole, to name the symbolic itself; the part is called to represent the whole of which it forms part. For example, the signifier 'Other' while belonging to the symbolic is called to name the whole to which it belongs. In other words, the problem, what introduces the incompleteness of the Other, is not that its name is absent from the symbolic itself but exactly the opposite: that it is impossible to find its proper name outside the symbolic; to return to our example, in order to name the symbolic it is necessary to use a signifier which is part of the symbolic. Consequently, what interrupts the closure of the symbolic, what makes the Other incomplete, is that its closure cannot be named and effected *per se*. It is necessary to represent this closure through the use of an ordinary signifier which is not designed *a priori* to perform this function.

In that sense the naming of the Other, the representation of its closure and fullness, is impossible without the introduction of a certain anomaly, without splitting the signifier called to perform this representation: on the one hand it is a particular signifier and on the other it has to be elevated beyond its particularity in order to represent the universality of the Other; on the one hand it is internal to the symbolic, but on the other, it has to be posited as the external element which fixes the meaning of the internal elements. It is in that sense that 'something anomalous always shows up in language, something unaccountable, inexplicable: an aporia. These aporias point to the presence within or influence on the symbolic of the real' (Fink, 1995a: 30). What is posited as an empty signifier, a pure, external signifier representing the closure and systematicity of the symbolic, cannot be dissociated from its concrete materiality as a signifier internal to the symbolic system. Simply put, the aspiration to fully represent and 'close' the Other leads to the emergence of anomalies and aporias which show the ultimate incompleteness of the Other.

10 In fact – and this is something which will be elaborated later on – it is due to the organisation of our desire around this object that the real becomes equivalent to fullness. It is because, as J.-A. Miller has put it, the object is a 'false' real, that is to say a part of *jouissance* as it is staged in fantasy (the fantasmatic or semantic, in other words the elaborated part of *jouissance*), which we retroactively project to our reflection on the pre-symbolic real – a real which is, as such, impossible to think.

11 This is true insofar as the real articulates the necessary with the impossible by repeatedly failing to be symbolised; the real 'doesn't stop not being written' (XX: 59). The same impossibility to 'know' the pre-linguistic state of the real can be encircled through the distinction between need and demand. The pre-linguistic state of the real corresponds to a state of pure need. Since, however, need is always articulated in language, thus being transformed into demand, it follows that a 'mythical' pre-linguistic state of need can only be hypothesised after it has been lost, that is to say articulated in demand; by this time, however, 'it is impossible to determine what that pure need would have been' (Evans, 1996a: 121–2).

12 Moreover, Lacanian ethics points to another way of constructing a political project beyond fantasmatic promise. This strategy will be developed in the last two chapters of this book.

13 In certain parts of his work Lacan implies that the subject can live but only temporarily, this forbidden enjoyment (we are referring to *jouissance*$_2$ in Fink's sense). During orgasm, for example, as Lacan points out in his seminar on *Identification*, the castrated subject is able for an instant to attain his identification, to make his demand coincide with his desire (seminar of 27 June 1962). This lasts only for an instant and is followed by a feeling of dissatisfaction. This is due to the fact that although desire is longing for continuity, *jouissance* can only be felt for one moment. After this particular instant the gap between desire and demand re-establishes itself and lack is reinscribed in the subjective level. For a detailed mapping of the nuances of the Lacanian conception of *jouissance* see Evans, 1998.

14 The argument for the social construction of reality is not disputing the existence of external reality, it is not a solipsistic argument. What it disputes is, first of all, our ability to access this reality outside discourse, our ability to gain definite access to the essence of things, to any pre-symbolic real. Humans are trapped within the universe of discourse. What that means is that it is impossible to conceive or articulate whatever is outside discourse without articulating it within the discursive field in one of its forms (political, scientific, etc.) (Barrett, 1991: 76–7). As Laclau and Mouffe point out, the fact that all objects are constituted as objects of discourse does not presuppose that the external world does not exist, it is not relevant for the realism/idealism opposition. An earthquake is an event which exists independently of our will, whether however, its specificity as

an object will be constructed within a scientific logic of 'natural phenomena' or as an expression of the will of God depends on the structuration of the particular discursive field in question (Laclau and Mouffe, 1985: 108). According to Castoriadis, whatever exists in 'objective reality' is accessible through the magma of socially instituted meaning, a meaning which transforms it ontologically. Nature poses limits or creates obstacles in the social institution of society but focusing on these natural obstacles does not reveal anything about human society exactly because our symbolic universe is not determined by any natural laws. What 'is' for society, what 'is' within our symbolic universe, may not correspond to any real or natural infrastructure and *vice versa* (Castoriadis, 1978: 336).

In Lacanian terms, something may thus 'be', without existing, may 'be' within our symbolic and imaginary world and through speech, without finding a support in the real (e.g. the complete Other) (Evans, 1996a: 16). We know, for example, that procreation presupposes sexual intercourse but that does not reveal anything about the vast alchemy of desire and sexuality marking human history. As it was so successfully pointed out in a recent title from the *Observer Review* 'Birds do it, bees do it, and rabbits are at it, well, like rabbits. But none of them dress up in rubber' (Diamond, 1997: 7). Natural support and natural limits are sometimes taken into account and others ignored, but in any case transformed by their insertion in the network of meaning and signification. This does not mean that everything is reduced to discourse but that even the real – what, for Lacan, remains outside symbolisation – is making its presence felt through the failure of this discursive universe. In other words, the attempts to symbolise the real are constant but never fully successful; something always escapes, but this escape is only shown through the disruption of symbolisation itself. Furthermore, one should not overlook the fact that in Lacan, as well as in a multitude of other thinkers such as Wittgenstein, Austin and Laclau, the discursive level is not reducible to the level of ideas, to the mental character which is usually attributed to it, as opposed to a certain material infrastructure. Lacan is stressing the materiality of the signifier (what he calls the 'Freudian materiality of the signifier') as Wittgenstein affirms the material dimension of language games, Austin the performativity of speech acts and Laclau the materiality of discourse.

15 As we have already pointed out, within fantasy, this illusion is articulated as a promise of attaining fullness in the future. What denies the realisation of fantasy in the present (the impossibility of fullness as such) is reduced to the intervention of a localised Other of prohibition. In other words, whenever we speak about 'covering over', 'suturing', etc. of the constitutive lack in the Other we are referring to a fantasmatic promise which even within the boundaries of fantasy is postponed. Only this postponement is not attributed to the constitutive impossibility of realising this promise; by always blaming 'someone else' fantasy attempts to transform impossibility to a prohibited possibility and thus sustain the hegemonic force of its promise.

16 The concept of the *point de capiton* is introduced by Lacan in his seminar of 6 June 1956 in an analysis of the role of the word *crainte* (fear) in Racine's play *Athalie*.

17 The *point de capiton* is necessary in the sense that without it there is no order; its function involves the introduction of a principle of ordering which makes possible the emergence of social meaning and the construction of reality. Without the intervention of the *point de capiton* the world collapses into a psychotic universe (it is no coincidence that the Name-of-the-Father functions as the prototype of the *point de capiton*).

18 This way a universal function (what determines global and planetic time) is assigned to a particular element (GMT). This particular element is emptied from its specific content and accepted as the embodiment of universality. It is transformed thus to an empty signifier. The relation between *points de capiton* and empty signifiers will be discussed in the following chapter.

19 This is only a provisional assumption which describes the strategy that has been dominant up to now. There exists, however, the possibility for a different strategy, traversing the fantasmatic illusions of the dominant reality constructions. This strategy will be explored, especially in its various political implications, in the last three chapters of this book.

20 The first approach is developed by Žižek in a variety of recent texts (Žižek, 1994b, 1995, 1996b). The second approach can be found throughout his *Sublime Object of Ideology* (Žižek, 1989).

21 What is problematic is not the tension itself but the fact that it remains concealed. According to a Lacanian approach this tension is unavoidable (since meta-language is both impossible and necessary) but has to be openly acknowledged and assumed.

22 This is a cause stimulating not only constructionist argumentation but social construction itself as a social process.

23 The question that remains open is the following: if no construction is capable of representing the real doesn't that mean that all constructions are equally valid? It is possible to provide two types of answer to this question. First of all, believing in the constructed nature of human reality does not entail believing that all constructions are equally valid, 'that conclusion [simply] does not follow. There are multiple realities because people differ in their situations and purposes...the reality a destitute black person constructs respecting the nature of poverty has little validity for a conservative political candidate or a conservative political scientist or even for the same black when he is trying to achieve high grades in a business school. Every construction of a world is a demanding activity. It can be done well or badly and be right or wrong...such understanding in no way suggests that every construction is as good as every other' (Edelman, 1988: 6). The success of a construction is primarily judged by its relevance for the social setting in which it is articulated. In other words the epistemological dimension of its validity is not always decisive.

How is it possible, though, to provide an epistemological answer to the aforementioned question? At this point the work of Katherine Hayles is extremely relevant. She is arguing, within the framework of a 'constrained constructivism', that although it is impossible to reach absolute and objective knowledge independently of our social and cultural positioning, this does not mean that all constructions share the same validity: our encounter with the unmediated flux of nature can guide us to reject certain constructions in favour of others, although not in an algorithmic way. According to her argument constrained constructionism is based on the recognition of the dialectic between the world of construction and social representation and the obstacles posed by the real of nature (Hayles, 1995: 53). Although human constructions do not reflect objective reality and nature, their survival and hegemonic appeal depends on their ability to withhold their encounter with the fluid and non-representable real of nature. Imagine, for example, a society in which the destructive force of a volcano is associated with the behaviour of a particular god. Thus the meaningless event of the volcanic eruption acquires a representation at the level of social construction. The result of this process is a particular symbolisation of nature as subject to the will of the god, a will which can be influenced through sacrifice, etc. If this will is not altered, and the volcano continues its destructive and destabilising course, it is conceivable that this construction will lose some of its hegemonic appeal and gradually be replaced by another. This is a process equivalent to the shift from one scientific paradigm to another in Thomas Kuhn's schema, to the transformative force of dislocation in Laclau's work. In our example, a particular construction of nature, although articulated in order to attach a meaning to the terror associated with a natural event, is not reflecting objective nature itself but nevertheless has to prove its relevance and validity in its interaction with the part of nature which escapes it, the part of reality that remains always 'outside', for ever unrepresentable, with the real of nature.

3 ENCIRCLING THE POLITICAL: TOWARDS A LACANIAN POLITICAL THEORY

1 The same applies to all the different levels used in our categorisations and constructions of reality, including the economy. For a first approach to the issue of the discursive construction of economic space, an issue falling outside the scope of this book, see Daly, 1991.

2 None of these poles exists as a self-contained or autonomous entity. Disorder always disrupts a field of partial fixation and order and is never itself absolute; it always leads to a new order, a new structuration of the social. Reality cannot master the real – and thus is always limited – on the other hand, however, the real cannot eliminate reality; its presence can only be felt within reality – when this reality is disrupted and the desire for a new symbolisation is starting to emerge.

3 To use Žižek's vocabulary, politics would correspond to the 'antagonistic fights as they take place in reality' (to the hegemonic struggle between already constructed political projects, between different symbolisations of reality) while the political would correspond to the moment of 'pure antagonism' which is logically prior to this externalisation (Žižek, 1990: 252–3): antagonism is not due to the empirical presence of the enemy but, prior to the development of our or his (the enemy's) identification or fantasmatic project forms the real blockage around which this and every identification is structured. It is the empirical trace of this ontological impossibility.

4 This also means that exclusion and difference are not produced solely on linguistic or semiotic grounds; they emerge at the intersection of the symbolic with the real: what is excluded from the representation of a nation, from the construction of what is usually called 'national identity', insofar as the articulation of this identity is attempted through symbolic and fantasmatic means, is a certain pre-symbolic real. No matter how much we love our national ways of enjoyment, our national real, this real is never enough, it is already castrated, it is the real as staged in fantasy, in national myths and feasts. This is never enough; there is a surplus which is always missing. Within the national fantasy, this loss can be attributed to the existence of an alien culture or people: the enjoyment lacking from our national community is being denied to us because 'they' stole it. They are to blame for this theft of enjoyment. They are fantasised as enacting in their own national rituals what they denied us. In the light of the analysis of social fantasy developed in Chapter 2, they are the symptom or (in a slightly modified reading which will be further developed in the next chapter) the horrific side of fantasy. It is not difficult to discern in this type of fantasmatic scenario the roots of nationalist and racist discourse. What is not realised within such a schema is the fact that, as Žižek points out, we never had at our disposal the surplus enjoyment that we accuse the Other of stealing from us. Lack is

originary; enjoyment constitutes itself as stolen from the beginning (Žižek, 1993, see especially the last chapter).

5 This is another characteristic uniting *points de capiton* and empty signifiers. Here I rely on the work of Žižek to suggest that this paradoxical confluence constitutes a defining mark of the *point de capiton* insofar as behind the dazzling splendour of the *point de capiton* ('god', 'country', 'party', 'class'), behind its fantasmatic fullness, it is possible to detect a self-referential contingent performative operation: the signifier without signified, the signifier of an emptiness (Žižek, 1989: 99).

6 This truth however is not something easy to accept: 'the dimension of truth is mysterious, inexplicable, nothing decisively enables the necessity of it to be grasped, since man accommodates himself to non-truth perfectly well' (III: 214). In other words, we should not underestimate the tendency of humans to prefer ignorance of this truth, of a possible danger they are not capable of manipulating (Douglas and Wildavsky, 1982: 26).

7 This is also ignored by Lacoue-Labarthe and Nancy when they argue that 'Lacan tirelessly adapts his discourse, in all sorts of ways, to the possibility of a representation, a *true adequate representation* of that very thing that exceeds representation' (Lacoue-Labarthe and Nancy, 1992: xxx; my emphasis).To the argument of Lacoue-Labarthe and Nancy we will return shortly.

8 These limits are transposed all the time as symbolisations replace one another, but this ontic dimension does not change the ontological causality of the real which does not stop inscribing itself through the failure of symbolisation.The causality of the real inscribes itself within symbolisation by not ceasing not being written, that is to say by remaining always outside the field of symbolic and fantasmatic representation and thus being capable of dislocating them by showing their internal lack, by revealing the fact that it cannot be domesticated.

9 As Laclau has put it, there is no direct way of signifying the limits of signification 'the real, if you want, in the Lacanian sense…except through the subversion of the process of signification itself. We know, through psychoanalysis, how what is not directly representable – the unconscious – can only find as a means of representation the subversion of the signifying process' (Laclau, 1996: 39).

10 Lacan's texts abound with references to art. For instance, he discusses Holbein's *Ambassadors* in his XI seminar and Munch's *Scream* in *Crucial Problems for Psychoanalysis*. He also refers to Magritte in his seminar on *The Object of Psychoanalysis* (seminar of 25 May 1966). Although J.-A. Miller has also referred to Magritte, for a Lacanian analysis of Magritte's work in general see Žižek, 1993 (especially pp. 103–8).

11 As Ernesto Laclau has put it, 'although the fullness and universality of society is unreachable, its need does not disappear: it will always show itself through the presence of its absence' (Laclau, 1996: 53). I want to suggest that what is at stake here is our ability to mark and to make visible this absence as the surfacing of a constitutive impossibility, without reducing it to the action of the Other; in short, to detect beyond the fantasmatic staging of castration the causality of a nondomesticated, non-imaginarised real.

12 The first part of their argument is already covered by our discussion in Chapter 1, so we will concentrate on the second part. However, for the sake of presenting their argument with a certain coherence, some repetition cannot be avoided. Keeping in mind our discussion of negative theology in note 4 of the first chapter will also be helpful for the reader.

4 BEYOND THE FANTASY OF UTOPIA: THE APORIA OF POLITICS AND THE CHALLENGE OF DEMOCRACY

1 This collapse is evident for example in the dislocation of most projects aiming at a global human emancipation (Laclau, 1996; especially Chapter 1, 'Beyond Emancipation').

2 It is not a coincidence that Aldous Huxley uses exactly this phrase as an epigraph in order to introduce his novel *Brave New World* (1932), a dystopian vision of the future in which the dark side of the realisation of 'utopia' is sketched, opening the road to a whole tradition of anti-utopian writing.

3 One might argue at this point that nobody really believes today in utopias; the whole discussion in this chapter might seem to some a bit outmoded. What I will try to show is that utopia is not that distant a way of understanding the world and organising our political praxis. This distance is only an illusion. In fact, beyond today's anti-utopian Western world, in the rest of the globe, nationalist and other utopian fantasies proliferate with an unprecedented rhythm. But even if, in some contexts, utopia is becoming distant, this is a danger we should not neglect. In the First World, for example, the crisis of utopian politics has not been channelled into a politically productive working-through, but remains a source of frustration, especially for the left. The result of this aporetic outcome is that utopian politics return to haunt our political theory and our political imagination. This fixation, which is mainly due to the continuing dominance of a utopian ethics of harmony, obscures a series of radical political possibilities which are located beyond fantasmatic politics. In that sense, settling our accounts with utopian discourse and its ethical foundations is crucial for the reinvigoration of our political thinking and our practical imagination.

4 For a recent review of Žižek's account of anti-Semitism see Santner's article 'Freud, Žižek and the Joys of Monotheism' (Santner, 1997).

5 This inherent contradiction of utopian mentality is very well depicted in Ambrose Bierce's definition of Harmonists as 'a sect of Protestants, now extinct, who...were distinguished for the bitterness of their internal controversies and dissensions'.

6 It is true that the neologism 'utopia' is introduced for the first time in 1516 with the publication of Thomas More's *Utopia*, a work exhibiting all the characteristics of utopian thought, such as the aspiration to eliminate dislocation and antagonism and create social harmony, etc. This does not mean, however, that More was the first to imagine such a utopian order, that is to say an order that after the publication of his book would be named utopian. In fact, he acknowledges himself that his enterprise is similar to Plato's in *Polity*, only better, because, as he points out, what in Plato was fantasy, in his *Utopia* is reality. In other words, his genius was 'to give to his imaginary world a local habitation and a name'. And although 'to name something is, in a sense, to create it' (Neville-Sington and Sington, 1993: 15) it is not illegitimate to trace the roots of this utopian way of thinking in the past.

7 The importance of revolutionary millenarianism for any study of utopia is supported by the hundreds of pages devoted to these movements in the work of Marx, Engels, Lukacs, Bloch, Debord and Vaneigem.

8 For a sympathetic critique of Sartre's overall analysis of anti-Semitism see Connolly, 1991: 99–107.

9 Nazi utopia was, unfortunately, not as optimistic as Bacon's *Nova Atlantis* (1627) in which Jews are reformed and instead of being exterminated stop 'hating Christ and the people that host them'.

10 Needless to say the prominence of antichrist and the end of the world were normally associated with social dislocation and political crisis: 'emphasis on

antichrist has its advantage in time of acute crisis because of the simple Manicheanism of the doctrine: the world is divided into black and white, Christian and Antichristian' (Hill, 1990: 170) and the solution becomes obvious: the elimination of the powers identified as antichristian.

11 One should not get the wrong impression, however, that the negativity of experience is always leading directly to the demonisation of a social category. This is clearly not the only way the encounter with the real can be administered. It is only the particular utopian administration of the fear or terror of experience that leads to the production of a scapegoat. Even in early modern society, a society that has been characterised as a society of omnipresent fear (although it now becomes evident that all historical periods can be so labelled), this fear did not always lead to the uniting of society against a common enemy, identified with a marginal social group. Although 'Jews, lepers, witches, vagrants, the poor, heretics and foreigners were all targeted as scapegoats at various points in the late medieval and early modern periods', on the other hand, 'only in the most extreme cases did the unifying power of fear result in the persecution of marginal groups' (Roberts and Naphy, 1997: 1–3). When, however, fear leads to persecution, the most unpredictable developments will follow. The choice of the group to be stigmatised is not determined by any reasonable connection. Instead it is determined, first, by its relatively marginal status: enemies are usually relatively powerless people. This displacement of enmity 'whether or not...justified it is gratifying, for it offers a way to vent discontents onto a target that can usually do little to retaliate' (Edelman, 1988: 78); and, second, by its visibility. This explains, for example, why, in early modern Europe, plague was combated by the large-scale slaughter of dogs, an animal species which had nothing to do with the plague. Huge numbers were killed, partly because dogs were extremely visible and because they were symbolically associated with a series of negative (human) qualities. Thus 'such creatures [could be singled out as]...a visible source of disorder' (Jenner, 1997: 55).

12 Of course, this way this same impossibility of utopia is ultimately inscribed within utopian discourse albeit in the form of a negation.

13 Here, instead of focusing on the relation between fantasy and symptom, we are prioritising an approach which highlights the dual nature of fantasmatic scenarios, the coexistence of their beatific and horrific sides.

14 On the issue of Habermas's utopianism see Jameson, 1991: 58–9.

15 It becomes clear now that the argument according to which the question of ethics is foreign to Laclau and Mouffe's political theory (Zerilli, 1998: 33), is completely misplaced. What is true, of course, is that their radical democratic project requires and can only be associated with a new conception of ethics. We shall argue that Lacanian ethics of the real are eminently qualified for this task.

16 Again, it would be unwise to suppose that the element of hope and passion could ever be eliminated from our culture, or that such a development would be a desirable one (Kolakowski, 1997: 221). Contrary however to what Kolakowski implies, when this hope is reduced to the utopian operation and this utopian operation comes close to its realisation, the only outcome can be catastrophe and anxiety, since anxiety, according to Lacan's seminar on *Anxiety*, is created by the lack of lack, a prospect entailed in the realisation of utopian blueprints. The possibility of a total filling of a void (which should be preserved) gives rise to anxiety (seminar of 12 December 1962). Yet, from this point of view, a full realisation of utopia is impossible because it would presuppose the regression to a pre-linguistic state (Kolakowski, 1997: 224) since it is language which introduces a structural lack to the human world. The only problem is that sometimes the realisation of this impossibility requires millions of victims.

17 See, in this respect, the whole discussion of representationalism in the first chapter.

18 The discussion of modernity in the second part of Chapter 3 is absolutely relevant here.

19 A more refined version of this critique is articulated by Whitebook. For Whitebook, Lacan 'absolutizes disunity and, in some sense, ceases himself to be a conflict theorist, which is to say, he assigns an unmitigated victory to Thanatos' (Whitebook, 1995: 129).

20 This is a thoroughly 'progressive' project. In that sense Homer should not 'get worried when radical politics can find itself agreeing with the Thatcherite right that there is no such thing as society' (Homer, 1996: 101) because it is his acceptance of left-wing fantasmatic politics that shares the same foundation with conservatism: a sort of *horror vacui* stimulated by the frightfulness of the lack in the Other leading both to the fantasies of the triumph of capitalism and to the new radical utopias of our age (ecotopias, etc.).

21 But let us give to Homer's quasi-utopian aspirations one more chance. Let us agree, for a moment, that we want to formulate a Lacanian quasi-utopian politics. Again, it is not necessary to 'reoccupy' the ground of traditional fantasmatic politics. Even Bruce Fink, who wants to retain a utopian element in his reading of Lacan, locates his 'utopian moment' beyond the level of fantasy. According to Fink the separation entailed in traversing fantasy leads the subject beyond neurotic alienation: 'subjectifying one's fate, that foreign cause (the Other's desire) that brought one into the world, alienation can be surpassed. A utopian moment of sorts in Lacan's later work, this passage beyond castration was, to the best of my knowledge, never recanted in Lacan's later work, unlike other utopian moments (e.g. full speech), which were implicitly critiqued in common instances of "Lacan against Lacan" (the late Lacan against the early Lacan)' (Fink, 1995a: 79). It is not articulating a new fantasy that is identified as a truly utopian moment. Articulating a new fantasy remains within the boundaries of neurosis. It is, on the contrary, 'the traversing of fantasy...[that] involves a going beyond of castration and a utopian moment beyond neurosis' (ibid.: 72). Articulating a new fantasy, although promising an encounter with our lost/impossible *jouissance*, although entailing a secondary gain (and here Homer is correct), cannot be truly utopian (in the positive sense of the term introduced by Fink); its consequences are elusive: 'The castrated subject is thus a subject who has not subjectified the Other's desire and who remains plagued by, and yet obtains a "secondary gain" from, his or her symptomatic submission to the Other....A kind of being is achieved through the first kind of separation: that provided by fantasy. Nevertheless, Lacan once again generally speaks rather of the "aphanisis" or fading of the neurotic subject in his or her fantasy as the object-cause steals all the limelight...the subject being eclipsed or overshadowed thereby. Thus the false being of the ego and the elusive being provided in fantasy are rejected, one after the other, by Lacan as lacking: neither can take the subject beyond neurosis. In both cases, the subject remains castrated, subjected to the Other. Lacan nevertheless maintains the notion of a being beyond neurosis' (ibid.: 72–3).

In that sense, even if it was possible and desirable to have a Lacanian utopia – if we thought that this concept could be purified from its incapacitating connotations – this utopia would be clearly located beyond the field of fantasy, beyond any 'reoccupation' of traditional politics. In fact, it would be possible to argue that even our own radical democratic project is based on a 'utopian' aspiration to do the impossible, to institutionalise social lack, to sediment the recognition of the impossibility of society. But this recognition is not conceived as a total enterprise and, besides, we all know that it can be realised, at least up to a certain extent: democracy is not only a project but also an everyday experience. In any case, even if it entails a quasi-utopian element we have to do with a realist utopia beyond fantasmatic politics; a quasi-utopia articulated around the idea of its own impossibility.

Freud was, in fact, the first to connect politics with the impossible. In his view, politics, together with psychoanalysis and education, constitutes an impossible profession. But if democratic politics is attempting something ultimately impossible, that is to say institutionalising social lack, in fact even if this is a quasi-utopian move, this is a quasi-utopia structured around its own negation; it negates the idea of its absolute realisation, in other words this is a 'quasi-utopia' beyond fantasmatic politics. If there is an *Aufhebung* in Lacan, it is one in which Hegel's progress is replaced by the anti-utopian 'avatars of a lack' (Lacan in Evans, 1996a: 43). This way, what is altered is not only the positive content of politics (utopian visions are replaced by the language games around a recognition of lack, which means that happiness is no longer a legitimate political objective although a better society definitely is) but also the support giving coherence to this positive content (the fantasmatic support is traversed by this recognition of lack). Moreover, if this is a quasi-utopian or utopian move, it can only be a utopian negation of utopia (remember Lacan's meta-linguistic negation of meta-language in the first note of the introduction). Perhaps the fantasmatic structure of utopia can only be traversed after we situate and orient ourselves within its dangerous ground; fantasy has to be constructed before it is traversed. In addition, one has to keep in mind that the crossing of utopian fantasy does not entail the disappearance of the social symptom but a new modality of interacting with it. To this we will return in the last chapter of this book. In any case, this new modality, even if one still wants to call it utopian, has important repercussions for our life: it neutralises the catastrophic effects or by-products of utopian visions. And this is something fundamental.

5 AMBIGUOUS DEMOCRACY AND THE ETHICS OF PSYCHOANALYSIS

1 As Lacan points out in *Transference*, concord can emerge out of discordance and conflict, and does not presuppose a harmonious foundation (seminar of 14 December 1960).

2 With democracy, on the other hand, all the dirt comes out, as Enzensberger has pointed out; but that dirt is ours, and we have to assume the responsibility of producing and dealing with it. The 'charm' of undemocratic rule is that it takes from us the burden of this responsibility.

3 It seems that today the future of political theory and effective political praxis depends on our ability to move beyond the previously hegemonic pessimism/optimism dichotomy. In fact, the irreducible interpenetration of these two poles means that pessimism itself is revealed as the condition of possibility for a certain optimism. For example, the irreducibility and constitutivity of dislocation, in other words the fact that no discourse or ideology can institute itself on the basis of total closure, constitutes the condition of the possibility of freedom; if closure was possible this would mean the end of history, our eternal entrapment within a certain discursive framework. For this play between pessimism and optimism see Laclau, 1990, especially the first part.

4 At first the idea of an institutionalisation of lack might seem absurd. In the context of this book, however, institutionalisation is understood as an act of post-fantasmatic discursive institution. Hence, institutionalisation of lack refers

to the recognition and preservation (of this recognition) of lack within a discursive or institutional framework. Simply put, institutionalisation of lack implies a symbolic gesture through which the lack that is always marking the symbolic – but which is usually masked by fantasy – is recognised in its irreducibility and preserved as such. In that sense, this ethical standpoint is not an ethics of a supposedly pure real but of the symbolic recognition of the structural causality of the real, not far away from what Lipowatz has called the ethics of the symbolic (Lipowatz, 1986).

5 Although, as Lacan makes clear, this does not necessarily entail the disappearance of all reference to sexuality as 'the foolish crowd thinks' (VII: 161).

6 As Kolakowski points out 'It is possible that from a historical perspective some important achievements of twentieth century science – Heisenberg's principle and Gödel's theorem – will be seen as contributions to the same antiutopian spirit of our age' (Kolakowski, 1997: 136).

7 It was Lacan, after all, who argued that 'atheism is tenable only to clerics' (XX: 108).

8 Once again, the question of meta-language is directly relevant to this whole discussion. It is precisely such 'impossible' utterances which keep the signifying process open and thus prevent us from assuming a meta-linguistic position. This impossibility is necessarily articulated in a meta-linguistic framework since meta-language is not a mere imaginary entity. It is real, in the strict Lacanian sense: 'That is, it is impossible to occupy its position. But, Lacan adds, it is even more difficult to simply avoid it. One cannot attain it, but one also cannot escape it' (Žižek, 1987: 34). In that sense, in order to avoid a fantasmatic meta-linguistic position (a meta-linguistic affirmation of meta-language) it is necessary to produce an utterance which shows the impossibility of occupying a pure meta-linguistic position through the failure of meta-language itself (a meta-linguistic negation of meta-language). One cannot escape the frame of symbolisation: what 'is' beyond symbolisation can only be shown within symbolisation, through the failure of symbolisation itself. The Lacanian solution then is to 'produce an utterance [or institutional setting] of pure metalanguage which by its patent absurdity, materializes its own impossibility; that is a paradoxical element which, in its very identity embodies absolute otherness, the irreparable gap, that makes it impossible to occupy a metalanguage position' (ibid.: 34).

9 It could also be argued that a system based on lot as in Ancient Athens would be much closer to an attempt to institutionalise such a recognition of social lack. In any case, the issue of Ancient Greek democracy and its relation to our understanding of modern democracy is not explored in this book. For an account of Ancient Greek democratic discourse and institutions which is relevant to our own account of modern democracy, I suggest Vernant, 1982.

10 This task should not be conceived as a pedagogical enterprise but as a hegemonic project. The application of pedagogy in politics is usually masking a totalitarian aspiration. Nonetheless, it might be possible to articulate a Socratic, democratic, political education that would escape such totalitarian aspirations. For such an attempt, see Euben, Wallach and Ober, 1994.

11 Naturally, it is not only psychoanalytic discourse that can work in such a way. In fact, as far as it concerns the political level, one cannot be over-optimistic regarding the hegemonic force of Lacanian psychoanalytic ethics, although this force may vary from context to context. In any case we wouldn't like an over-psychoanalyticisation to couple an over-philosophisation which, as Rorty points out, has created in the United States and Britain 'a self-involved academic left which has become increasingly irrelevant to substantial political discussion' (Rorty, 1996: 69). In fact, the problem with psychoanalytic discourse may be

more serious than that of philosophisation. It can be articulated in these terms: if it is so difficult to bring particular subjects to cross their fundamental fantasy within the analytic context, on what grounds can one be proposing such a change in the socio-political level where, as the politics of the psychoanalytic communities itself reveals, this crossing might be even more laborious? However, difficulty is not an adequate deterrent for assuming a political ethics and acting in politics. Besides, the change in question should not necessarily be envisaged as a radical break or a moment of total transgression; it can be a gradual process: imagine, for instance, someone walking on a moebius strip – the topological structure praised by Lacan – thus passing, without changing his or her pace, from its first to its second side.

12 It has to be recognised though that Whitebook is not using the word 'imaginary' as defined by Lacan. He is closer to the definition of Castoriadis. However, it is doubtful whether this undermines at all the validity of our comments.

13 Insofar as real lack can be symbolically encircled, the *point de capiton* in democracy can only be the signifier of the lack in the Other. In democracy the point of reference which totalises social meaning is occupied by a detotaliser, a symbolic recognition of the impossibility of any final totalisation.

14 Although Derrida's 'democracy to come' has been described as utopian (by Rorty and Critchley, among others) Derrida points out that when he speaks of 'democracy to come' 'this does not mean that tomorrow democracy will be realized, and it does not refer to a future democracy...this is not utopian, it is what takes place here and now, in a here and now that I regularly try to dissociate from the present' (Derrida, 1996: 83).

15 For a more detailed exposition of the project of radical democracy see Laclau and Mouffe, 1985 (especially Chapter 4); Mouffe, 1992; Trend, 1996a, 1996b.

BIBLIOGRAPHY

Adorno, T. (1993) *The Authoritarian Personality*, New York: Norton.

Alcorn, M. (1994) 'The Subject of Discourse' in Alcorn, M., Bracher, M., Corthell, R. and Massarder-Kenney, F. (eds) *Lacanian Theory of Discourse*, New York: New York University Press.

Anderson, B. (1991) *Imagined Communities*, London: Verso.

Anderson, P. (1992) *A Zone of Engagement*, London: Verso.

Apollon, W. (1996) 'Introduction II' in Apollon, W. and Feldstein, R. (eds) *Lacan, Politics, Aesthetics*, Albany: SUNY Press.

Arditi, B. (1993) 'Tracing the Political', unpublished paper.

Arendt, H. (1979) *The Origins of Totalitarianism*, San Diego: Harvest.

Armstrong, J. (1982) *Nations Before Nationalism*, Chapel Hill: University of North Carolina Press.

Badiou, A. (1996) 'Philosophy and Psychoanalysis', *UMBR(a)*, one $\{\varnothing\}$: 19–26.

Barker, K. (1993) *Michel Foucault*, London: Penguin.

Barrett, M. (1991) *The Politics of Truth*, Oxford: Polity.

Barthes, R. (1973) *Elements of Semiology*, New York: Hill and Wang.

—— (1990) *S/Z*, Oxford: Blackwell Publishers.

Baudrillard, J. (1996) *The Transparency of Evil*, trans. Z. Sarikas, Athens: Exantas (in Greek).

Bauman, Z. (1989) *Modernity and the Holocaust*, Cambridge: Polity Press.

Beardsworth, R. (1996) *Derrida and the Political*, London: Routledge.

Beck, U. (1997) *The Reinvention of Politics*, trans. M. Ritter, Cambridge: Polity.

Bellamy, J. E. (1993) 'Discourses of Impossibility: Can Psychoanalysis be Political?', *Diacritics*, 23, 1: 24–38.

Benjamin, W. (1968) *Illuminations*, Arendt, H. (ed.) with Introduction, trans. H. Zohn, New York: Schocken Books.

Benveniste, E. (1966) *Problems in General Linguistics*, trans. M. E. Meek, Coral Gables: University of Miami Press.

Benvenuto, B. and Kennedy, R. (1986) *The Works of Jacques Lacan: An Introduction*, London: Free Association Books.

Benvenuto, S. (1996) 'Lacan's Dream', *Journal of European Psychoanalysis*, 2: 107–31.

Berger, J. and Luckmann, T. (1967) *The Social Construction of Reality*, London: Allen Lane.

Berneri, M. (1971) *Journey Through Utopia*, New York: Shocken Books.

164

Blumenberg, H. (1985) *The Legitimacy of the Modern Age*, trans. R. Wallace, Cambridge, Mass.: MIT Press.

Boothby, R. (1991) *Death and Desire: Psychoanalytic Theory in Lacan's 'Return to Freud'*, New York: Routledge.

Borch-Jacobsen, M. (1991) *Lacan, The Absolute Master*, Stanford: Stanford University Press.

—— (1997) '*Basta Cosi*! Mikkel Borch-Jacobsen on Psychoanalysis and Philosophy, Interview by Chris Oakley' in Dufresne, T. (ed.) *Returns of the 'French Freud': Freud, Lacan and Beyond*, New York: Routledge.

Bourdieu, P. (1991) *Language and Symbolic Power*, Cambridge: Polity.

Bowie, M. (1991) *Lacan*, London: Fontana.

Bracher, M. (1993) *Lacan, Discourse and Social Change*, Ithaca: Cornell University Press.

—— (1994) 'Introduction' in Alcorn, M., Bracher, M., Corthell, R. and Massarder-Kenney, F. (eds) *Lacanian Theory of Discourse*, New York: New York University Press.

—— (1997) 'Always Psychoanalyze! Historicism and the Psychoanalysis of Culture and Society', *Journal for the Psychoanalysis of Culture and Society*, 2, 1: 1–16.

Brennan, T. (1993) *History after Lacan*, London: Routledge.

Butler, J. (1993) *Bodies That Matter*, New York: Routledge.

—— (1997) *The Psychic Life of Power*, Stanford: Stanford University Press.

Castoriadis, C. (1978) *The Imaginary Institution of Society*, Athens: Ραππας.

—— (1991) *The Cross-roads of the Labyrinth*, Athens: Υπσιλον.

Chaitin, G. (1996) *Rhetoric and Culture in Lacan*, Cambridge: Cambridge University Press.

Cohen, A. P. (1989) *The Symbolic Construction of Community*, London: Routledge.

Cohn, N. (1993a) *Cosmos, Chaos and the World to Come: The Ancient Roots of Apocalyptic Faith*, New Haven: Yale University Press.

—— (1993b) *Europe's Inner Demons: The Demonization of Christians in Medieval Christendom*, London: Pimlico.

—— (1993c) *The Pursuit of the Millennium: Revolutionary Millenarians and Mystical Anarchists of the Middle Ages*, London: Pimlico.

—— (1996) *Warrant for Genocide: The Myth of the Jewish World Conspiracy and the Protocols of the Elders of Zion*, London: Serif.

Collier, A. (1998) 'Mind, Reality and Politics', *Radical Philosophy*, 88: 38–43.

Collingwood, R. G. (1945) *The Idea of Nature*, Oxford: Clarendon Press.

Connolly, W. (1987) *Politics and Ambiguity*, Madison: University of Wisconsin Press.

—— (1991) *Identity/Difference: Democratic Negotiations of Political Paradox*, Ithaca: Cornell University Press.

Conway, D. (1997) *Nietzsche and the Political*, London: Routledge.

Copjec, J. (1994) *Read my Desire: Lacan against the Historicists*, Cambridge, Mass.: MIT Press.

Coward, R. and Ellis, J. (1977) *Language and Materialism*, London: Routledge and Kegan Paul.

Critchley, S. (1992) *The Ethics of Deconstruction*, Oxford: Blackwell.

Culler, J. (1989) *On Deconstruction*, London: Routledge.

Daly, G. (1991) 'The Discursive Construction of Economic Space', *Economy and Society*, 20, 1: 79–102 .

Delanty, G. (1997) *Social Science: Beyond Constructivism and Realism*, Buckingham: Open University Press.

Demertzis, N. (1996) *The Discourse of Nationalism*, Athens: Σακκουλας.

Derrida, J. (1981) *Positions*, trans. A. Bass, Chicago: University of Chicago Press.

—— (1988) 'The Purveyor of Truth', trans. A. Bass, in Muller, J. and Richardson, W. (eds) *The Purloined Poe: Lacan, Derrida and Psychoanalytic Reading*, Baltimore: Johns Hopkins University Press.

—— (1990a) *Of Grammatology*, trans. K. Papagiorgis, Athens: Γνωση.

—— (1990b) 'Force of Law: The 'Mystical Foundation of Authority', *Cardozo Law Review*, 11, 5–6: 919–1045.

—— (1992) 'How to Avoid Speaking: Denials' in Coward, H. and Foshay, T. (eds) *Derrida and Negative Theology*, Albany: SUNY Press.

—— (1995a) *On the Name*, Dutoit, T. (ed.), trans. D Wood, J. Leavey, Jr and I. McLeod, Stanford: Stanford University Press.

—— (1995b) 'For the Love of Lacan' in *Cardozo Law Review*, 16, 3–4: 699–728.

—— (1996) 'Remarks on Deconstruction and Pragmatism' in Mouffe, C. (ed.) *Deconstruction and Pragmatism*, London: Routledge.

Dervin, D. (1997) 'Where Freud Was, There Lacan Shall Be: Lacan and the Fate of Transference', *American Imago*, 54, 4: 347–75.

Diamond, J. (1997) 'Birds Do It, Bees Do It, and Rabbits Are At It, Well, As Rabbits. But None of Them Dress Up in Rubber', *Observer Review*, 6 July: 7.

Dor, J. (1985) *Introduction á la lecture de Lacan: 1. L'inconscient structuré comme un langage* (*Introduction to the Reading of Lacan: 1. The Unconscious Structured as a Language*), Paris: Denoël.

—— (1992) *Introduction á la lecture de Lacan: 2. La structure du sujet* (*Introduction to the Reading of Lacan: 2. The Structure of the Subject*), Paris: Denoël.

—— (1997) *The Clinical Lacan*, Northvale: Jason Aronson.

Douglas, M. and Wildavsky, A. (1982) *Risk and Culture*, Berkeley and Los Angeles: University of California Press.

Dreyfus, H. L. and Rabinow, P. (1982) *Michel Foucault*, London: Harvester Wheatsheaf.

Dunn, J. (1979) *Western Political Theory in the Face of the Future*, Cambridge: Cambridge University Press.

Dyrberg, T. B. (1997) *The Circular Structure of Power*, London: Verso.

Eco, U. (1995) *The Search for the Perfect Language*, trans. A. Papastavrou, Athens: Ελληνικα Γραμματα.

Edelman, M. (1988) *Constructing the Political Spectacle*, Chicago: Chicago University Press.

Eder, K. (1996) *The Social Construction of Nature*, trans. with introduction M. Ritter, London: Sage.

Eliade, M. (1989) *The Myth of the Eternal Return*, trans. W. Trask, London: Arkana.

Elliott, A. (1992) *Social Theory and Psychoanalysis in Transition*, Oxford: Blackwell.

—— (1994) *Psychoanalytic Theory: An Introduction*, Oxford: Blackwell.

Elliott, A. and Frosh, St. (eds) (1995) *Psychoanalysis in Contexts*, London: Routledge.

Etchegoyen, R. H. and Miller J.-A. (1996) 'Interview with Juan Carlos Stagnaro and Dominique Winterbert' in *Vertex, Revista Argentina de Psiquiatria*, VII, 26: 260–74 (in Spanish).

Euben, P., Wallach, J. and Ober, J. (1994) *Athenian Political Thought and the Reconstruction of American Democracy*, Ithaca: Cornell University Press.

Evans, D. (1996a) *An Introductory Dictionary of Lacanian Psychoanalysis*, London: Routledge.

—— (1996b) 'Historicism and Lacanian Theory', *Radical Philosophy*, 79: 35–40.

—— (1997) 'The Lure of the Already There and the Lure of the Before: Psychoanalytic Theory and Historiography', *Journal for the Psychoanalysis of Culture and Society*, 2, 1: 141–4.

—— (1998) 'From Kantian Ethics to Mystical Experience: An Exploration of Jouissance' in Nobus, D. (ed.) *Key Concepts of Lacanian Psychoanalysis*, London: Rebus Press.

Evernden, N. (1992) *The Social Creation of Nature*, Baltimore: Johns Hopkins University Press.

Feher-Gurewich, J. (1996) 'Toward a new Alliance between Psychoanalysis and Social Theory' in Pettigrew, D. and Raffoul, F. (eds) *Disseminating Lacan*, Albany: SUNY Press.

Fink, B. (1995a) *The Lacanian Subject, Between Language and Jouissance*, Princeton: Princeton University Press.

—— (1995b) 'The Real Cause of Repetition' in Feldstein, R., Fink, B. and Jaanus, M. (eds) *Reading Seminar XI: Lacan's Four Fundamental Concepts of Psychoanalysis*, Albany: SUNY Press.

—— (1995c) 'Science and Psychoanalysis' in Feldstein, R., Fink, B. and Jaanus, M. (eds) *Reading Seminar XI: Lacan's Four Fundamental Concepts of Psychoanalysis*, Albany: SUNY Press.

—— (1997) *A Clinical Introduction to Lacanian Psychoanalysis: Theory and Techinque*, Cambridge, Mass.: Harvard University Press.

Forrester, J. (1990) *The Seductions of Psychoanalysis*, Cambridge: Cambridge University Press.

Foucault, M. (1983) *This is not a Pipe*, trans. with Introduction J. Harkness, Berkeley: University of California Press.

—— (1984) *The Foucault Reader*, London: Penguin.

—— (1989) *The Order of Things*, trans. A. Sheridan-Smith, London: Routledge.

Freud, S. (1973) *New Introductory Lectures on Psychoanalysis*, Pelican/Penguin Freud Library, 2, London: Pelican.

——(1982) *Civilization and its Discontents*, London: The Hogarth Press and the Institute of Psycho-analysis.

—— (1991a) *The Interpretation of Dreams*, London: Penguin.

—— (1991b) *Group Psychology and the Analysis of the Ego, Pelican/Penguin Freud Library*, 12, London: Penguin.

Freud, S. and Bullitt, W. (1967) *Thomas Woodrow Wilson, Twenty-eighth President of the United States: A Psychological Study*, London: Weidenfeld and Nicolson.

Frosh, S. (1987) *The Politics of Psychoanalysis: An Introduction to Freudian and Post-Freudian Theory*, Houndmills: Macmillan.

Gadet, F. (1986) *Saussure and Contemporary Culture*, trans. G. Elliott, London: Hutchinson Radius.

Geuss, R. (1981) *The Idea of a Critical Theory*, Cambridge: Cambridge University Press.

Glejzer, R. (1997) 'Lacan with Scolasticism: Agencies of the Letter', *American Imago*, 54, 2: 105–22.

Gramsci, A. (1975) 'Universal Language and Esperanto' in Cavalcanti, P. and Piccone, P. (eds) *History, Philosophy and Culture in the Young Gramsci*, Saint Louis: Telos Press.

Hall, St. (1988) 'The Toad in the Garden: Thatcherism among the Theorists' in Nelson, G. and Grossberg, L. (eds) *Marxism and the Interpretation of Culture*, London: Macmillan.

Harkness, J. (1983) 'Translator's Introduction' in Foucault, M. *This is not a Pipe*, Berkeley: University of California Press.

Hegel, G. (1991) *The Philosophy of History*, trans. J. Sibree, Amherst: Prometheus Books.

Heidegger, M. (1972) *On Time and Being*, trans. J. Stambaugh, New York: Harper and Row.

Hill, C. (1984) *The World Turned Upside Down*, London: Peregrine Books.

—— (1990) *Antichrist*, London: Verso.

Holzner, B. (1968) *Reality Construction in Society*, Cambridge, Mass.: Shenkman.

Homer, S. (1996) 'Psychoanalysis, Representation, Politics: On the (Im)possibility of a Psychoanalytic Theory of Ideology?', *The Letter*, 7: 97–109.

Jakobson, R. (1998) *Essays on the Language of Literature,* trans. with introduction A. Berlis, Athens: Εστια.

Jameson, F. (1982) 'Imaginary and Symbolic in Lacan: Marxism, Psychoanalytic Criticism, and the Problem of the Subject' in Felman S. (ed.) *Literature and Psychoanalysis*, Baltimore: Johns Hopkins University Press.

—— (1991) *Postmodernism or the Cultural Logic of Late Capitalism*, London: Verso.

Jenner, S. R. (1997) 'The Great Dog Massacre' in Roberts, P. and Naphy, W. G. (eds) *Fear in Early Modern Society*, Manchester: Manchester University Press.

Jonas, H. (1992) *The Gnostic Religion*, London: Routledge.

Joy, M. (1992) 'Conclusion: Divine Reservations' in Coward, H. and Foshay, T. (eds) *Derrida and Negative Theology*, Albany: SUNY Press.

Julien, P. (1994) *Jacques Lacan's Return to Freud: the Real, the Symbolic and the Imaginary*, New York: New York University Press.

Kant, E. (1963) *On History*, L. W. Beck (ed.) with introduction, trans. L. W. Beck, R. Anchor and E. Fackenhem, London: Macmillan.

Kateb, G. (1963) *Utopia and its Enemies*, London: The Free Press of Glencoe.

Keane, J. (1995) *The Media and Democracy*, trans. P. Hatzipanteli, Athens: Πατακις.

Kelsen, H. (1946) *Society and Nature*, London: Kegan Paul, Trench, Trubner and Co.

Klotz, J. P. (1995) 'The Passionate Dimension of Transference' in Feldstein, R., Fink, B. and Jaanus, M. (eds) *Reading Seminar XI: Lacan's Four Fundamental Concepts of Psychoanalysis*, Albany: SUNY Press.

Kolakowski, L. (1978) *The Main Currents of Marxism*, vol. I, Oxford: Oxford University Press.

—— (1997) *Modernity on Endless Trial*, Chicago: Chicago University Press.

Kuhn, T. (1962) *The Structure of Scientific Revolutions*, Chicago: Chicago University Press.

Kurzweil, E. (1998) *The Freudians, a Comparative Pesrpective*, New Brunswick: Transaction Publishers.

Lacan, J. (1953–4) *The Seminar. Book I. Freud's Papers on Technique, 1953–4*, Miller, J.-A. (ed.), trans. with notes J. Forrester, Cambridge: Cambridge University Press, 1987.

—— (1954–5) *The Seminar. Book II. The Ego in Freud's Theory and in the Technique of Psychoanalysis*, Miller, J.-A. (ed.), trans. S. Tomaselli, with notes J. Forrester, Cambridge: Cambridge University Press, 1988.

—— (1955–6) *The Seminar. Book III. The Psychoses 1955–6*, Miller, J.-A. (ed.), trans. with notes R. Grigg, London: Routledge, 1993.

—— (1957–8) *The Formations of the Unconscious*, unpublished, trans. C. Gallagher.

—— (1958–9) *Desire and its Interpretation*, unpublished, trans. C. Gallagher.

—— (1959–60) *The Seminar. Book VII. The Ethics of Psychoanalysis 1959–60*, Miller, J.-A. (ed.), trans. with notes D. Porter, London: Routledge, 1992.

—— (1960–1) *Transference*, unpublished, trans. C. Gallagher.

—— (1961–2) *Identification*, unpublished, trans. C. Gallagher.

—— (1962–3) *Anxiety*, unpublished, trans. C. Gallagher.

—— (1964) *The Four Fundamental Concepts of Psychoanalysis*, Miller, J.-A. (ed.), trans. A. Sheridan, London: Penguin, 1979.

—— (1964–5) *Crucial Problems for Psychoanalysis*, unpublished, trans. C. Gallagher.

—— (1965–6) *The Object of Psychoanalysis*, unpublished, trans. C. Gallagher.

—— (1972–3) *The Seminar. Book XX. Encore, On Feminine Sexuality, The Limits of Love and Knowledge, 1972–3*, Miller, J.-A. (ed.), trans. with notes Br. Fink, New York: Norton, 1998.

—— (1972) 'Of Structure as an Inmixing of an Otherness Prerequisite to any Subject Whatever' in Macksey, R. and Donato, E. (eds) *The Structuralist Controversy: The Languages of Criticism and the Sciences of Man*, Baltimore: Johns Hopkins University Press.

—— (1977) *Écrits, A Selection*, trans. A. Sheridan, London: Tavistock/Routledge.

—— (1977) 'Preface' in Lemaire, A., *Jacques Lacan*, trans. D. Macey, London: Routledge and Kegan Paul.

—— (1978) *Replies*, trans. P. Kalias, Athens: Ερασμος.

—— (1987) 'Television', trans. D. Hollier, R. Krauss and A. Michelson, *October*, 40: 7–50.

—— (1988) 'Logical Time and the Assertion of Anticipated Certainty: A New Sophism', trans. B. Fink, *Newsletter of the Freudian Field*, 2, 3: 4–22.

—— (1988c) 'Seminar on the *Purloined Letter*', trans. J. Melhman, in Muller, J. and Richardson, W. (eds) (1988) *The Purloined Poe: Lacan, Derrida and Psychoanalytic Reading*, Baltimore: Johns Hopkins University Press.

—— (1989a) 'Science and Truth', trans. Bruce Fink, *Newsletter of the Freudian Field*, 3, 1 and 2: 4–29.

—— (1989b) 'Kant with Sade', trans. J. Swenson Jr, *October*, 51: 55–104.

—— (1995) 'Position of the Unconscious', trans. Br. Fink, in Feldstein, R., Fink, B. and Jaanus, M. (eds) *Reading Seminar XI: Lacan's Four Fundamental Concepts of Psychoanalysis*, Albany: SUNY Press.

—— (1996a) 'A Theoretical Introduction to the Functions of Psychoanalysis in Criminology', trans. M. Bracher, R. Grigg and R. Samuels, *Journal for the Psychoanalysis of Culture and Society*, 1, 2: 13–25.

—— (1996b) 'On Freud's *TRIEB*' and on the Psychoanalyst's Desire', trans. B. Fink, in Feldstein, R., Fink, B. and Jaanus, M. (eds) *Reading Seminar I and II: Lacan's Return to Freud*, Albany: SUNY Press.

Lacan, J. and the École Freudienne (1982) *Feminine Sexuality*, Mitchell, J. and Rose, J. (eds), trans. J. Rose, London: Macmillan.

Laclau, E. (1977) *Ideology and Politics in Marxist Theory*, London: Verso.

—— (1988a) 'Politics and the Limits of Modernity' in Ross, A. (ed.) *Universal Abandon?*, Minneapolis: University of Minnesota Press.

—— (1988b) 'Metaphor and Social Antagonisms' in Nelson, G. and Grossberg, L. (eds) *Marxism and the Interpretation of Culture*, London: Macmillan.

—— (1990) *New Reflections on the Revolution of our Time*, London: Verso.

—— (1991) 'God only Knows', *Marxism Today*, December: 56–9.

—— (1993) 'Power and Representation' in Poster, M. (ed.) *Politics, Theory and Contemporary Culture*, New York: Columbia.

—— (1994) 'Introduction' in Laclau, E. (ed.) *The Making of Political Identities*, London: Verso.

—— (1996) *Emancipation(s)*, London: Verso.

Laclau, E. and Mouffe, C. (1985) *Hegemony and Socialist Strategy*, London: Verso.

Laclau, E. and Zac, L. (1994) 'Minding the Gap: The Subject of Politics' in Laclau, E. (ed.) *The Making of Political Identities*, London: Verso.

Lacoue-Labarthe, P. (1997) 'On Ethics: A propos of Antigone', *Journal of European Psychoanalysis*, 3–4: 55–71.

Lacoue-Labarthe, P. and J.-L. Nancy (1992) *The Title of the Letter*, trans. with introduction Fr. Raffoul and D. Pettigrew, Albany: SUNY Press.

—— (1997) *Retreating the Political*, Sparks, S. (ed.), London: Routledge.

Lane, C. (1996) 'Beyond the Social Principle: Psychoanalysis and Radical Democracy', *Journal for the Psychoanalysis of Culture and Society*, 1, 1: 105–21.

Laplanche, J. and Pontalis, J. B. (1988) *The Language of Psychoanalysis*, trans. D. Nicholson-Smith, London: The Institute of Psychoanalysis/Karnac Books.

Laurent, E. (1995) 'Alienation and Separation', parts I and II in Feldstein, R., Fink, B. and Jaanus, M. (eds) *Reading Seminar XI: Lacan's Four Fundamental Concepts of Psychoanalysis*, Albany: SUNY Press.

Leader, D. (1996) *Lacan for Beginners*, London: Icon Books.

Lee, J. S. (1990) *Jacques Lacan*, Amherst: University of Massachusetts Press.

Lefort, C. (1986) *The Political Forms of Modern Society*, (ed.) with introduction J. Thompson, Cambridge: Cambridge University Press.

—— (1988) *Democracy and Political Theory*, trans. D. Macey, Oxford: Polity.

Leledakis, K. (1995) *Society and Psyche: Social Theory and the Unconscious Dimension of the Social*, Oxford: Berg.

Lemaire, A. (1977) *Jacques Lacan*, trans. D. Macey, London: Routledge and Kegan Paul.

Levitas, R. (1990) *The Concept of Utopia*, Syracuse University Press.

Lipowatz, T. (1982) *Diskurs und Macht. J. Lacans Begriff des Diskurses. Ein Beitrag zur politischen Psychologie* (*Discourse and Power. J. Lacan's Concept of Discourse. A Contribution to Political Psychology*), Marburg: Guttandin und Hoppe.

—— (1986) *Die Verleugnung des Politischen. Die Ethik des Symbolischen bei J. Lacan* (*The Disavowal of Politics. The Ethics of the Symbolic in J. Lacan*), Weinheim: Quadriga.

—— (1993) 'The Real, the Symbolic, the Imaginary in Political Theory', unpublished paper.

—— (1995a) *Against the Wave*, Athens: Πλεθρον.

—— (1995b) 'Ethics and Political Discourse in Democracy', *Acta Philosophical/Filozofski Vestnik*, 2: 135–43.

—— (1998) *Politik der Psyche* (*Politics of the Psyche*), Vienna: Turia und Kant.

Lowenthal, D. (1985) *The Past is a Foreign Country*, Cambridge: Cambridge University Press.

Löwith, C. (1949) *Meaning in History*, Chicago: Chicago University Press.

Luhmann, N. (1990) *Political Theory in the Welfare State*, trans. with introduction J. Bednarz Jr, Berlin: De Gruyter.

Lyotard, J. F. (1983) *Le Différend* (*The Different*), Paris: Éditions de Minuit.

Macey, D. (1988) *Lacan in Contexts*, London: Verso.

McIntyre, A. (1968) *Marxism and Christianity*, London: Duckworth.

Maier, C. (ed.) *Changing Boundaries of the Political*, Cambridge: Cambridge University Press.

Mannheim, K. (1991) *Ideology and Utopia*, London: Routledge.

Marin, L. (1984) *Utopics: Spatial Play*, New Jersey: Humanities.

Marquand, D. (1998) 'The Blair Paradox', *Prospect*, May: 19–24.

Marx, K. and Engels, F. (1983) *The Communist Manifesto*, London: Lawrence and Wishart.

Michelman, S. (1996) 'Sociology before Linguistics: Lacan's debt to Durkheim' in Pettigrew, D. and Raffoul, F. (eds) *Disseminating Lacan*, Albany: SUNY Press

Miller, J.-A. (1977–8) 'Suture: Elements of the Logic of the Signifier', *Screen*, 18, 4: 24–34.

—— (1987) Interview in *Le Matin, Newsletter of the Freudian Field*, 1, 1: 5–10.

—— (1988) 'Another Lacan', *Lacan Study Notes*, 6–9: 266–71.

—— (1989) 'To Interpret the Cause: From Freud to Lacan', *Newsletter of the Freudian Field*, 3, 1 and 2: 30–50.

—— (1991) 'The Analytic Experience: Means, Ends and Results' in Ragland-Sullivan, E. and Bracher, M. (eds) *Lacan and the Subject of Language*, New York: Routledge.

—— (1992) 'Duty and the Drives', *Newsletter of the Freudian Field*, 6, 1 and 2: 5–15.

—— (1995) 'Context and Concepts' in Feldstein, R., Fink, B. and Jaanus, M. (eds) *Reading Seminar XI: Lacan's Four Fundamental Concepts of Psychoanalysis*, Albany: SUNY Press.

—— (1996a) 'An Introduction to Seminars I and II: Lacan's Orientation Prior to 1953', parts I, II and III, in Feldstein, R., Fink, B. and Jaanus, M. (eds) *Reading Seminar I and II: Lacan's Return to Freud*, Albany: SUNY Press.

—— (1996b) 'An Introduction to Lacan's Clinical Perspectives' in Feldstein, R., Fink, B. and Jaanus, M. (eds) *Reading Seminar I and II: Lacan's Return to Freud*, Albany: SUNY Press.

—— (1997) 'The Flirtatious Remark' in *UMBR(a)*, one {∅}: 87–102.

Monchi, V. (1997) 'Previous Conviction' in *Prospect*, March: 80.

171

Mouffe, C. (1992) 'Preface: Democratic Politics Today' in Mouffe, C. (ed.), *Dimensions of Radical Democracy*, London: Verso.
—— (1993) *The Return of the Political*, London: Verso.
—— (1996) 'Radical Democracy or Liberal Democracy?' in Trend, D. (ed.) *Radical Democracy*, New York: Routledge.
—— (1996) 'Deconstruction, Pragmatism and the Politics of Democracy' in Mouffe, C. (ed.) *Deconstruction and Pragmatism*, London: Routledge.
—— (ed.) (1996) *Deconstruction and Pragmatism*, London: Routledge.
Muller, J. and Richardson, W. (1982) *Lacan and Language: A Readers Guide to the Écrits*, New York: International Universities Press, Inc.
—— (eds) (1988) *The Purloined Poe: Lacan, Derrida and Psychoanalytic Reading*, Baltimore: Johns Hopkins University Press.
Nasio, J. D. (1996) 'The Concept of the Subject of the Unconscious' in Pettigrew, D. and Raffoul, F. (eds) *Disseminating Lacan*, Albany: SUNY Press.
—— (1997) *Hysteria: The Splendid Child of Psychoanalysis*, trans. S. Fairfield, Northvale: Jason Aronson.
Neville-Sington, P. and Sington, D. (1993) *Paradise Dreamed*, London: Bloomsbury.
New, C. (1996) *Agency, Health and Social Survival: The Ecopolitics of Rival Psychologies*, London: Taylor and Francis.
Nobus, D. (1998) 'Life and Death in the Glass: A New Look at the Mirror Stage' in Nobus, D. (ed.) *Key Concepts of Lacanian Psychoanalysis*, London: Rebus Press.
Norval, A. (1996) *Deconstructing Apartheid Discourse*, London: Verso.
Pécheux, M. (1988) 'Discourse: Structure or Event?' in Nelson, G. and Grossberg, L. (eds) *Marxism and the Interpretation of Culture*, London: Macmillan.
Pippin, R. (1991) *Modernism as a Philosophical Problem*, Oxford: Blackwell.
Post, J. (1996) 'The Loss of Enemies, Fragmenting Identities, and the Resurgence of Ethnic/Nationalist Hatred and Anti-Semitism in Eastern Europe', *Journal for the Psychoanalysis of Culture and Society*, 1, 2: 27–33.
Potter, J. (1996) *Representing Reality: Discourse, Rhetoric and Social Construction*, London: Sage.
Ragland-Sullivan, E. (1991) 'Introduction' in Ragland-Sullivan, E. and Bracher, M. (eds), *Lacan and the Subject of Language*, New York: Routledge.
Rajchman, J. (1991) *Truth and Eros: Lacan, Foucault and the Question of Ethics*, London: Routledge.
Ranciere, J. (1992) 'Politics, Identification and Subjectivization', unpublished paper.
Richards, T. (1993) *The Imperial Archive: Knowledge and the Fantasy of Empire*, London: Verso.
Richardson, W. (1988) 'Lacan and the Problem of Psychosis' in Allison, D., Oliveira, P., Roberts, M. and Weiss, A. (eds) *Psychosis and Sexual Identity*, New York: SUNY Press.
Ricoeur, P. (1986) *Lectures on Ideology and Utopia*, Taylor, G. (ed.), New York: Columbia University Press.
Roazen, P. (1969) *Freud, Political and Social Thought*, London: The Hogarth Press.
Roberts, P. and Naphy, W. G. (1997) 'Introduction' in Roberts, P. and Naphy, W. G. (eds) *Fear in Early Modern Society*, Manchester: Manchester University Press.
Rodriguez, L. (1990) 'Fantasy, Neurosis and Perversion', *Analysis*, 2: 97–113.
Rorty, R. (1980) *Philosophy and the Mirror of Nature*, Oxford: Blackwell.

—— (1996) 'Response to Ernesto Laclau' in Mouffe, C. (ed.) *Deconstruction and Pragmatism*, London: Routledge.

Roudinesco, E. (1990) *Jacques Lacan & Co.: A History of Psychoanalysis in France, 1925–1985*, trans. with foreword J. Mehlman, London: Free Association Books.

—— (1997) *Jacques Lacan*, trans. B. Bray, Cambridge: Polity.

Roustang, F. (1982) *Dire Mastery: Discipleship from Freud to Lacan*, Baltimore: Johns Hopkins University Press.

—— (1990) *The Lacanian Delusion*, trans. G. Sims, New York: Oxford University Press.

Rustin, M. (1995) 'Lacan, Klein and Politics' in Elliott, A. and Frosh, S. (eds) *Psychoanalysis in Contexts*, London: Routledge.

Samuels, R. (1993) *Between Philosophy and Psychoanalysis*, New York: Routledge.

—— (1997) 'Lacan and Ethics and Adam and Eve', *UMBR(a)*, 1: 117–19.

Santner, E. (1997) 'Freud, Žižek, and the Joys of Monotheism', *American Imago*, 54, 2: 197–207.

Sartre, J.-P. (1995) *Anti-Semite and Jew, An Exploration of the Etiology of Hate*, preface M. Walzer, trans. G. Becker, New York: Shocken Books.

Saussure, F. de (1983) *Course in General Linguistics*, Bally, C. and Sechehaye, A. (eds), with the collaboration of A. Reidlinger, trans. R. Harris, London: Duckworth.

Schneiderman, S. (1983) *Jacques Lacan: The Death of an Intellectual Hero*, Cambridge, Mass.: Harvard University Press.

Schurmann, R. (1990) *Heidegger, on Being and Acting: From Principles to Anarchy*, Bloomington: Indiana University Press.

Scott, A. (1990) *Ideology and New Social Movements*, London: Unwin Hyman.

Scott, C. (1989) 'The Pathology of the Father's Rule: Lacan and the Symbolic Order' in Wyschogrod, E., Crownfield, D. and Raschke, C. (eds) *Lacan and Theological Discourse*, Albany: SUNY Press.

Simons, J. (1995) *Foucault and the Political*, London: Routledge.

Sloterdijk, P. (1988) *Critique of Cynical Reason*, trans. M. Eldred, London: Verso.

Smith, J. (1991) *Arguing with Lacan: Ego-Psychology and Language*, New Haven: Yale University Press.

Smith, P. (1996) *Disraeli: A Brief Life*, Cambridge: Cambridge University Press.

Sobel, D. (1996) *Longitude*, London: Fourth Estate.

Soler, C. (1991) 'Literature as Symptom' in Ragland-Sullivan, E. and Bracher, M. (eds), *Lacan and the Subject of Language*, New York: Routledge.

—— (1995) 'The Subject and the Other', parts I and II, in Feldstein, R., Fink, B. and Jaanus, M. (eds) *Reading Seminar XI: Lacan's Four Fundamental Concepts of Psychoanalysis*, Albany: SUNY Press.

Stavrakakis, Y. (1997a) 'Ambiguous Democracy and the Ethics of Psychoanalysis', *Philosophy and Social Criticism*, 23, 2: 79–96.

—— (1997b) 'Green Fantasy and the Real of Nature: Elements of a Lacanian Critique of Green Ideological Discourse', *Journal for the Psychoanalysis of Culture and Society*, 2, 1: 123–32.

—— (1997c) 'Field Note on Advertising', *Journal for the Psychoanalysis of Culture and Society*, 2, 1: 139–41.

—— (1997d) 'Ambiguous Ideology and the Lacanian Twist', *Journal of the Centre for Freudian Analysis and Research*, 8 and 9: 117–30.

—— (1997e) 'Green Ideology: A Discursive Reading', *Journal of Political Ideologies*, 2, 3: 259–79.

—— (1997f) 'On the Political Implications of Lacanian Theory: A Reply to Homer', *The Letter*, 10: 111–22.

—— (1998) 'Laclau mit Lacan: Zum Verhältnis von Politischer Theorie und Psychoanalyse' ('Laclau with Lacan: On the Relation between Political Theory and Psychoanalysis') in Marchart, O. (ed.) *Das Undarstellbare der Politik* (*The Unrepresentability of the Political*), Vienna: Turia und Kant.

Stephens, A. (1987) 'The Sun State and its Shadow: On the Conditions of Utopian Writing' in Kamenka, E. (ed.) *Utopias*, Melbourne: Oxford University Press.

Szerszynski, Br. (1996) 'On Knowing What to Do: Environmentalism and the Modern Problematic' in Lash, S., Szerszynski, B. and Wynne, B. (eds) *Risk, Environment and Modernity*, London: Sage.

Tallis, R. (1997) 'The Shrink from Hell', *The Times Higher Education Supplement*, 31 October: 20.

Talmon, J. L. (1971) 'Utopianism and Politics' in Kateb, G. (ed.) *Utopia*, New York: Atherton Press.

Taylor, G. (1986) 'Editor's Introduction' in Ricoeur, P., *Lectures on Ideology and Utopia*, New York: Columbia University Press.

Thompson, J. (1995) *The Media and Democracy*, Cambridge: Polity.

Thurston, L. (1998) 'Ineluctable Nodalities: On the Borromean Knot' in Nobus, D. (ed.) *Key Concepts of Lacanian Psychoanalysis*, London: Rebus Press.

Touraine, A. (1991) 'What Does Democracy Mean Today?', *International Social Sciences Journal*, 128: 259–68.

—— (1994) 'Democracy', *Thesis Eleven*, 38: 1–15.

—— (1997) *What is Democracy?*, trans. D. Macey, Boulder: Westview Press.

Trend, D. (1996a) 'Introduction' in Trend, D. (ed.) *Radical Democracy*, New York: Routledge.

—— (1996b) 'Democracy's Crisis of Meaning' in Trend, D. (ed.) *Radical Democracy*, New York: Routledge.

Turkle, S. (1992) *Psychoanalytic Politics*, London: Free Association Books.

Vattimo, G. (1988) *The End of Modernity*, trans. with Introduction J. Snyder, Cambridge: Polity.

—— (1993) *The Transparent Society*, trans. D. Webb, Cambridge: Polity.

Vergotte, A. (1983) 'From Freud's other Scene to Lacan's "Other" ' in Smith, J. and Kerrigan, W. (eds) *Interpreting Lacan, Psychiatry and the Humanities*, Vol. 6, New Haven: Yale University Press.

Verhaeghe, P. (1994) 'Psychotherapy, Psychoanalysis and Hysteria', *The Letter*, 2: 47–68.

—— (1995) 'From Impossibility to Inability: Lacan's Theory of the Four Discourses', *The Letter*, 3: 76–99.

—— (1997) *Does the Woman Exist?*, London: Rebus Press.

—— (1998) 'Causation and Destitution of a Pre-ontological Non-entity: On the Lacanian Subject' in Nobus, D. (ed.) *Key Concepts of Lacanian Psychoanalysis*, London: Rebus Press.

Vernant, J.-P. (1982) *The Origins of Greek Thought*, Ithaca: Cornell University Press.

Vincent, J. (1990) *Disraeli*, Oxford: Oxford University Press.

Wallace, R. (1985) 'Translator's Introduction' in Blumenberg, H., *The Legitimacy of the Modern Age*, Cambridge, Mass.: MIT Press.

Weale, A. (1995) *The New Politics of Pollution*, Manchester: Manchester University Press.

Weber, S. (1991) *Return to Freud*, Cambridge: Cambridge University Press.

Whitebook, J. (1995) *Perversion and Utopia*, Cambridge, Mass.: MIT Press.

Widmer, P. (1995) 'Freud und die Demokratie' ('Freud and Democracy'), *Riss*, 29/30: 67–90.

Wilden, A. (1968) *Jacques Lacan: Speech and Language in Psychoanalysis*, Baltimore: Johns Hopkins University Press.

Williams, R. (1988) *Keywords*, London: Fontana Press.

Wittgenstein, L. (1988) *Tractatus Logico-Philosophicus*, London: Routledge.

—— (1992) *Philosophical Investigations*, Oxford: Blackwell.

Worster, D. (1993) *The Wealth of Nature*, New York: Oxford University Press.

—— (1994) *Nature's Economy*, second edn, Cambridge: Cambridge University Press.

Wrong, D. (1994) *The Problem of Order: What Unites and Divides Society*, Cambridge, Mass: Harvard University Press.

Wyschogrod, E., Crownfield, D. and Raschke, C. (eds) (1989) *Lacan and Theological Discourse*, Albany: SUNY Press.

Zeitlin, M. (1997) 'The Ego Psychologists in Lacan's Theory', *American Imago*, 54, 2: 209–32.

Zerilli, L. (1998) 'This Universalism Which is not One', *Diacritics*, 28, 2.

Žižek, S. (1987) 'Why Lacan is not a Post-structuralist?', *Newsletter of the Freudian Field*, 1, 2: 31–9.

—— (1989) *The Sublime Object of Ideology*, London: Verso.

—— (1990) 'Beyond Discourse Analysis' appendix in Laclau, E. *New Reflections on the Revolution of Our Time*, London: Verso.

—— (1991a) *Looking Awry*, Cambridge, Mass.: MIT Press.

—— (1991b) *For They Know Not What They Do*, London: Verso

—— (1992) *Enjoy your Symptom*, New York: Routledge.

—— (1993) *Tarrying with the Negative*, Durham: Duke University Press.

—— (1994a) *The Metastases of Enjoyment*, London: Verso.

—— (1994b) 'Between Symbolic Fiction and Fantasmatic Spectre: Towards a Lacanian Theory of Ideology', *Analysis*, 4: 9–62.

—— (1995) 'Introduction: The Spectre of Ideology' in Žižek, S. (ed.) *Mapping Ideology*, London: Verso.

—— (1996a) 'I Hear you with my Eyes' in Žižek, S. and Salecl, R. (eds) *Gaze and Voice as Love Objects*, Durham: Duke University Press.

—— (1996b) 'Invisible Ideology: Political Violence Between Fiction and Fantasy', *Journal of Political Ideologies*, 1, 1: 15–32.

—— (1997a) 'The Abyss of Freedom' in Žižek, S. and Schelling, F. W. J. *The Abyss of Freedom/Ages of the World*, Ann Arbor: University of Michigan Press.

—— (1997b) *The Plague of Fantasies*, London: Verso.

—— (1998) 'The Seven Veils of Fantasy' in Nobus, D. (ed.) *Key Concepts of Lacanian Psychoanalysis*, London: Rebus Press.

Žižek, S. and Schelling, F. W. J. (1997) *The Abyss of Freedom/Ages of the World*, Ann Arbor: University of Michigan Press.

INDEX

language 13, 22, 23, 37, 53, 84; analysis operates through 21; Augustinian picture of 25; central feature of 52; child becomes a subject in 20; common 80, 115; diachronic axis of 57; emphasis on 14; introduction of 46; laws of 20, 32, 33; objectivity of 28; paradigmatic axis of 57, 76; perfect 115; poles of 76; primary status of 22; reality and 34, 66; something missing in 28, 52; structure of 59; subject emerges in 42; synchronic axis of 57; syntagmatic axis of 57, 76; universality of 28, 42, 115, 116; what cannot be articulated in 56; words signify 25; *see also* linguistics; meaning; meta-language; words
Laplanche, Jean 16, 30
Law(s) 20, 31, 59; ethical 128; moral 128; rule of 122; of signifier 57; symbolic 32, 43, 46; universal 125
Leader, Darian 53
League of Nations 2
Lee, Jonathan Scott 84, 85, 130, 131
Lefort, Claude 72–3, 79, 123, 124, 125, 138
legitimacy 125
Leledakis, Kanakis 38, 52
Lévi-Strauss, Claude 2, 11
Levitas, Ruth 99, 100
libido 130, 131–2
linguistic(s) 2, 18, 19, 23, 26, 57, 58; disturbances noticed in psychotics 33; diversion of 90, 91; psychoanalysis and 21, 22; structural 11, 21, 22
Linnaeus, Carolus 63
Lipowatz, Thanos 109, 130
literature 6
Locke, John 123
Loewenstein, Rudolph 10
logic 4, 7, 20, 34, 42, 43, 76; innovative 123; political, metonymic 77; of signifier 91; utopian 101
logocentrism 127
longitude problem 60–1
loss 82
love 38, 115
Lovelock, James 63
Lowith, Karl 117
Luckmann, Thomas 54, 56, 67
Luhmann, Niklas 138

Magritte, René 85
Mannheim, Karl 110
Marcuse, Herbert 114
Marin, Louis 100, 101, 107, 111
Marx, Karl 113, 117, 118, 123
Marxism 14, 72
materialism 14, 17
meaning 53; based on semblance 39; community of 32; decontestation of 120; eschatological 136; fantasmatic 87; fixation of 44, 60; lack of 137; lost 22; metaphoric and metonymic production of 76; network of 55; nodal point that fixes 80; postmodern conceptions of 60; reality and 54; sedimentation of 67; signifier creates 26, 60; social 54, 55, 86; stable 27, 60; symbolic 67, 69; syntagmatic pole of 77; theory of 24, 25, 27, 57, 58; unending fluidity of 59; utopian 70, 100
méconnaisance 30
memory 85
Merleau-Ponty, Maurice 10
meta-discourse 8
meta-language 66, 84, 93
meta-narratives 99
metaphor 32, 42, 47, 50, 62, 74, 75, 79, 81; creative, inability to construct 33; logic of 76, 77; metonymy and 57–9
metaphysics 15, 16, 63, 93; rigid 94; subversion of 91
metonymy 26, 45, 50, 75–6, 77, 81; metaphor and 57–9; telos of 91
Michelman, Stephen 37, 39
millenarianism 52, 76, 82, 103
Miller, Jacques-Alain 1–2, 12, 47–8, 62, 130
Milton, John 106
mirror stage 6, 17, 18–19, 30, 31
modernity 87, 89, 97, 103, 104, 117; ageing 96; political 98
moments 79

Monchi, Valerie 134
Montaigne, Michel de 97
moralities 128
More, St Thomas 100
mortification 28
mother 20, 31, 33, 34, 128; primordial
    42; prohibited 45; sleeping with 43;
    unity between child and 48
Mouffe, Chantal 36, 41, 72, 73, 76, 77,
    79, 95, 111–12, 125, 126, 127
Mukhina, V. 114
myth(ology) 42, 47, 56, 87, 88–9; family
    19

Name-of-the-Father 31–2, 33, 42, 44–5
Nancy, Jeab-Luc 2, 16, 37, 90–4
narcissism 3, 18
nationalism 82
nature 54–5, 65, 67, 69–70, 86;
    conservation of 64; construction of
    63; symbolisation of the real of 87
Nautical Almanac 61
Nazis 100, 103, 104, 105, 108, 109
need 68; becomes demand 34; fulfilment
    of 53, 60
negativity 67, 81, 87, 100, 101;
    irreducible 107; proliferation of 108;
networks: of meaning 55; symbolic 19
neurosis 32, 33, 58
'New Labour' 77, 78
Newton, Sir Isaac 63
Nietzsche, Friedrich 4
Nilus 104
nodal points 79, 80, 114, 135
Norval, Aletta 74
nothingness 48, 73

objective 1, 9, 39, 74; lacking 40–5; role
    of 37; understanding of 4
objectivism 93
objectivity: fantasmatic 68; of language
    28; sedimented forms of 73; socio-
    political 8, 9, 37; *see also* social
    objectivity
object 25, 40–70; beautiful 132;
    imaginary 131; impossible 113;
    signified 26; socially-constructed 30;
    socio-political 37; symbolic 131

objet petit a 45, 47, 49, 50, 51, 81, 134
obscurantism 5, 6
Odum, Eugene P. 63
Oedipus complex 31, 34, 43
ontology 91, 123
optimism 96, 104, 111, 122
order 16, 27, 116; collapse of 135;
    contingency of 110; discursive 68;
    harmonious 117; natural 32; political
    111; social 32, 37, 65, 136; socio-
    ideological 110; socio-symbolic 37;
    structural 61; symbolic 31, 32, 35, 38,
    44, 68, 84
organisation 79, 104, 136, 138; of
    enjoyment 109
orthopaedics 30, 92
Other(ness) 34, 40, 47, 62, 128, 135, 139;
    lack in 41, 46, 51, 117, 129, 134;
    foreclosure of Name-of-the-Father in
    place of 32; no Other of 53; pre-
    symbolic 86; radical 86; social 41;
    something missing in 39, 49; symbolic
    19, 21, 32
Owen, Robert 100

paradigms 55, 8, 76, 87, 133
paradox 34, 42, 69, 82–3, 94, 122, 131;
    study of 85; tragic 108
paranoid culture 1
paranoid-schizoid states 119
parents 19, 20; relations to 37
Paris International Exhibition (1937)
    114
particularism 10, 125, 137
particularity 33, 40, 108, 133
pathos 37
perfection 104
personalisation 20
personality: constituted and specified 30;
    unity of 15
pessimism 95, 99, 118
phallus 50, 51
phenomena 103, 124; first order 48;
    ideological 36; political 36;
    psychological 1; second order 48;
    social 1, 3, 102
philosophy 15, 94, 95, 113, 117;
    humanist tradition 14; Lacanian

CPSIA information can be obtained at www.ICGtesting.com
Printed in the USA
BVOW08s1336280416

445992BV00008B/37/P